# DATE DUE

JAN 2 5 2010

BRODART, CO.                    Cat. No. 23-221-003

# Advance Praise for *Paths to Power*

"*Paths to Power* got it right in looking at the factors of an individual's background that tend to lead to business success. Fortunately, there has been enormous change over the last century, which provides increasing opportunity based on merit for getting to the top of U.S. business."

—Stephen A. Schwarzman, Chairman, CEO, and Cofounder,
The Blackstone Group

"The book contributes significantly to leadership literature by providing, in one place, a fascinating set of stories about the lives and experiences of a broad swath of American business leaders. It offers a valuable antidote to the data-light analyses that often masquerade as scholarship in the field of leadership."

—Robert Thomas, Executive Director, Accenture's Institute
for High Performance Business

"This book is beautifully written and fully engaging. It is based on substantial analytical work, and it gives this work many human faces. Moreover, it teaches its readers social and business history and geography lessons as well as information about leaders' paths to power. It is thought provoking and very stimulating."

—Jean M. Bartunek, Professor of Organization Studies,
Boston College

# Paths to Power

# Paths to Power

*How Insiders and Outsiders*

*Shaped American Business*

*Leadership*

Anthony J. Mayo

Nitin Nohria

Laura G. Singleton

Harvard Business School Press

*Boston, Massachusetts*

Printed in the United States of America

10  09  08  07  06      5  4  3  2  1

978-1-4221-0198-8 (ISBN 13)

**Library of Congress Cataloging-in-Publication Data**

Mayo, Anthony J.
   Paths to power : how insiders and outsiders shaped American business leadership / Anthony J. Mayo, Nitin Nohria, Laura G. Singleton.
         p. cm.
   Includes bibliographical references.
   ISBN 1-4221-0198-3 (alk. paper)
   1. Executives—United States—History.   2. Leadership—United States—History.   3. Success in business—United States—History.   I. Nohria, Nitin, 1962–   II. Singleton, Laura G.   III. Title.
   HD38.25.U6M345 2006
   338.092'273—dc22

                                                                      2006019977

The paper used in this publication meets the minimum requirements of the American National Standard for Information Sciences—Permanence of Paper for Printed Library Materials, ANSI Z39.48-1992.

*For our parents*

*Earl and Cecile Mayo*

*Kewal and Guddi Nohria*

*Julius and Marjorie Singleton*

# [ CONTENTS ]

Contents

Who reaches the top of a nation's premier institutions is an ageless question, and it is one that is endlessly discussed and dissected—for good reason. In answering it we come to better appreciate what values as a nation we hold dear. We come to better understand who presides over our dominant organizations. And we come to know better which pathways lead to the apex—or which do not.

In their masterful account of the paths to power in America's foremost institutions, Tony Mayo, Nitin Nohria, and Laura Singleton tell us how the leaders of big business came to lead their businesses during the twentieth century. They assess how religion, class, education, and other demographics served to powerfully advantage or disadvantage some over others. Through painstaking research, the authors have constructed a richly nuanced portrait of the nation's one thousand most influential business leaders. Since these careers span the century, *Paths to Power* also reveals how the principles of ascent have profoundly evolved over the decades, and how our societal values have been altered as well.

Studies of the social origins of America's business elite have been a long-standing research tradition, dating to such classics as W. Lloyd Warner and James Abegglen's *Big Business Leaders in America* and Mabel Newcomer's *The Big Business Executive*, both published in 1955. We have not had the benefit of a truly comprehensive portrait since those works of more than fifty years ago; now Mayo, Nohria, and Singleton have not only updated the picture but also produced the definitive portrait of our time.

What they find is both compelling and sobering. Religious advantage has been in sharp decline for the past hundred years. The authors note that "the overall picture presented by our leaders leaves little doubt that religious affiliation played an important role at the start of the twentieth century in facilitating the personal networking that opened doors to business success." At that time, Protestants, especially Episcopalians and Presbyterians, reached the pinnacle of business success far more often than members of any other faith. By the end of the century, by contrast, a substantial majority of the nation's top executives no longer proclaimed any religious affiliation at all. Many were observant in their faith, of course, but their public silence on the issue reveals, the authors conclude, that religious affiliation "no longer served as a public and widely appreciated signal of legitimacy" for careers in business.

In religion's place, the authors report, is a great new differentiator, higher education. Less than a fifth of the business leaders in 1900 had completed college; today, less than a tenth have not. And within that world, the most privileged track has lost much of its luster. Prior to 1950, better than two-fifths of the college-educated business executives had attended Ivy League institutions; since 1950, however, this proportion has fallen by half. At the same time, the MBA degree has risen from no presence at all to a commanding platform. Among those business leaders born before 1900, only one had earned an MBA degree. Of those born since 1930, well over a quarter had completed an MBA program. The first MBA holder reached the corner office in 1931; of those reaching the corner office in the 1990s, by contrast, more than half featured an MBA on their résumés. The MBA, the authors found, has risen from "non-existent to standard equipment."

The declining rule of religion and rising authority of education in defining the paths to power suggests that performance has increasingly taken precedence over pedigree when it comes to promotion. Certainly the relative weight of these two factors has tilted significantly toward the former. That is one of the compelling themes of this volume, and it is consistent with what we have seen at so many American firms during the past several decades. Individual results have increasingly come to overshadow seniority and other demographic advantages when it comes to promotion.

Yet at the same time, a sobering message of *Paths to Power* is that class still matters, albeit more indirectly through the educational credentials it bestows, and so do race and gender. At the start of the century, half of the top executives came from families in which the father held middle-class jobs, and another fifth came from even more affluent heritages. That fraction has remained relatively constant over the entire century. For women and African Americans, the upward ascent has been and still remains very challenging.

In looking ahead, Mayo, Nohria, and Singleton anticipate both "open doors" and "glass ceilings" for those who aspire to reach the peak of the business world. An increasingly critical career credential, the MBA degree, was once the preserve of men but today some 40 percent of all new degree recipients are women. If that door is opening, modest family origins still constitute a ceiling, albeit a semipermeable one; a few of those with such a background move up but most never obtain the educational qualifiers that have come to constitute the essential stepping stones. Now "no less than at any time during the twentieth century," the authors conclude, "only an exceptional individual can break through socioeconomic barriers and rise to business leadership."

The side-by-side persistence of both open and closed paths to power is not surprising, given the nation's overarching commitment to equality of opportunity but frequent shortfall in achieving it. In *An American Dilemma* (1944), his classic account of race in the United States, Gunnar Myrdal wrote that although we value personal performance over family pedigree, that commitment has been unevenly applied to African Americans. Myrdal concluded on an optimistic note, however, predicting that our transcendent belief in open opportunity would eventually triumph over lingering bias. The authors of *Paths to Power* cautiously conclude much the same, providing that "business practices, public policies, and philanthropic activities" work to remove the persisting demographic barriers so that demonstrated performance finally prevails.

The overarching trends captured by the authors' statistical patterns are wonderfully illuminated by dozens of portraits. One of the most revealing is their account of Irving Shapiro, born in Minneapolis to Lithuanian immigrants. Upon his graduation from law school in 1941, friends and faculty urged him to change his last name; because of his refusal to do so he received no offers from Minneapolis law firms that still put religious preference ahead of individual potential. Nevertheless, an attorney who had come to appreciate Shapiro's talents regardless of his disadvantaged demographics brought him into the legal department of DuPont Corporation.

Even then, DuPont management had a lingering reputation for anti-Semitism, but Shapiro's exceptional abilities brought him to the attention of top management, and by 1973 he had joined their ranks—despite his disadvantages of family and faith. Shapiro described his new life in the corner office: "You are accepted for what you achieve and judged by your performance, regardless of how you pray." By the 1970s, the American business community had moved in much the same direction, and one of its preeminent organizations, the Business Roundtable, elected Shapiro as its leader. There, he came to serve as the public face of the private sector. Performance had indeed prevailed over pedigree.

The paths-to-power story is all here, and Tony Mayo, Nitin Nohria, and Laura Singleton tell it with a compelling narrative. And it is a story that tells us as much about American culture as big business. Personal background has been remarkably persistent in defining who reaches the corporate apex, but over time, individual performance is gradually but relentlessly displacing it. The intensifying competition of a flattening world—where results matter above all else—is sure to hasten the final triumph of performance.

—MICHAEL USEEM

A key lesson from our analysis of access to power and opportunity in American business leadership is the importance of strong personal networks and connections. Through the process of researching one thousand business leaders and writing *Paths to Power*, we have been fortunate to have developed a strong network of support and encouragement for which we are deeply grateful.

As for our first book, *In Their Time: The Greatest Business Leaders of the 20th Century*, the motivation for *Paths to Power* came from Richard Tedlow's study "The Chief Executive Officer of the Large American Industrial Corporation in 1917," published in *Business History Review*. We were intrigued by his comparison of CEOs from two distinct points in history and sought to better understand the evolving portrait of the CEO in the twentieth century. We also drew inspiration and insights from previous studies of access and opportunity in American business, including "The American Business Elite: A Collective Portrait" by C. Wright Mills, *The Journal of Economic History* (1945); *The Big Business Executive: The Factors That Made Him, 1900-1950* by Mabel Newcomer (1955); *American Business Leaders: A Study of Social Origins and Stratification* by F. W. Taussig and C. S. Josyln (1932); "Pathways to Top Corporate Management" by Michael Useem, *American Sociological Review* (1986); and *Big Business Leaders in America* by W. Lloyd Warner and James C. Abegglen (1955).

Our inspiration found traction through the generous support and encouragement of Harvard Business School's Leadership Initiative led by Professor Linda Hill and the Division of Research under the direction of Professors Krishna Palepu and Debora Spar. We also wish to acknowledge the support of other members of the Division of Research, including Research Director Geoff Jones, Ann Cichon, and Steve O'Donnell. We are privileged to be a part of the HBS community and wish to extend our gratitude to Deans Kim Clark and Jay Light for their commitment to our research endeavors.

"The Great American Business Leaders of the 20th Century" database that was used as the analytical foundation for *Paths to Power* was created through the work of a number of individuals associated with the HBS Leadership Initiative from 2001 to 2004. We are particularly grateful to Bridget Gurtler. who supported the data-gathering efforts at the outset of this project, and to Lisa Pode, who helped finalize the data-collection process. In addition, we are grateful for the administrative support and research efforts of Chris Allen, Alison Comings, Lindsay Greene, KC Hazarika, Albert Jiménez Howell, Kyle Klopcic, Eva Maynard, Patrick Regan, Agata Mazurowska-Rozdeiczer, Nicolay Siclunov, Monica Mullick Stallings, Jennifer Suesse, Emily Thompson, Sarah Woolverton, and James Zeitler. We especially want to recognize Kyle Klopcic for his significant contributions in fact checking and securing additional source data for the various business leaders who are profiled in the pages of *Paths to Power*, as well as for numerous other leaders whose stories fell victim to the editing process. His overall efforts deepened our understanding of typical leader profiles and definitely helped improve the book. Patrick Regan, who succeeded Kyle in this data-collection assignment, also merits our particular appreciation. Finally, we are indebted to the staff of Baker Library, especially the Historical Collections Department, for their patience and assistance with our numerous archival requests.

Throughout the process of researching and writing *Paths to Power*, we have benefited from the support, encouragement, and fresh perspective of a number of colleagues, including Warren Bennis, Linda Hill, Rakesh Khurana, John Kotter, Joshua Margolis, Lisa Pode, Mark Rennella, Scott Snook, and Michael Useem. We also wish to thank our editors at HBS Press—Melinda Merino and Julia Ely—who helped us shape and frame the overall flow of the book. In addition, we are grateful for the efforts of the production and design teams at HBS Press including Jennifer Waring, Patricia Boyd, and Mike Fender.

The photos that accompany this book were selected based on the research efforts of Lisa Pode and Abby Lorenz. Though archival photo research can be an arduous process, Lisa was undeterred, and *Paths to Power* has been enhanced through her dedication and enthusiasm.

I (Tony Mayo) wish to thank my coauthors Nitin and Laura for their brilliant insights, their collaborative spirit, and mostly for their friendship. Nitin has been a tremendous mentor for me in my role at Harvard Business School. His thoughtful guidance and unwavering support have enabled me to realize many of my personal and professional goals. Through this project, I have also been fortunate to reconnect with my former classmate Laura, whose dedication, thoughtfulness, and perseverance were instrumental in the shaping of *Paths to Power*. As ever, I am grateful to my family (my wife Denise and our three children, Hannah, Alex, and Jacob) for their uncompromising love and support. On a final note, I wish to thank my parents Earl and Cecile Mayo whose love, guidance, and faith helped me find and carve out my own path in life.

It has been a privilege for me (Nitin Nohria) to work with Tony Mayo and Laura Singleton on this project. Tony has been a remarkable force of energy in advancing an idea I had more than five years ago that we could learn a lot about leadership by studying business leaders historically over the course of a century. But for his indefatigable energy, this idea would never have taken off, let alone result in two books. Laura has been a prime driver of this project, and I admire her for taking on this daunting project, placing her mark on it, and working relentlessly to transform it from a mass of data and a set of interesting ideas into a coherent and compelling book. As this book shows, our families can have a profound influence on our lives. I owe the greatest debt to my parents Kewal and Guddi Nohria, who have given me everything a son could ever ask. I am equally grateful to my wife Monica and my daughters Reva and Ambika, who continue to be patient and loving as I keep working on projects that inevitably take time that could have been theirs.

I (Laura Singleton) am very grateful to Nitin and Tony for granting me the extraordinary opportunity to join them in shaping this book, following their successful collaboration on *In Their Time*. I should also acknowledge Tony's and my mutual friend from Section I of our MBA days, Sue Thirlwall, who helped us connect for this project. Personally, I'm thankful, as always, for the love and encouragement of my mother Marjorie and sisters Gretchen, Becky, and Sarah, who were ever-enthusiastic in their reviews of early chapter drafts. I also could not have gotten through the project's challenges without the prayerful support of my "other" family—past and present members of Cambridgeport Baptist Church, among whom Katrina Poirier, Joy Jordan-Lake, Carol Freeman, Jan and Paul Bothwell, and Dan and Kathy Szatkowski deserve my special thanks. I thank my fellow doctoral students and faculty in the Organizational Studies group at the Carroll School of Management, Boston College, especially cohort-mates Rick Cotton, Michael Krot, and

Reut Livne-Tarandach, for their good cheer to sustain the final push of editing. Finally, like my coauthors, I acknowledge in this book a debt to my parents—my mother and my late father, Julius Singleton. The research I did for this project deepened my appreciation for how many changes have occurred in America over the course of their lives and how much my own life has been blessed by their unchanging, loving, and ever-generous support.

# Paths to Power

# ONE

# Paths to Power

## Tracing a Full Century
## of Changing Access

*"Isn't it just a bunch of white men?"*

A S AUTHORS OF A BOOK discussing the demographic characteristics of top U.S. business leaders of the twentieth century, we've heard this question, or variations on the theme, quite a bit. Judging that there is little suspense regarding the point, we fearlessly disclose in the first paragraph of this book that, yes, the vast majority of individuals in top leadership of U.S. businesses over the course of the past century were white men. Through at least the 1970s, only exceptional circumstances provided any opportunity for a woman or person of color to gain leadership of a significant business enterprise. It may therefore come as a surprise when we suggest that, over the century, there have nevertheless been significant changes in the country's paths to power in business leadership. To support this contention, we begin by presenting briefly two prominent U.S. business leaders, James Stillman and Sanford "Sandy" Weill. Each occupied the helm of the nation's largest financial enterprise, with a century separating their tenures. In 1900, the enterprise was known as National City Bank, and in 2000, many mergers and several corporate name changes later, the same company, still the largest of its kind, was known as Citigroup.

## A Tale of Two White Guys

James Stillman was born in 1850 in Texas to parents who hailed from Connecticut. His father was a cotton merchant who had settled in the frontier territory to seek his fortune. Prior to the Civil War, James and his mother returned to the Northeast for the boy's education. Stillman's ancestors had fought in the Revolutionary War, and the family tree extended back to a George Stillman, who was born in England and had arrived in Hadley, Massachusetts, in 1690. The Stillman lineage thus enjoyed a heritage of almost two full centuries in the United States, and the Northeast in particular, by the time James entered adulthood.

Sandy Weill, by contrast, was born in 1933 in Brooklyn to parents who had emigrated from Poland. His father, an entrepreneur of modest scale, was in the dressmaking business and later owned a company that imported steel. The senior Weill sold the steel company just as Sandy, the first in his family to earn a college degree, was graduating from Cornell University. With the sale of his father's company, the job Sandy had expected to take after graduation vanished, and he was left to hit the streets of New York City looking for work. Although a New Yorker himself, he had no legacy connecting him to the local business elite. In fact, Weill learned through numerous rejections from Wall Street firms that the more prestigious companies were largely averse to hiring Jews. Or, if a company did hire Jews, it discriminated against Eastern European Jews like Weill, preferring descendants of the earlier German Jewish immigrants. Weill finally found his first job in 1955 as a messenger for Bear Stearns, a second-tier Wall Street brokerage at the time.

James Stillman, who was an Episcopalian, encountered no difficulties with religious prejudice, of course. He obtained his schooling in Westchester County, New York, and had his first job at sixteen in his father's cotton business, an enterprise prominent enough that the senior Stillman sat on several boards of directors, including that of National City Bank. With his father in failing health, James was granted power of attorney and headed up the family's business interests by age twenty-two. He grew close to Moses Taylor, then president of National City Bank, who became a key professional mentor. Taylor encouraged Stillman's involvement in railroad interests and helped further his business connections. Not that Stillman needed much help—

William Rockefeller, a brother of the famous John D. and a friend of Stillman's through common board memberships and family connections, was also prominent on National City's board. Stillman's sister had married a Rockefeller, and his daughters would each marry one of William's sons. In 1891, Taylor's son-in-law, Percy Pyne, president of National City Bank, died, purportedly having personally designated Stillman as his successor. At that time Stillman, just forty-one, took over the leadership post.

Weill, on the other hand, did not reach the top of Citigroup until age sixty-five. From that first job after college, he worked his way up to become a broker at Bear Stearns and then chipped in with friends to start a small brokerage house. Over some twenty years of mergers, it grew into one of the largest U.S. securities firms, Shearson Loeb Rhoades, which was sold to American Express in 1981. Weill became an executive at American Express as part of the deal, but lost the battle for CEO succession there and wound up quitting in 1985. At age fifty-two, he was looking for another chance at a top post, dangling his now significant financial assets to sweeten the package. He soon got his opportunity with Commercial Credit, which was being spun off by a troubled parent company. Weill invested some $7 million of his own money in the deal. Starting in 1986, when he took over the firm, he pursued steady growth through mergers and acquisitions that included Travelers Insurance, Salomon Brothers, and Smith Barney. In 1998, Weill, as CEO of Travelers, sought and negotiated a merger with Citicorp, the modern incarnation of National City Bank.

Admittedly, both Stillman's and Weill's successes extended to their offspring. Stillman's son, James Alexander Stillman, was president of National City from 1919 through 1921, and a grandson, James Stillman Rockefeller, had an even lengthier run heading the bank in the 1950s. Weill's son also worked for Citigroup during Weill's tenure, but Sandy's daughter, Jessica, has been the one with the higher-profile career. Cornell University–educated like her father, she became an executive in the brokerage industry, working on Wall Street for several years before joining Smith Barney, a Travelers subsidiary, in 1992. She left five years later to head a smaller brokerage house and in 2003, as CEO, took a start-up financial services company public. The following year, the enterprise, built through acquiring private financial-planning firms, showed over $600 million in income.

*James Stillman (left) headed the largest financial institution in America, National City Bank, at the turn of the twentieth century. Sandy Weill (right) led the present-day version of National City Bank under the name Citigroup at the turn of the twenty-first century.* (Sources: left, Picture History; right, Mark Peterson/CORBIS)

To recap our stories: one white man was an Episcopalian son of Colonial-era stock, with Rockefellers for in-laws; the other, a Jewish son of Polish immigrants, began his career armed only with a college degree. One had a son and grandson who ran the business after him, and the other had a daughter who, some people thought, might have done so, but who went on instead to develop a significant business of her own. A couple of white guys, yes, but do you still think that nothing has changed?

## The Myths and Changing Realities of Access

Hopefully, the sagas of Weill and Stillman suggest that the paths to power in U.S. business leadership have indeed changed over the past century. What appears closed today is significantly more open than before, but in respects not always apparent to the eye. In the past, moreover, some impressions of openness masked a significant degree of closure. Consider, for instance, the works of Horatio Alger.

"I hope, my lad, you will rise and prosper in the world. You know in this free country poverty in early life is no bar to a man's advancement," says the benevolent Mr. Whitney to a scrappy bootblack, Ragged Dick, the star of the 1868 Alger novel of the same name. By the end of the saga, young Dick, through honesty, courage, industriousness, and several incredibly fortunate encounters with patrons like Mr. Whitney, has risen to a clerk's job, now styling himself Richard Hunter, Esquire, described by a friend as "a young gentleman on the way to fame and fortune." Alger closes the book on a triumphant note: "He is Ragged Dick no longer. He has taken a step upward, and is determined to mount still higher."[1] Dick's tale was just the first of many Alger stories chronicling poor boys whose journeys to respectability took a similar path involving a heroic if unlikely mix of pluck and luck. The corpus is commonly cited, even by those who have never read a word of Alger, as the archetypal conception of American rags-to-riches mobility. Alger's books undeniably helped institutionalize a notion that has a mythical hold on American consciousness—the idea that anyone, anywhere, who makes an effort to advance in this nation can find success.

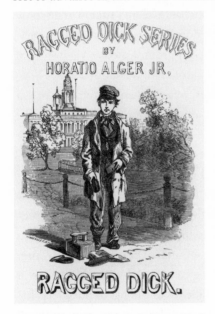

*Title-page book illustration of Horatio Alger's inspirational stories about Ragged Dick, a hard-working young man who rises from poverty to become wealthy and successful. Alger's stories contributed to the belief that in America anything is possible with hard work and determination.* (Source: CORBIS)

The stories also prove the point, however, that openness is a matter of perspective. A closer examination of Alger's first book reveals that this promise of mobility explicitly extends to a group of rather narrow scope. It's true that Alger tutored the children of Jewish financier Joseph Seligman in New York and purportedly found much inspiration for his stories in the rags-to-riches success of his employer.[2] But although Ragged Dick is dirt poor, orphaned, and uneducated when the story starts, there are several things he is definitely not. He is not Irish, Italian, Jewish, or Catholic. He is not from the South, nor is he African American, and he is most evidently not a woman. He is a nominally Protestant white male whose command of English grammar may be weak, but whose accent invokes no origin other than the New York streets. In short, no characteristics of race, sex, birthplace, or religious affiliation separate him from the mass of successful American business leaders of his day. After a series of incredibly fortunate encounters with kindly benefactors, a few grammar lessons, a good washing, and a new suit of clothes, Ragged Dick would face no particular barriers to traveling in the same company as James Stillman.

Imbedded deeply in the nation's most powerful parables about the society's openness to all comers is ironic testimony of its closure to many. As inspiring as Alger's stories were, they largely sidestepped the uncomfortable possibility that there existed barriers even harder to overcome than humble beginnings. This tension between the idealized openness and real closure in American social structure has continued to attract chroniclers on both sides in the 150 years since the Alger stories were first published. From Pitirim Sorokin's study of America's millionaires in the 1920s, to C. Wright Mills's identification of the Power Elite in the 1950s and Digby Baltzell's characterization of the Protestant establishment in the 1960s, to Michael Useem's Inner Circle study in the 1970s and 1980s, the suspicion that a dominant elite controls U.S. society, and U.S. businesses in particular, has been promulgated as vigorously as the rags-to-riches tales and melting-pot reputation of the United States.[3]

The issue's continued salience, moreover, reflects the presumption that it *matters* who leads businesses. Indeed, as the title of our book indicates, the paths to business leadership facilitate access not just to individual prosperity but to power—power that in this case includes the opportunity to shape industries, to control and allocate scarce resources, and, what is most important, to influence others' lives. Businesses have had such an impact on the literal and figurative landscape of America that we, like the scholars who preceded us, believe it is critically important to understand how this power was attained and who was able to grasp it. The identities of business leaders matter because of the expectation that those of a given class or category will favor their own in further business dealings, to the disadvantage of outsiders. Indeed, the democratic and egalitarian American ideals of opportunity for all have been consistently confronted by studies showing the reality of the country's class structure, societal prejudices, and the perpetuation of advantages, as well as disadvantages, over generations. The widening gap between the incomes of rich and poor in the nation is yet another indication that the barriers of power and class may become too great for the have-nots to overcome in search of opportunity.

Assertions of societal closure have prompted responses, of course. It seems no coincidence that clusters of scholarly studies on the composition of U.S. business leadership occurred in the wake of significant social upheaval in Russia. Marxist arguments, of course, provided the ultimate anti-Alger voice by emphasizing class rigidity rather than permeability as a consequence of capitalism. First, the Bolshevik Revolution spawned the era of Sorokin and F. W. Taussig and C. S. Joslyn. Sorokin, on the basis of a study of America's millionaires, asserted that America's wealthy class constituted a "caste-like group" (see chapter 6). Taussig and Joslyn undertook a study that, they claimed, produced results rebutting Sorokin's assertions. They nevertheless concluded that a caste-like class system as they defined it, while not yet in existence, appeared imminent in the United States.

Later, the early years of the Cold War produced the work of W. Lloyd Warner, James Abegglen, and Mabel Newcomer. Warner and Abegglen rebutted Taussig's and Joslyn's conclusions with statistics showing an increased openness in business leadership to individuals from working-class backgrounds (see chapter 6). Newcomer's findings generally agreed with Warner and Abegglen's, and she pointed to education's likely role in continuing to increase this openness of leadership to all social classes in coming generations (see chapter 5). Scholarly studies at different times thus have also reached different conclusions about whether access to leadership and power has become more or less open in the United States as time goes by.

With the close of the century came an apt moment to reexamine the picture and to gain, with a view stretching over multiple generations, an appreciation for the trends that have held and those that did not continue as predicted. In *Paths to Power*, we are particularly interested in how much the path has changed over the last hundred years and what that evolution portends for the future. Undeniably, certain individuals still traverse an inside track to business leadership while others outside the core group face a harder path to entrance, a path that tends to result in greater attrition of these outsiders' numbers along the way. External phenomena—legislation, economic upturns or downturns, wars, or cultural shifts—may facilitate changes in the lines of demarcation, but there is also evidence that change occurs organically and endogenously. Outsiders who penetrate the insider group are assimilated into it in some ways but also adulterate its uniformity by their presence, giving rise to increased openness for those who fit the profile of these *nouveau* insiders. Indeed, the extent of such changes over the century has, ironically, helped produce the contemporary viewpoint that race and sex, the most persistent parameters of insider-outsider demarcation, are the only distinctions relevant to a discussion of diversity.

For as much as three-quarters of the twentieth century, though, factors such as where you were born, who your parents were, and where you went to church were distinctions that mattered, and mattered very much, in the selection of business leadership. Some, if not all, appear to matter significantly less today. Do they really matter less? If so, how did this change happen? The questions remain important because any such changes have affected only the rules for entry, not the game itself, and the game is still one whose winners occupy dominant roles in society. A new and different kind of insider may emerge, but the advantages one holds over an outsider remain, and understanding the changes of the past can shed important light on the dilemmas of the present.

## Tracing the Paths of the Past

To provide new and worthwhile input into this conversation about the paths to U.S. business leadership, we wanted to compare not only statistics but individual stories of successful leaders over the past century. Following a sweep of careers and lives over several generations was, we felt, critical for the observation of meaningful change, because a career length extending twenty years or more after college, and, increasingly, graduate study, has become the typical prerequisite for success at the highest levels of business. Legislative initiatives of the 1960s and 1970s, along with changing attitudes toward women and racial minorities, are only beginning to show impact on the composition of top leadership. Focusing analysis solely on the dimensions of race and sex effectively limits consideration of change to little more than one generation. But insiders are still insiders, and outsiders are still outsiders, so the issues of today and yesterday share enough parallels to make comparisons with the past valuable and allow for some transfer of insights. The data we present illuminate not only how insiders and outsiders have been defined, but how those critical barrier-breaking journeys happened.

To conduct our exploration, we began with the thousand-member database, "Great American Business Leaders of the 20th Century," whose members were selected by researchers in the Harvard Business School Leadership Initiative. The database also served as the basis for our previous book, *In Their Time: The Greatest Business Leaders of the Twentieth Century*. While *In Their Time* tells the story of context-based leadership by analyzing how great leaders harnessed the macro-level environmental factors of their times to develop, grow, or reinvent businesses, *Paths to Power* explores the personal backgrounds of great business leaders to paint an evolving portrait of that leader over time. The perspectives complement each other by respectively articulating the *how* (*In Their Time*) and the *who* (*Paths to Power*) of American business leadership over the past century. The database and qualifications for leaders who were selected are described in more detail in the appendix.

Our candidate selection process provided a starting point different from prior studies of the demographics of business leaders. Earlier studies have tended to focus on those heading up America's largest corporations at one or more distinct points in time.[4] Our list casts a broader net for candidates by including a variety of enterprise sizes, but is also narrower in that it focuses on achievement rather than simple advancement. Many of those identified inherited a leadership role in the family business, for example, but they did not likewise inherit their places on this list—they earned the recognition by producing successful results. The individuals selected did not just happen to lead or found companies, but did so with distinction. While the list includes many who headed companies outside the *Fortune* 100 or its equivalent in their time, it in turn does not include all one hundred people on any such list. The level of selectivity results in a culling of approximately the top 10 to 20 percent of business leaders over the century.

By setting excellence as the key criterion rather than size of enterprise, we lost the ease of an objective bar for inclusion but gained the opportunity to examine characteristics of successful business leaders in America across time and across all roads to distinction. One person might start a company that, while small, endures and produces innovations that seed other companies; another person climbs a corporate ladder over several decades while turning competitive peers into cooperative colleagues; a third transforms a sleepy, maturing family business into a growth engine with a dramatically new focus, to name just a few possibilities. Each of these endeavors demands diverse qualities such as technical acumen, charisma, boldness, drive, patience, and business savvy, with different capabilities emphasized in the mix in each case. No single personality type is the obvious fit, for no one personality is likely to do all these things well.

In recognizing diverse paths to success, we have broadened the diversity of leaders considered for selection. Our list includes, along with prototypical business insiders, a good sampling of outsiders to common channels for business success. This combination allowed us to observe trends in access for groups with even marginal levels of inclusion in business, such as women and minorities. At the same time, the list does not ignore the firms and individuals most widely associated with American business success. In short, while the process identified more than just the usual suspects, the majority of these exceptional leaders still come from large industrial firms, reflecting the prominent place such companies held and still hold in the country's business structures. The increased variety of paths to success offers valuable ways to compare leader characteristics, but it by no means misrepresents the typical leader profile.

## Finding the Factors That Matter

In describing this profile, we focused on the dimensions of birthplace, religious affiliation, education, socioeconomic class, race, and sex. These factors commonly distinguished outsiders from insiders in U.S. business leadership over the century. With the exception of race and sex, our focal dimensions are virtually identical to those used in studies of prior eras. Consequently, some of our results can be compared with earlier studies, which can help validate our findings. The factors also match contemporary formulations for nondiscrimination in U.S. policy enactments—the classic "race, color, religion, sex, or national origin" language found in the Civil Rights Act of 1964, for instance. These factors have been acknowledged by the nation as being a basis of past discrimination, and have been banned from use in further discrimination. Although more recent antidiscrimination statutes may present new elements in the list (sexual orientation or disability status, for example), the markers that we analyze have the advantage of historical and public recognition. Because of that recognition, most of these characteristics may be obtained through biographical records even for persons long deceased.

Taking this range of factors into account, we argue that there have indeed been significant changes in the profile of business leaders during the twentieth century, even though, as acknowledged, most of the leaders throughout this period were white men. Percolating beneath the surface were the kinds of changes hinted at in the contrasting profiles of James Stillman and Sandy Weill. Figure 1-1, which groups leaders in rough generational increments on the basis of when they began their tenures as CEO (or started their companies, if entrepreneurs), offers one look at the century's dynamics by focusing on the occupations of the fathers of leaders across the eras.

FIGURE 1-1

## The changing picture of the occupations of the business leaders' fathers

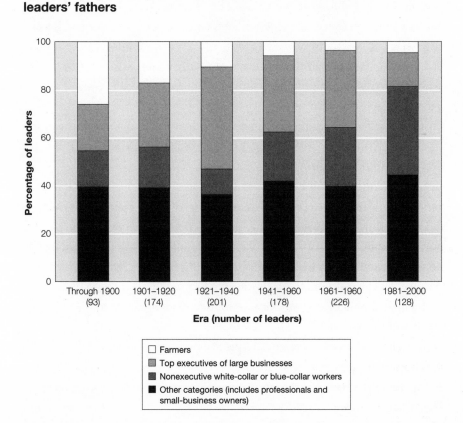

*Source*: HBS Leadership Initiative's "Great American Business Leaders of the 20th Century" database.
Data shown for leaders whose father's occupation is known; approximately 70–85 percent of leaders, depending on era.

The century's early leaders, including those who arose in the mid- to late nineteenth century, were predominantly entrepreneurs with fathers in small businesses and farming. Rather quickly, however, the foundational era of enterprise building gave birth to a legacy system that produced a significant share of the next generation's leaders. Well-established fathers who themselves had succeeded in business began to pass their own businesses, or at least the connections developed through those successes, to their offspring, providing head starts that brought significant advantages. With the rise of these well-ensconced fathers in the 1920s, we see a simultaneous trough in the proportion of leaders coming from more modest backgrounds. Almost as quickly, however, a new trend emerges at mid-century: leaders from working-class families begin to increase in representation while those with executive fathers plateau and ultimately diminish in percentage. For leaders emerging in the last two decades of the century, the children of workers outnumber the children of large-company executives. Alger's outlook notwithstanding, most leaders had middle-class backgrounds in every era but the first, when slightly more leaders were disadvantaged. Small-business owners and professionals continued to be represented in steady proportions of about 20 percent and 10 percent, respectively, throughout the eras. Still, by the century's end, there was a perceptible dilution in the pattern of "hand-me-down success" from top executive fathers to aspiring corporate leaders.

Other markers of this dilution, and the origins of it, are suggested by key variables for the leaders presented in figure 1-2. Without question, as the stories of Weill and Stillman reinforce, religion helped exclude (in the case of non-Protestants) or ratify (in the case of members of "prestige" denominations such as Episcopalians) candidates for business leadership during the century. As figure 1-2 indicates, however, education, notably the MBA, overtook religious affiliation in significance for determining access to leadership as the century progressed.

This chart provides a different perspective on the trip we just took through the century's leaders. At the beginning of the century, we see, as before, those entrepreneurs who formed the foundations of the country's often-characterized Protestant establishment. More specifically, Episcopalians and Presbyterians constitute the largest block of those for whom religious affiliation is known. During this era, even though most leaders were entrepreneurs, Jewish or Catholic leaders were very much on the outside of dominant leadership

FIGURE 1-2

## Education supplants religious status indicators

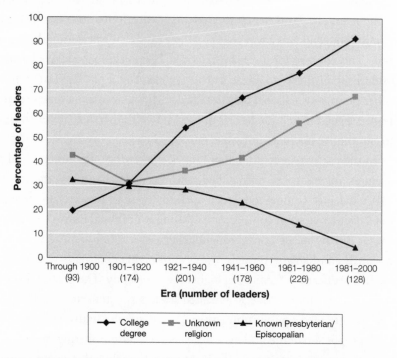

**Era (number of leaders)**

| College degree | Unknown religion | Known Presbyterian/ Episcopalian |

*Source*: HBS Leadership Initiative's "Great American Business Leaders of the 20th Century" database.

networks, and one's religious affiliation was a prominent part of one's public image, easily accessible to researchers looking for the information a century or more later. Though relatively few leaders were college graduates, those who were had mostly attended the Ivy League institutions, a natural outgrowth of their relatively prestigious roots.

The steep uptick in college education for leaders from 1921 to 1940 signals the new era of more affluent leaders, many of them second-generation heads of family businesses. This era also matches the peak in leaders who were children of executives, as shown in figure 1-1. Many of these leaders were the sons of entrepreneurs who lacked college education themselves but saw it as the way to establish their sons as part of the business elite that they themselves had entered through perseverance and prosperity. The prototypical "professional manager"—that is, a CEO who rose within a company without being part of its founding family—was also emerging in this period, and college was typically part of such a leader's background. The prerequisites for a professional manager's path tended to be credentials that matched the profile of existing managers. This match in credentials substituted for the previous era's family connections as a way to precertify a candidate's fit within the organization. This concern for fit meant that mid-century leaders were educated not exclusively in the Ivy League but in a wider blend of "Big Ten" schools or other prestigious regional colleges. These Midwestern alma maters made the leaders a good match for careers in the Midwest's then-expanding businesses in automotive manufacturing and fabricated goods.

In the last two generational groups of the century, the professional management role was well entrenched, and fast on its heels was the rise of the MBA, a degree coming to be seen as certifying not just a socially desirable fit but a distinctive set of competencies. Rising educational norms spurred on by the GI Bill in the late 1940s brought college educations to more and more individuals and likewise brought those multiplying collegians within reach of graduate education, facilitating higher levels of study. The greater diversity of backgrounds among college-educated leaders was reflected in the kinds of colleges attended—public universities of no particular status made up a significant proportion of the undergraduate degrees, outnumbering the Ivy League schools in representation. At the same time, though, MBA degrees at prestigious schools often supplemented less-prestigious undergraduate degrees. Apparently, high-status graduate degrees now provided the kinds of alumni networks enjoyed by those with undergraduate Ivy educations earlier in the century. The increasing detachment of professional networks from religious institutions was unmistakable—two-thirds of leaders had no identifiable religious affiliation. Jewish and Catholic leaders were now mixing into management circles with little or no evidence of the outsider status that previously limited their involvement.

## What Paves the Avenues of Access?

This quick scan over the century helps explain our conclusion that U.S. business leadership is in a continuing state of flux regarding these attributes of openness and closure. Those who stress the societal openness described by Alger and those who emphasize the closed nature of the business elite have each persisted in their stories for a reason. The picture of access we find is time-sensitive and contingent rather than uniformly progressive or retrogressive. At any time, the answer to whether a person with a given set of characteristics could succeed in business was neither yes nor no, but rather "Yes, if . . ." Yes, if the aspiring leader found a way around whatever obstacles those characteristics created in the path to success. Discovering the enabling contingencies—the stories behind the ifs—allows us to move beyond generalizations and statistics to reveal the evolution of American business leadership and America itself during the twentieth century.

To get at these stories, as well as to capture the sense of the century as it unfolds, our chapters focus on the selected dimensions in turn: birthplace within the United States (chapter 2), nationality for those born outside the U.S. (chapter 3), religious affiliation (chapter 4), education (chapter 5), and socioeconomic class (chapter 6). Chapter by chapter, we share stories that illustrate when and where each of these aspects of personal background mattered most and how transitions occurred. The chapter order reflects the trend of each characteristic's impact and persistence as a factor in the composition of business leadership. Birthplace and religious affiliation were important factors early in the century and became less important over time, whereas education showed the opposite pattern, becoming significantly more important as the century went along. Finally, socioeconomic class has had a remarkably consistent level of impact—its role was neither as extreme as predicted by the trends early in the century nor fully neutralized by the century's end. In chapter 7, we turn to the situation of women and racial minorities, the ultimate outsiders whose progress inward can mainly be traced over just the last few decades. We close with chapter 8—an assessment of what the future may hold for U.S. business leadership.

Understanding the evolving characteristics of leaders tells us not just about these people but about America, because, of course, any leader needs followers. Across the array of industries and firms, this need remains a unifying factor: to attain excellence, leaders need others willing to follow them or offer support. While we selected leaders for this study on the basis of merit, opportunity was a prerequisite for their careers. To attain success, leaders required a lot more than the new suit of clothes that paved Ragged Dick's way, and benefactors, for leaders who had them, were not provided by a helpful author to secure a happy ending. Access to something—a job at minimum, plus maybe some training or capital—was the first step toward realizing the promise of their talents. The ease with which such access was gained differentiates an insider's road to success from an outsider's. Prejudice was obviously a relevant factor in making access more difficult.

The country's educational shifts, economic development, military activities, and domestic policy initiatives have all played their part in shaping the leadership pipeline, often helping outsiders to overcome the prejudices working against them. Education could blur differences in background by providing insiders and outsiders with the common credential of a college degree or an MBA. Geographic areas where rapid economic development was under way, as it was in the West early in the century, tended to present lower barriers against outsiders seeking to enter business. The need to harness the efforts of *all* citizens during wartime meant that factors such as religious affiliation and parental status were minimized in favor of finding the most capable individuals to meet the country's needs. The ties formed among diverse individuals who were mingled by necessity during a war effort often translated to professional networks after the war ended. Finally, the GI Bill after World War II is an example of a domestic policy initiative that made college degrees and postgraduate study affordable for veterans from all socioeconomic classes, improving their access to leadership networks.

Although U.S. history formed a common backdrop for leaders over the century, the contingencies that supported access to opportunity can be most clearly seen at an individual level. In the stories of leaders, we identified four key themes shaping their paths to power: place, personal networks, professional credentials, and perseverance. Not every story displays every theme, but the themes tend to operate in a compensatory way. Lack of any single theme in a given leader's rise to power is usually made up for by increased reliance on one of the other three.

### Place

For the insider, *place* generally meant having been born in an area where numerous strong and thriving businesses already existed. Early in the century, there was a striking correlation between the distribution of leader birthplaces and existing concentrations of U.S. industry, with both centered in urban areas of the Northeast and Midwest (see chapter 2). Being an established native in these regions, even for those not fortunate enough to find success within a family business, offered the chance to exploit existing local affinities or the network of connections with immediate family and friends. The more well-to-do the family, of course, the greater the benefit of such connections, but relatively modest local ties might still provide sufficient credibility to get an entry-level job, a start-up loan, or an appointment to make a sales pitch. Over two-thirds of our leaders whose tenures began in 1900 or earlier established themselves in the regions where they were born. Movement from the South to the North, given that the Civil War was only a generation or two past, was particularly rare, and Southerners needed strong personal connections to pave the way for any such transition.

Those born outside the opportunity hubs of the Northeast or Midwest, including those born outside the United States entirely, typically followed one of two alternative paths to success. The first was to start operating as a big fish in a small pond, leveraging status in a region with minimal developed industry to build a business that could ultimately transcend local boundaries or provide a launching point into higher business circles. This path suited some Southerners or rural Midwesterners and attracted early immigrants to those same regions. The second path required finding a frontier: outsiders fared best in rapidly developing locations, particularly in the West. There, the growth of opportunity left so much open turf, it could not be bounded by effective barriers to entry. Such frontiers presented the greatest possibilities for immigrants (see chapter 3). Whether in a small pond or expanding frontier, once an outsider attained a significant degree of material prosperity, the credential of wealth was potent enough to qualify that person as an insider in at least some measure. As a result, the individual gained passage on previously closed avenues of access into the social and business circles of established industrial centers.

### Personal Networks

For the true insider, the benefit of personal networks is obvious. The most advantaged players were born into or married into families that already controlled a successful business or were otherwise wealthy or influential. While we can readily track the parentage of leaders, their marital networks are virtually impossible to map fully—marital networks played a role in many stories we tell and doubtless figured in many others. Marriage could expand a leader's personal network, but because, particularly early in the century, marriage partners were typically chosen from others of similar status and religion, marriage was unlikely to turn an outsider into an insider overnight. In other words, marriage was mostly an avenue that helped the rich get richer. Not surprisingly, individuals with high-status backgrounds and personal networks commensurate with that status showed signs of dominating business interests by the 1920s (chapter 6). Family ties and money even constituted barrier breakers powerful enough to bring leadership opportunities to relative outsiders such as foreign-born men (chapter 3) and white women (chapter 7) in eras when the presence of either group in top corporate circles was quite extraordinary.

For a person without the advantage of blood ties to powerful networks, links to success might be made in other ways. The exceptionally bright student might attend a prestigious educational institution, even on scholarship, thus winning classmates as friends and gaining credibility with fellow alumni. During both world wars, military service mixed individuals of different classes in ways that promoted such networks of loyalty and helped break through religious or status barriers (chapters 4 and 6). Involvement in politics at a grassroots level, where the field is open to volunteers from a variety of backgrounds, could result in friends in high places for those lucky enough to back a winning candidate. All these upward paths into networking, however, were decidedly more open to, and in the earlier part of the century almost exclusively benefited, native-born white men who shared the religious affiliation and ethnic characteristics of the insider majority.

At first it may appear that outsiders had no networks to leverage, except networks formed with insiders through schooling, wartime service, or political involvement. The stories of those who found success suggest otherwise, however. As we discuss in chapters 3 and 4, immigrants or members of religious minorities often capitalized on contacts and business partnerships within networks of their coaffiliated communities. African Americans also began businesses by offering products or services to members of their minority group who were underserved or not served at all by established companies (chapter 7). Female entrepreneurs early in the century paralleled this practice, marketing in sectors where women were the primary consumers. The profit potential of a niche business was limited, however, by the prospects for widespread adoption of its products and services. If the offerings suited the needs of those in the majority culture, and if the outsider status of those who sold them posed little deterrent to majority acceptance, large-scale success was possible. Among outsider groups, white women thus generally faced the best possibilities to establish prominent businesses, and did so in arenas like cosmetics, food, and fashion. The constraints on the reach of businesses started by Jewish, Catholic, or foreign-born leaders likewise diminished over the century, but enterprises begun by African Americans were most likely to be restricted in size by this barrier.

### Professional Credentials

Becoming a business leader in the early part of the century was, unlike practicing law or medicine, a pursuit that required no training or credentials. As will be discussed in chapter 5, college educations were then atypical among businessmen and, when attained, functioned more as a signal of parental status or a vehicle for accessing peer networks than a verification of skills needed in the business world. Specialized training, particularly in law, science, or engineering, did offer a path into business success, as those skills brought recognizable value in certain settings. Professionals who gained influential corporate posts on the basis of their area of expertise could, over time, leverage those roles to gain general management positions. For outsiders, education was more important, as the credibility it offered seemed particularly critical in overcoming resistance to their entry. Foreigners who succeeded had much higher education levels, on average, than did the mass of immigrants, and African American leaders were proportionately more educated than even successful white insiders. Rather than being a luxury, educational credentials may have been a necessity for an outsider to offset other traits that stigmatized him or her in the eyes of insiders.

As the century progressed and educational levels in the United States rose overall, however, graduate business education emerged as a norm for successful leaders. Our analysis shows that, within a few decades of the establishment of graduate business schools, the MBA degree became a key professional credential in business. By the end of the century, evidence suggested the formation of a new insider status conferred by this degree—one powerful enough to supersede some of the barriers against previous outsider groups.

The solidification of this norm, however, places a new focus on access to the MBA itself, which is a point we address in our final chapter.

## Perseverance

Perseverance constituted the final means by which those striving for success could make up for disadvantages in place, personal networks, or professional credentials. High levels of effort and endurance, often beyond all reasonable expectation, were much more common in the stories of outsiders than in those of insiders. Perseverance figures prominently in the successes of immigrants (chapter 3), non-Protestant religious affiliates (chapter 4), those of lower socioeconomic classes (chapter 6), and, of course, women and African Americans (chapter 7). This perseverance was primarily manifested through entrepreneurship—those facing a difficult path in established businesses took on the added challenge of building one from the ground up, which required a greater commitment of time and resources and entailed a higher risk of failure. The degree of outsider stigma attached to a particular group is often indicated by the extent to which its members' paths to success involved business start-ups—African American women on our list win the dubious prize in this case, as every one of them succeeded through entrepreneurship. Perseverance might require not just starting new businesses but breaking ground on new industries, which foreign-born leaders in particular did to a noteworthy degree (chapter 3). Similar to territory on a geographic frontier, the boundaries of an industry in the process of formation are more permeable to outsiders. At the same time, such pursuits involve yet more risk and effort for the potential reward.

Perseverance was not a quality exclusive to entrepreneurs, however. The growth of large industrial companies in the second half of the century prompted the formation of career ladders for systematic management development that allowed certain kinds of outsiders to accumulate insider status through the course of long advancement in a single company. The entry point was typically a low-level job that required no prestigious family connection or Ivy League degree. This was a case where, as with the tortoise and the hare, slow and steady wins the race. Nevertheless, the race remained a venue that for many years explicitly, and for a longer time implicitly, included only white men who already matched at least the surface-level insider characteristics. The rules for success on this path were weighted rather heavily in favor of those who could fit in well, meaning the path primarily helped break barriers for white men with the relatively invisible disadvantage of lower socioeconomic backgrounds (chapter 6). Moreover, persevering to win this particular race to the top generally delivered access only to a company-specific, or at best an industry-specific, scope of opportunity for one's pains.

## Signposts for Future Access Trends

In the end, whether their access to opportunity was hand-delivered or hard-won, all of our subjects managed to gain some payoff of success, which brought them happy endings of the kind Alger might have written. Regardless of origins, religion, race, sex, or creed, *yes* was ultimately the answer to the question of whether business leadership was open to them, even when the initial *if* attached to the answer imposed conditions that amounted to Herculean labors. These individuals either had credibility or earned it, and they found ways to prosper. Recognizing the reality of both the successes and the associated struggles neither trumps Alger nor trumpets his stories as anything other than fiction. The significance of our exercise is, rather, to explore how the characteristics of these highly successful leaders may have affected their journeys and how these men and women found advantages or overcame disadvantages in drawing on the factors of place, personal networks, professional credentials, and perseverance.

However they got there, the leaders on our list became members of an elite and powerful element in society. By the end of the twentieth century, many of those aspirants who had climbed the corporate career ladder rung by rung were finding that the distinctions that had mattered when they were at the bottom had blurred once they reached the top. True, the group's homogeneity in terms of race and sex displays only slight changes, but religion and birthplace, to name two previously salient factors, have largely vanished from conversations about leader selection. The MBA credential shows signs of becoming a new cloak of uniformity behind which, in terms of leadership access, other differences might be rendered almost invisible. Late-century trends showing broader access to graduate degrees in business, particularly by women, are only starting to bear fruit as a new century begins. The benefits of this new ticket for admission may still be distributed unevenly for different socioeconomic groups, however, and we can expect that sources of leverage other than professional credentials will continue to matter and may even increase in importance as the MBA becomes ubiquitous. For those who desire to see the diversity in American business leadership grow even greater, discovering just how leadership composition has developed to this point gives insights into the next leg of the journey. The story, we believe, is indeed worth telling and reading, as the questions we consider for the twentieth century may offer answers for the twenty-first.

# TWO

# Birthplace

## Exploiting the Power of Place

*"Have you always lived in New York, Dick?" asked Frank, after a pause.*
*"Ever since I can remember."*

—Horatio Alger, Jr., *Ragged Dick*

UNDERSTANDING the distinctions created by one's birthplace, even within the United States, provides a powerful starting point for considering the framework that separated outsiders from insiders in business leadership in the twentieth century. It's easy to forget both how divided the country was by the Civil War and how different the various regions still were in terms of population and industrial development in the early 1900s. By beginning our story with this consideration of place, we'll establish how each of the country's major regions—Northeast, Midwest, West, and South—offered advantages or disadvantages to leaders who were born there. This process will also provide an overview of the distinctions among the various regions as sites for success, in that a region's characteristics are revealed not just through the experiences of its own natives, but through the characteristics of those who were from other parts of the United States and who were able to succeed there. The Northeast was in general a seat of opportunity, but mainly for its own natives or for those from well-established families in the similarly industrialized Midwest. The West, with less-formalized social and business structures, plus rapid growth, proved a wide-open magnet for all comers, particularly entrepreneurs. The South, with little industrial development and a weaker economic foundation earlier in the century, tended to lag in the production of leader successes.

Given his start in the Northeast, therefore, we find that Alger's hero, Ragged Dick, is at least in this respect by no means disadvantaged. More particularly, his New York roots gave him something in common with a significant share of the prominent leaders on our list. More leaders were born in New York than the next two highest states (Pennsylvania and Illinois) combined. The U.S. West and all foreign countries put together did not produce as many leaders as New York did, and even more surprising, the state's total exceeded that of the entire South. In all, 16 percent of our successful leaders were born in New York.

Interpreting the significance of statistics such as these regarding our set of leaders is admittedly speculative—after all, we are examining a group of individuals who attained success and we are attempting, post hoc, to understand what aspects of their background were linked to that achievement. Without a control group of individuals matched to them in relevant factors such as birth year, it's impossible to confirm the qualities that most distinguished our successful individuals from their peers. New York, for instance, was and is a very populous state—can we be sure that the distribution of our leader births is even unusual? For the sake of exploratory comparison in this study, we will commonly draw on census statistics to offer at least one reference point regarding how much the characteristics of this leader group differ from the likely representation if a sample had been drawn at random from a comparable general population. These directional differences suggest the kinds of attributes that set our leaders apart and that thus might be associated with their success.

Applying this kind of comparison, we discover that, while New York was indeed the country's most populous state from the 1830s through the 1960s, at no time after the 1880s did it contain much more than 10 percent of the U.S. population, making it decisively overrepresented on this basis among leaders on our list.[1] About a quarter of the businesses represented by these leaders overall were, admittedly, based in New York, which presents one explanation for the state's prominence as a birthplace. However, both this proportion and New York's share of population display a slight downward trend over the century, while the proportion of leaders from New York, despite an early dip, appears reinvigorated at the century's end (figure 2-1).

**FIGURE 2-1**

## New York's prominence in leadership not a passing phenomenon

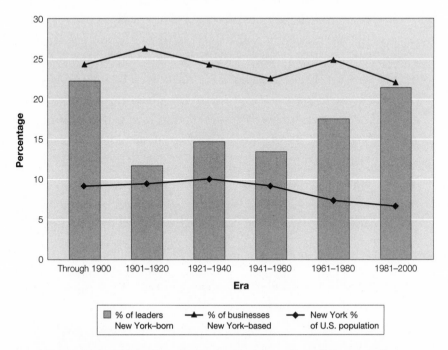

*Source*: HBS Leadership Initiative's "Great American Business Leaders of the 20th Century" database.

Percentages calculated by era for ascending leaders and businesses they led; population figures for close of era.

The most self-evident conclusion from this observation is that opportunity begets opportunity. New York's business base attracted many newcomers, but it primarily supplied an edge for its own natives in leadership. In fact, the match of successful business leaders' origins with regions of established business is a phenomenon observable outside New York as well. The distribution of birthplaces of U.S.-born leaders in the early part of the century corresponds most strikingly with the country's industrialization, not its population. Of the U.S. leaders ascending before 1950, a little over 17 percent were born in New York; in 1880, the median birth year of these leaders, this state housed just under 17 percent of the country's manufacturing establishments.[2] While not all the state-by-state comparisons align that closely, the pattern holds remarkably well for the five census divisions providing the largest share of business leaders in this period (figure 2-2).

This pattern of successful business leaders emerging from the shadow of established enterprise left the more industrialized states comparatively overrepresented at the expense of rural regions, particularly the South. This region, of course, included in its population a significant proportion of African Americans, who were largely disenfranchised as candidates for business leadership at the time. Still, the origins of pre-1950s leaders correspond more closely with the distribution of manufacturing establishments than even with the distribution of native white adult males of prime working age at the turn of the century.[3]

FIGURE 2-2

### Origins of early U.S.-born leaders conform to manufacturing regions

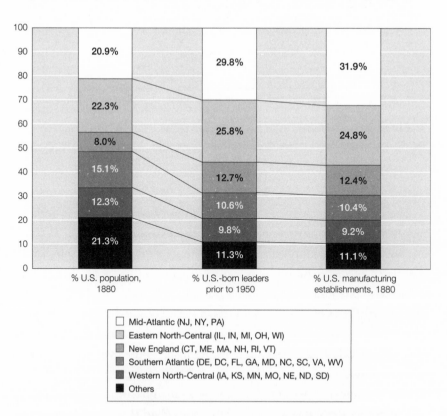

| | | |
|---|---|---|
| □ Mid-Atlantic (NJ, NY, PA) | | |
| ▨ Eastern North-Central (IL, IN, MI, OH, WI) | | |
| ▨ New England (CT, ME, MA, NH, RI, VT) | | |
| ▨ Southern Atlantic (DE, DC, FL, GA, MD, NC, SC, VA, WV) | | |
| ▨ Western North-Central (IA, KS, MN, MO, NE, ND, SD) | | |
| ■ Others | | |

*Source*: HBS Leadership Initiative's "Great American Business Leaders of the 20th Century" database.

## New Yorkers in an Advantaged Place

Virtually all the paths to success in business—inheriting business leadership, being hired as a manager into an existing business, and even founding a business—are more likely to be available to those born in areas where businesses are already concentrated. New York was the natural winner of this geographic lottery at the start of the twentieth century, but the victory was by no means confined to New York City, the metropolis that a current-day reader would consider the business nexus of the state. On the contrary, New York's prosperity as a site for leaders from the earliest part of the century was driven by a wave of industrialization in the upper middle portion of the state, occasioned by the development of the Erie Canal, which opened in 1825. The canal, of course, also channeled trade down the Hudson River and through New York City, bringing the city to prominence as an East Coast port. As proof of the advantage that the canal helped bring to New York State, close to 64 percent of our native New York State leaders who ascended to success in the first half of the century did it via an enterprise in that state. Such home-state success was enjoyed by only about 35 percent of other U.S.-born leaders in that era. The proportion of in-state success drops to just over half for New Yorkers ascending in 1950 or later, but this figure still well exceeds the comparable proportion for other U.S.-born leaders—a figure that remained around one-third. For the century as a whole, only the states of California and Texas bettered New York's proportions of stay-at-home success. These two states, much larger geographically, offered their own significant pockets of opportunity but also were relatively remote from other options. Combined, they still produced only about a third as many leaders as New York did.

A classic illustration of the process by which industry begets industry and existing business begets leaders is provided in the emergence of typewriter manufacturing in upstate New York, a story that features multiple links to the Erie Canal. The typewriter industry placed six leaders on our list, four of them New York born, and all associated with New York enterprises. The story of the typewriter began, however, not in New York but in Milwaukee, where Christopher Latham Sholes, the man generally credited with creating the first practical typewriter, was living in the late 1860s. Sholes was born in Pennsylvania but was of New England ancestry extending back to the iconic Pilgrim couple, Priscilla and John Alden.[4] He had moved westward and built a career

*The Erie Canal played an integral role in the development of industry throughout New York.* (Source: CORBIS)

as a newspaper publisher before becoming intrigued with the possibility of creating a new, automated printing device.

Sholes and his financial backer, James Densmore, struggled to develop an efficient production environment in the Midwest for the promising invention. Attempts to set up manufacturing in both Chicago and Milwaukee failed, as the workers available could only handcraft machines, making production too costly. Urged by G. W. N. Yost, a former business partner of Densmore's, Sholes and Densmore looked for help at the Remington Arms company, a business that arguably constituted the era's hub of manufacturing innovation. These advantages of industrialization thus served to pull Sholes's valuable business opportunity from the Midwest back to the Northeast. The Remington plant was in Ilion, New York, situated right on the Erie Canal, and Yost had grown up in Yates County, about 125 miles southwest of Ilion in the Finger Lakes region of waterways that were also linked to the canal.[5] Remington Arms had prospered in weapons sales during the Civil War, and the company's expertise in mechanical tools and mass production—capabili-

ties developed in the production of rifles—offered possibilities for the manufacture of other goods. Ongoing attempts to diversify into agricultural tools
and sewing machines, among other items, had as yet garnered only modest
success.

It was therefore with some eagerness that a young Remington executive,
Henry H. Benedict, examined a piece of correspondence from Densmore
concerning Sholes's invention. The letter itself, naturally, provided eye-
catching testimony of the breakthrough nature of the machine, as it was rendered in printed type. In 1873, mechanical printing was used only for books,
periodicals, and advertisements—correspondence was always handwritten.
Benedict, a local boy born within a few miles of Ilion, was well educated for
his era, having attended seminary courses and the Eastman Business College
in Poughkeepsie before graduating from nearby Hamilton College in 1869,
upon which he immediately began working for the Remingtons, advancing
into management in their sewing-machine business.[6] Seeing the unique missive in Philo Remington's office, Benedict encouraged the company president
to follow up regarding the device. Densmore and Yost brought a working
typewriter to the Remingtons for demonstration and, in no small part because of Benedict's enthusiasm, the company took on production of the machines, under the leadership of a key sewing-machine engineer. The earliest
Remington model betrays his influence on its design: the typewriter, enclosed
in a metal casing painted with floral decoration, was affixed to a small work-
table with wrought-iron legs. A round dial on the right side, looking almost
identical to a sewing-machine wheel, operated the carriage return via a cord
attached to a foot treadle.[7]

Acceptance of the new device by the public was slow. At a price tag of $125,
the machine was expensive, and a trained operator was considered necessary
for its use. Densmore and Yost initially served as sole sales agents, with discouraging results. The Remingtons began driving sales in 1875, first outsourc-
ing the task to the Fairbanks Company, a highly successful manufacturer of
commercial scales, and then forming an in-house sales team in 1881. Clarence
Seamans, the young manager heading the sales effort at Fairbanks, was then
hired by the Remingtons in an appointment championed by Benedict. Seamans, an Ilion native, had taken his first job at age fifteen in the Remington
gun factory, working alongside his father.[8] In 1882, Benedict and Seamans

*An 1870s version of the E. Remington
& Sons typewriter sat on a cast-iron
stand and included a foot treadle (similar to sewing machines of the same era)
to operate the carriage return.* (Source:
Getty Images)

purchased the contract for sales of the Remington machine, forming a partnership with another zealous typewriter salesman, William Wyckoff of
Ithaca (a city on the tip of Cayuga Lake, yet another of the "fingers" linked to
the canal). The troika made great strides, steadily increasing annual unit sales
from under twenty-three hundred in 1882 to almost four thousand by 1884.[9]

In 1886, however, as Remington became weighed down by financial troubles, Benedict got wind that the company might sell the typewriter business.
He traveled to Ilion and, by his own account, tried, out of loyalty to his old
employer, to convince Philo Remington that the asset held too much promise
to be sold.[10] When it became clear that Remington had his mind set on selling
and would not be persuaded otherwise, Benedict made an offer to buy the
business. Under this new ownership, Remington-branded typewriters found
both the manufacturing stability and marketing acumen to attain lasting popularity and lead the field in both the United States and Europe, assuring
Benedict and Seamans of their places on our list of successful leaders. Indeed,
Benedict's prophecy to Remington would be proven right, as the typewriter
company prospered while the remaining Remington Arms business went into
bankruptcy and was sold by the family in 1888.[11]

In 1893, Remington Typewriter became the anchor for a "trust" of smaller producers organized as the Union Typewriter Company, headed by Seamans. Among the manufacturers encompassed by the trust was the Smith-Premier Typewriter Company, a family typewriter enterprise based in Syracuse, about seventy miles due west of Ilion, on a spur of the Erie Canal. Like the Remingtons, the Smiths began in gun manufacture and branched out to produce other machinery. In 1903, the Smith brothers, restless to develop their own machine so they could offer a visible typing display (early typewriters printed on paper as it passed within the machine's casing), broke from the Union fold and reestablished an independent business.[12] In 1920, the Smiths merged with the maker of Corona portable typewriters, forming Smith-Corona Typewriters, another long-term industry success. Both Wilbert and Hurlburt Smith, the latter born in New York after the family moved from Connecticut, appear on our list. A company brochure of the 1930s would emphasize the firm's manufacturing heritage, noting that "men in whose blood runs the very instinct of generations of fine work—men whose fathers and grandfathers engraved the gunstocks of the famed Smith guns" were the ones now skillfully making its typewriters.[13]

In 1927, Remington Typewriter merged with the Rand Corporation, a maker of registers and ledger systems for business recordkeeping. Rand originated as a family business near Tonawanda, New York, a town situated at the western end of the Erie Canal along the Niagara River. The merged company was called Remington-Rand and was led by James Rand, another New Yorker on our list. When he announced the Remington-Rand electric typewriter in 1948, Rand invoked the company's historic regional legacy: "The future of the typewriter will be guided not only by the inspiring example of Christopher Latham Sholes, but also by the tradition of E. Remington & Sons and their ingenuity in manufacturing."[14] In 1955, Remington-Rand merged with Sperry Products, one of several technology-related businesses started by New Yorker Elmer Sperry, yet another of our leaders. As the Sperry-Rand Corporation, the company would be an early participant in the computer industry, linking the typewriter to a new wave of technology that would ultimately carry Sholes's distinctive keyboards into the twenty-first century. Thus continued the chain of one successful enterprise after another, all in New York, and mostly run by New Yorkers. Such stories as these helped maintain the prominence of New York business leaders for over a century.

## Privileged Outsiders Gain Northeastern Access

As helpful as it was to be born in New York, and perhaps especially along the Erie Canal, the region also offered more than enough opportunity for new-comers—about 43 percent of the leaders in our database succeeded in compa-nies based in the Northeast, more than half of those in New York, meaning that a goodly proportion of outsiders succeeded there in addition to locals. In the Northeast, there were more successful leaders who had been born outside the region than the total number of leaders succeeding in either the South or the West. Breaking into business leadership in the hub of activity, and hence social structure, wasn't always easy, however. A certain level of prosperity, ac-companied by personal connections, understandably might enhance one's chances. As a result, many leaders who succeeded in moving into the North-east from elsewhere in the United States were the product of families that had attained some status in a less competitive region. These transplants found their springboard into the Northeast in the second or third generation of business success. Nearly two-thirds of newcomers to the Northeast had wealthy or middle-class backgrounds, while less than 59 percent of U.S.-born newcomers to the South, Midwest, or West were as prosperous.[15] Well over half of the U.S.-born outsiders who succeeded in the Northeast originated in the next-most-industrialized Midwestern states—of these business leaders, more than 70 percent were from middle-class or wealthy backgrounds.

Two Midwesterners who led businesses in the Northeast have a unique claim on our list: they are brothers who succeeded in distinct businesses and industries, neither one a family concern. Gordon and Frederick Rentschler were sons of a prosperous patriarch who positioned them to become big fish in an even bigger pond than he had to offer. Though one biographical re-source calls Gordon an "Ohio farm boy," his father, George Rentschler, a German immigrant who entered America with his family at age six, had started a successful foundry and machine manufacturing business in Hamil-ton, Ohio, a town some forty miles southwest of Dayton along the Great Miami River.[16] Hamilton, not unlike the towns of upstate New York, had prospered industrially in the mid-nineteenth century as a result of canal building. It was served by a spur of Ohio's Miami-Erie Canal, which allowed northward navigation that had been impossible on the Great Miami. Once the spur canal was built, goods from the region could safely travel either south to the Ohio River or north to Lake Erie and further east via the Erie Canal it-self, maximizing available markets and suppliers. Gordon and Frederick were born in the 1880s. They were children of their father's second marriage, when he was around forty and his business career was in full blossom.[17] Accordingly, by the time the boys were ready for college, the elder Rentschler's resources were sufficient to send both to Princeton University. Gordon graduated in 1907 as president of his class, and Frederick graduated two years later. Each son returned to the family business in Ohio to start his career.

For Gordon, his ties back East came into play after the catastrophic Ohio floods of 1913, which caused extensive damage to Dayton, Hamilton, and other towns along the Great Miami River. In the aftermath of the disaster, the state instituted a conservancy program to help develop regional infra-structure for flood prevention. In 1915, Gordon, who at age thirty was just as-suming the presidency of the family's foundry and machinery business, was appointed one of three project trustees.[18] He became instrumental in secur-ing over $30 million in bond financing for the work, working closely with National City Company, a securities affiliate of New York's National City Bank. Charles Mitchell, newly minted president of National City Company at the time, would become president of the bank in 1921. That same year, 1921, when the bank's sugar interests in Cuba fell into financial turmoil, Mitchell turned to Gordon for help, remembering Rentschler's familiarity with sugar mill machinery, one of the lines manufactured by his family's business. So valuable did Gordon Rentschler's industry connections and knowledge prove to be that he was made the youngest member of National City's board of directors in 1923. It wasn't long before these New York busi-ness activities began to dominate Rentschler's time, and by 1925, he became a vice president of the bank, assistant to Mitchell and the recognized heir apparent. After just four years—a meteoric rise in the eyes of contempo-raries—Rentschler, forty-three, assumed the bank presidency when Mitchell ascended to chairman.[19] The bond between Rentschler and his mentor tight-ened further when Gordon and Frederick's younger brother, George, mar-ried Mitchell's daughter in 1936.[20] Gordon served as president until 1940, when he likewise became chairman, holding that post until his death in 1948. His end came, ironically enough, in the place where his success with Na-tional City began—he died on vacation in Havana shortly after returning from a visit to a sugar mill.[21]

Gordon's brother Frederick also leveraged machinery expertise for success in the Northeast, but in a very different field. In 1917, he enlisted in the war effort for World War I, inspecting aircraft engines for the army at a New Jersey plant of Wright-Martin, the firm that continued the legacy of aviation pioneers Orville and Wilbur Wright and Glenn L. Martin. Frederick became engrossed in the study and development of aircraft engines, and after the war, he headed up a reconstituted Wright Aeronautical Corporation, also in New Jersey. He resigned in 1924, however, frustrated with financial backers unwilling to invest at the level he felt was necessary to create a next generation of lighter, air-cooled (rather than liquid-cooled) aircraft engines.

In 1925, as Gordon was settling into his work at National City, Frederick Rentschler plunged into entrepreneurship, starting Pratt & Whitney Aircraft Engines. His family business ties provided a crucial jumpstart in making the connection with the source of his seed capital and initial manufacturing plant. Pratt & Whitney, in Hartford, Connecticut, was a subsidiary of toolmaker Niles-Bement-Pond, which had its roots in Niles Tool Works, a company based in Hamilton, Ohio, since the 1860s.[22] The president of Niles-Bement-Pond, James K. Cullen, was an old family friend, and Gordon was a recently elected board member. Frederick approached Pratt & Whitney with a letter of introduction from Cullen, and the deal was quickly done. The younger

Rentschler then attracted some of the best engineers from Wright to join him in his new venture, and that same year, the first "Wasp" air-cooled engine was developed. Along with its more powerful sister, the "Hornet," the "Wasp" and its successor models quickly became engines of choice for civilian and military aircraft. In 1928, Pratt & Whitney Aircraft was merged with Boeing Airlines and Chance Vought into United Aircraft, with Frederick at its head. In 1931, he turned several acquisitions in air transport into the United Air Lines subsidiary, the first transcontinental airline, although just three years later, legislation breaking up the aviation conglomerates forced its spin-off.

*Frederick B. Rentschler, chairman of United Aircraft, displaying part of the Turbo Wasp engine in 1950.* (Source: Time Life Pictures/Getty Images)

By the dawn of World War II, investments in emerging helicopter technology added a key component to United's arsenal of engines and aircraft. Frederick had the know-how and connections to capitalize on military contracts, both from his own army service and through acquaintances like his younger brother George's Princeton classmate James Forrestal. After working in military procurement, Forrestal served as secretary of the navy under Roosevelt and as secretary of defense under Truman. Frederick kept close ties with Gordon, too, as the National City executive served on United Aircraft's board, and after Gordon's death, Frederick served on National City's. The Rentschler brothers from Ohio in this way influenced Northeastern business connections even into the twenty-first century: the chief executive of United Technologies Corp. still serves on the board of Citigroup, and the relationship remained reciprocal until 2002, when scrutiny of board interlocks prompted Sandy Weill to resign from United Technologies' board.[23]

## Midwesterners Own the "Company Man" Era

In the late 1920s, when the Rentschlers ascended to their top leadership roles, they were part of an advance guard of Midwesterners who began to surpass the dominance of Northeasterners in leadership on our list. Indeed, Midwesterners owned the century's middle decades, building from the 1920s to a peak in the 1950s, when over 45 percent of ascending leaders had Midwestern roots versus just over 20 percent from the Northeast. It is no coincidence that the rise of the Midwestern leader occurs almost in lockstep with the growth of the professional management model; during these decades, large companies started hiring managers-in-training on the basis of considerations of fit that favored a middle-class, cookie-cutter candidate. Prospects were weeded out and fine-tuned through a long series of steppingstone assignments that developed productive "company men."

Illustrating the lengths to which companies went to assess suitability for such a path, a 1951 *Fortune* survey revealed that about half of the responding firms regularly screened the *wives* of candidates for executive jobs, with one company indicating it rejected some 20 percent of prospective management trainees solely on this basis.[24] Editors of *Fortune* observed, with definite trepidation, "What more and more modern corporations want is 'group integration;' to them, the good wife is the wife who subordinates her own individuality and aspirations to the smooth functioning of the system; the wife, in short, who 'adapts.'"[25] The author of the *Fortune* article was William H. Whyte Jr., who went on to write *The Organization Man*, a seminal work on the group-think psychology of his era's corporate executive. Emphasizing the zeal of companies for individuals with the "right" profile, Whyte noted that one-third of corporations used personality testing on prospective employees in 1952; by 1954, 60 percent of a group of sixty-three large corporations he consulted did, and he estimated that the number of blank psychological testing forms sold had risen 300 percent in the first half of the 1950s.[26]

For the large manufacturing enterprises of this era, many of them based in the Midwest, the malleable men from the region matched the desired profile quite well. In the late 1950s, one Manhattan-based corporate search executive said he had met a company president who openly stated his preference for Midwesterners, asserting that they were "physically stronger than men produced by any other part of the country."[27] Not quite so hard-charging as their Eastern-born compatriots, men of the Midwest also paced themselves more comfortably through the tenures of twenty years or more that typically preceded CEO roles at established firms. In some companies, in fact, the internal succession sequence became almost a science, with one successful long-term leader following on the heels of another in neatly arranged cycles, each man serving six to ten years at the top. Without a doubt, the premier practitioner of this method was Minnesota Mining and Manufacturing, the diversified Midwestern growth engine more familiarly known as 3M. Though 3M did not supply the largest overall number of leaders on our list (DuPont and General Electric had more), in the category of company men, 3M takes the top prize, delivering from the 1950s through the 1980s five successful ascending leaders, who each served in the company for more than twenty years before reaching the top. Among them, Herbert Buetow, Bert Cross, Raymond Herzog, Lewis Lehr, and Allen Jacobson headed the company for all but six of the years between 1953 and 1991. The only leader not on our list from that period was Harry Heltzer, who succeeded Cross but resigned after being implicated in an embarrassing incident regarding illegal political contributions.[28]

That Buetow, Cross, Herzog, Lehr, and Jacobson all made our list is a by-product of 3M's phenomenal success during the era. The firm grew at a steady clip from some $18 million in annual profits when Buetow's tenure began to over $1 billion by the end of Jacobson's. Indeed, the very elements of 3M's formula for success helped make the firm a fruitful incubator of company men. In the late 1940s, 3M head William McKnight, who had himself served over twenty years in the top spot and made our list, had laid the groundwork for a decentralized management approach that fostered the development of leaders in the company and generated enough opportunity to keep many employees loyal to a noteworthy degree.[29] The company emphasized research and new-product innovation as the pathway to growth and, to facilitate this, opened the door to leadership for anyone who came up with a winning idea. Any scientist or salesman could thus be running his own "enterprise" within 3M in short order if his innovation found a market. These independent business silos gave rise to entrepreneurial opportunities and multiplied the possibilities for advancement. Policy norms against outside hiring and an ironclad rule against nepotism gave employees good reason to feel that loyalty would be rewarded.[30] A worldwide "personnel inventory" was continually maintained to ensure managers were up-to-date on qualified internal candidates for any position they needed to fill. By making those inside the company the true *insiders* and rewarding innovation and competence rather than bloodlines, 3M not only grew but maintained turnover rates so low that its competition doubted the veracity of the figures.[31]

It's not hard to see, though, that prohibiting nepotism and even guaranteeing opportunity for merit-based advancement are measures that, while favorable to current employees, would not necessarily lead to diversity at the top of the company. Buetow, Cross, Herzog, Lehr, and Jacobson offer strong indications that the results were just the opposite. All five men were born in the northern Midwest and graduated from Midwestern colleges, with the exception of Cross, who began working for 3M as an undergraduate and didn't finish his studies at the University of Minnesota, because the company sent him on an assignment to England. Buetow, Lehr, and Jacobson all attended state universities, and although Herzog graduated from the more prestigious private Lawrence University, it was nonetheless a hometown school for a boy raised in Appleton, Wisconsin. None of the five earned MBAs or other graduate degrees. Herzog, a physics major in college, had taught high school science before joining 3M. Lehr and Jacobson, both company lifers, were trained as engineers. Buetow, the only one of the group who rose through finance, had started in bookkeeping jobs for the city of Saint Paul and the state of Minnesota and, perhaps as a result, was the only one with fewer than thirty years of service when he became CEO. The three out of five whose religious affiliation could be identified were Presbyterians. None of the leaders seemed to have come from elite family stock—Lehr's father, for example, was a haberdasher.[32] And while Jacobson's father eventually became the head of Northwestern Bell in Omaha, he achieved that office just as his son did, working his whole career there and advancing through the ranks.[33] All were in their mid- to late fifties when they got the top job, and none but Buetow served more than ten years. Each, a loyal company man to the end, stepped down at or shortly before age sixty-five. Part of keeping the chain of succession intact obviously meant knowing when to move on.[34]

## Western Opportunities Lure Many

While the Northeast and the Midwest were the regions of established opportunity, the West offered the enticement of a fast track to riches. No area acted as a greater magnet for leaders (figure 2-3). The West had by far the greatest proportion of outsider leaders succeeding there, while at the same time it kept home its own leaders at a proportion rivaling that of the opportunity-rich Northeast. Factors that helped create this hospitable environment for success were the rapid development of the region in the early twentieth century and a pioneering business climate permeable to outsiders—after all, almost everyone there already *was* an outsider in some way.

The magnetism of the West is apparent in the story of Elbridge Stuart, whose enterprising life displays a steady westward mobility in search of opportunity. Born in North Carolina in 1856, Stuart was the twelfth of thirteen children in a devout Quaker family. As the hostilities of the Civil War began to percolate, the peace-minded Stuarts moved to Indiana. There Elbridge was educated through the equivalent of eighth grade, earning a diploma in bookkeeping. At fifteen, he attempted his first business venture, pooling his and a brother's savings with a contribution from their father to bring the total capital to three hundred dollars. The young entrepreneurs used this to open a storefront selling farm produce in Indianapolis, and they experienced a few months of success. Unfortunately, however, a relapse of rheumatism, from which he had suffered as a child, put Elbridge in bed for months. His brother then fell ill with typhoid fever, and the business folded.[35]

**FIGURE 2-3**

## Western region a magnet for leaders

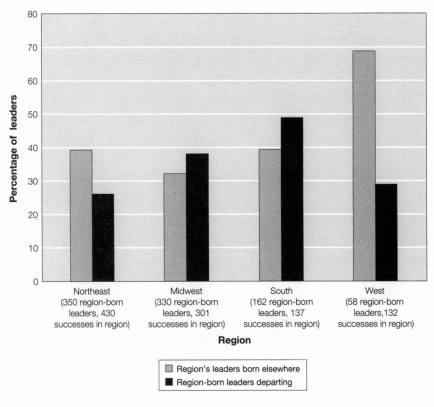

*Source*: HBS Leadership Initiative's "Great American Business Leaders of the 20th Century" database.

Elbridge rallied and went to work as a wagon driver the following year, but another attack of rheumatism left him determined to find his fortune in a warmer and less humid climate, prompting the first of his significant moves west. At seventeen, he went to join his brother Jehu, who was working in Lawrence, Kansas, as a physician. Jehu hoped Elbridge might follow in his professional footsteps, but the teenager's queasiness at an autopsy put that out of the question. He instead took a disparate series of jobs, the steadiest being as a dry-goods clerk. The advancing railroads and fast-moving expansion further west fueled ambition in him and three of his fellow clerks, and they combined their savings to buy a mule team, joining the work of laying track for the Santa Fe Railroad. Eight months at this grueling endeavor convinced them that clerking wasn't so bad, and they sold off the mules. Stuart headed for Albuquerque, where an interview with a grocery wholesaler led to a job managing a commissary for another railroad contractor. After two workers died in a gunfight outside his tent, however, Stuart retreated from the frontier and returned, somewhat abashed, to Kansas.

He was back at his old job in the dry-goods store when a contact from the Albuquerque wholesaler walked in and rekindled Stuart's dreams, encouraging him that the town of El Paso was ripe for a boom when the railroad arrived. The contact offered to loan half the money to start a general store there if Stuart and one of his clerk friends provided the rest. Stuart and his partner gathered supplies and arrived in El Paso in January 1881.[36] The Southern Pacific Railroad followed in May and the Santa Fe on July 1, so the partners' timing was perfect. The store proved by far the most successful of Stuart's ventures to date. Outlasting two different partners who each sold out and moved on, he was sole proprietor of the prosperous business by 1889. Four years later, now thirty-seven and married with two children, Stuart found incentive to move still further west. His wife's health had deteriorated after the birth of their second child, and doctors thought the coastal climate of Southern California might bring about a recovery. The family's restorative trip took a business turn, as a salesman whom Stuart knew from his calls at the El Paso store persuaded Stuart to become his partner in starting up a grocery wholesale business in Los Angeles. Stuart sold his El Paso business and moved to California. After five years, the new business was making a tidy profit, but investors intent on higher returns bought out Stuart's one-third stake, binding him by a noncompetition agreement from starting a similar business locally.

Now almost forty-three, Stuart again did what he seemed to do best— move and start over. Once more he was invited into partnership by an old acquaintance, this one a Midwestern grocery wholesaler who was pursuing new prospects in California.[37] The acquaintance persuaded Stuart to join him in buying out a bankrupt milk cannery located in Kent, Washington, south of booming Seattle. They founded the Pacific Coast Condensed Milk Company, soon to be known as producers of Carnation Cream. Stuart cultivated relationships with the local dairy farmers and soon had an ample supply of raw milk. Meanwhile, the Swiss-born dairyman they had brought in to run their operations was perfecting a preservation process that utilized heat rather than the previously customary practice of adding sugar. The resulting long-lived evaporated milk was just the product for men on their way to even more far-flung opportunities—Klondike gold rushers who had started heading for Alaska and the Yukon in the late 1890s. Prospectors even appreciated the butterfat that typically separated to the top of the can, a phenomenon that homemakers regarded as a defect. The miners, however, welcomed it as a token of the richness of the product and the closest thing to butter that they were likely to find up north!

Klondike fever had almost run its course by 1899, though, and the business did not grow quickly enough for Stuart's partner, who was ready to sell his share after two years. Rather than give up, Stuart bought him out and persevered in building a wider market for canned milk. In 1910, he made his only remaining relocation, necessitated by a local labor dispute, when he reestablished his main factory and dairy farm in Tolt, Washington, a little over thirty miles northeast of Kent.[38] By 1916, the fame of the company's flagship brand was such that the company was renamed Carnation Milk Products, and the town of Tolt likewise exuberantly renamed itself after its premier employer the following year.[39] Finally, in the town of Carnation, Washington, Stuart stayed put—for generations, in fact, as his son and grandson ran his company after him, both making our list for their success as leaders. Around the time of his death in 1944, Carnation operated plants throughout the United States and internationally and was the largest-selling brand of evaporated milk in the world.[40]

Stories like Elbridge Stuart's didn't end with the gold rush, the completion of the railroads, or even the advent of air travel. The West in fact increased its cachet as a source of outsider opportunity in the latter half of the twentieth century, hosting close to 30 percent of the U.S.-born leaders who succeeded outside their home region in that period, second only to the Northeast. Leaders born in the Northeastern business hub also went west themselves at rates that suggest the region was no longer so much a haven for outsiders as a preferred destination of power players. More than half of New York–born leaders and close to 45 percent of Northeasterners overall who uprooted themselves in this period chose, rather than sticking in the neighboring Midwest as they had earlier in the century, to vault across the country to the West to seek their fortunes.

One might guess that technology was at the heart of all these westward moves. With financial success being one of the criteria for our selection of leaders, however, precious few Internet pioneers qualified. Some Northeastern-bred software and hardware leaders like New Yorkers Larry Ellison of Oracle and John Sculley of Apple did, to be sure, but a similar number of Northeasterners made their mark in entertainment or media-connected businesses, which likewise thrived in the West. One of those, whose hard-charging tactics in the cable industry would be characterized as befitting an outlaw's Wild West mentality, was the nevertheless Connecticut-born John Malone.[41]

Malone's childhood in Milford, Connecticut, is sometimes offhandedly characterized as upper-crust or affluent, but in fact his upbringing was essentially middle class. His father, an engineer with General Electric, spent most of his week at a facility in Syracuse, returning to Milford on weekends and also tinkering in his home workshop with inventions, some of them early GE television prototypes. Malone likewise showed an early aptitude for gadgets and engineering, running a radio repair business at age eight. In the post-Sputnik rush to develop young U.S. science talent, his skills helped win him a scholarship to the tony Hopkins Grammar School in New Haven, to which he commuted for high school.[42] From there, he earned an engineering degree at Yale and then started work at the era's classic research post, AT&T's Bell Laboratories, in 1963. AT&T would finance his multiple graduate degrees, including a PhD in operations research at Johns Hopkins University, a degree he zipped through, completing in 1967.

At Bell Labs, however, Malone also came face-to-face with the company-man persona, and he didn't like it at all. "The odds were that you were going to spend your whole life writing memos and making basically no impact on anything," he recalled in a 1994 interview.[43] Itching for a faster pace, he took a position with McKinsey's New York office in 1968. Here, however, the pace, or at least the speed with which he was sent on the road to please consulting clients, proved *too* fast, and he rankled at the toll that incessant travel was taking on his marriage. Changing jobs yet again, he joined General Instrument Corporation in 1970, becoming president of its Jerrold Electronics division, which sold cable television equipment. To sell products for use in the young cable industry was inescapably also to be involved in financing—the buyers were largely undercapitalized, to say the least. Though Malone was just turning thirty at the time, his smarts and creativity, plus the loan programs he administered, won him favor with clients, and he rapidly developed connections in the industry.[44]

By 1972, Malone had job offers from not one but two nascent cable entities—both Steve Ross of Warner Communications and Bob Magness of Tele-Communications Inc. (TCI) were inviting him to run their respective cable operations. The prominence of the Warner name is obvious, but TCI's name seemed rather more auspicious than the firm warranted. Magness, a client of Malone's at Jerrold, had begun his enterprise in the 1950s in tiny Memphis, Texas, running cable lines himself and funding the effort with proceeds from the sale of cattle from his ranch. The company had expanded significantly and was now based in Denver but still serviced mostly small communities in the Rocky Mountain states. Malone, however, chose to head west, a decision he later pinned on his wife's desire to leave the East Coast—he promised her they'd lead a different, more laid-back lifestyle in Colorado.[45] He took a 50 percent pay cut to become CEO of TCI, with Magness remaining chairman. Unfortunately for Malone and his wife, that laid-back lifestyle did not materialize at first, as he spent most of his time back East in Boston and New York, wooing bankers and trying to help TCI out of a financing crunch. A breakthrough came in 1978, when he persuaded a consortium of insurance companies to grant TCI longer-term financing, clearing away much of the bank debt burden. Malone also became an early client of junk-bond pioneer Michael Milken of Drexel Burnham Lambert, even doing an endorsement video for the high-interest, high-risk financing format.[46] In the early 1980s, with HBO and Showtime well established and icons-in-the-making like ESPN and CNN coming online, cable's content was becoming attractive to a growing market—industry stock prices began ticking upward, and TCI began to gain financial flexibility.

As his cash resources grew, Malone built up the company "in little bites rather than big swallows"—he acquired smaller providers at a rate approaching one every two weeks.[47] With the numbers of households served by TCI rising rapidly, Malone took advantage of this leverage to negotiate rock-bottom prices with content providers, further improving his cost position. Playing both sides of the street, he also invested some of TCI's resources in

*Raymond W. Smith (left), chairman and CEO of Bell Atlantic, and John C. Malone, president of TCI and chairman and CEO of Liberty Media Corporation, announce their corporate merger agreement in October 1993. This merger culminated Malone's career at TCI, passing on control of the cable empire he had built.* (Source: AFP/Getty Images)

content providers like Turner Broadcasting and the Discovery Channel. By 1986, just months after cable-industry deregulation had taken effect, he could boast that one dollar invested in TCI in 1977 was now worth four hundred.[48] TCI was growing by leaps and bounds, but Malone was winning no popularity contests. During this period, he gained a reputation as a cutthroat competitor and borderline monopolist, being famously termed Darth Vader by then-Senator Al Gore.[49] The power of TCI was such, however, that it converted even Malone's enemies into business partners. In 1993, Sumner Redstone of media conglomerate Viacom filed an antitrust suit filled with scathing rhetoric about TCI's activities. By 1995, Viacom had cut a deal to sell its own cable holdings to TCI and simultaneously dropped the lawsuit. Malone's final act of a long and successful run at TCI was to work one last deal that effectively brought things full circle with his first employer. In 1998, he sold out the company to AT&T, retaining control of just one key asset— Liberty Media, its content arm, for which he garnered favorable provisions to continue its operation.⁵⁰ The adventure out West was unquestionably a profitable one for Malone, though the assets he built wound up, for the most part, back under a Northeastern company's control.

## The West Spawns Entrepreneurs

Not surprisingly, given the growth of the West's economy during the century and the extent to which the region's settlers were also outsiders to most established business sectors, Western-born leaders gravitated toward entrepreneurship at proportions higher than any other region. More than half the leaders born there found their way to success through starting their own business (figure 2-4). Again, it's tempting to assume this is all a product of the technology boom of the late twentieth century, but an entrepreneurial spirit

**FIGURE 2-4**

**West gives rise to entrepreneurs**

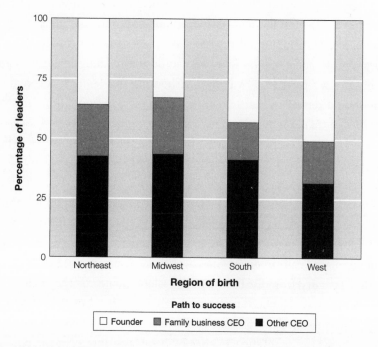

*Source*: HBS Leadership Initiative's "Great American Business Leaders of the 20th Century" database.

was on the rise out West long before anyone had ever heard of Silicon Valley. Only about one-fifth of the ventures started by these Western-born leaders were related to technology. The rest spanned a diverse array of industries, from financial services and retail to fast foods and transportation.

Eagerness for entrepreneurship would seem to come naturally to those born in the West in the early twentieth century. These leaders were mostly products of families willing to set off in search of once-in-a-lifetime opportunities. The California gold rush inspired the migration of James Casey's father, a prospector living in a mining town in western Nevada when James was born in the 1880s. Actual riches materialized for few, of course, and families like Casey's kept on the move. They soon came to Seattle, and James had to go to work to help support his family, starting at age eleven, when his father fell seriously ill and died not long afterward. Casey's first jobs were in making store deliveries and then delivering messages for a telegraph service. As a messenger, he did much more than deliver telegrams, answering calls to transport beer, restaurant meals, or even a desperate addict's opium fix.[51] By age fifteen, he'd weathered enough adventures to feel confident in striking out with partners in a messenger service. He started in Seattle, but a year or so later, he and a friend headed back to the state of his birth, drawn to the booming prospector's town of Goldfield, Nevada. A friend of Casey's father introduced him to the local sheriff, and the boys soon were in business. Things went well for a time, but Casey's partner fell victim to a shooting and James was convinced that he should retreat to Seattle, which, opium addicts and all, nevertheless represented a tamer environment.[52] In 1907, now nineteen, Casey, his brother, and a couple other teenage partners used one hundred dollars in borrowed start-up funds to start American Messenger Service.

The shoestring enterprise helped bridge a gap in the limited communication services offered by two competing but unconnected telephone companies. Casey's group subscribed to telephone lines from both providers and posted information about the company near public phones, where people commonly placed calls to dictate messages for delivery. A band of boy bicyclists, they operated from the basement of a saloon owned by the uncle of one of Casey's partners. The headquarters was unimpressive, but the young men rapidly proved themselves reliable. Well before the days of round-the-clock business, their firm established an edge by being available 24/7; the boys accomplished this by making a bed of the top of the saloon counter, resting the pillow next to the phones.[33] They also delivered packages, a service not yet offered by the U.S. Post Office. In just over five years, they had a staff of one hundred messengers and several leading Seattle merchants as customers. In 1913, they expanded through a merger with a local motorcycle carrier and bought their first car. Casey and company were progressively mastering a centralized delivery approach to serve multiple merchants in a city, improving cost efficiency and customer convenience. He surveyed competitors offering similar services in other cities, and their discouraging reports only made him more confident that his methods would succeed where theirs had failed. He thus proceeded with a conviction that the field was wide open.[54] Expansion to San Francisco followed with the acquisition of an Oakland delivery firm in 1919, which also occasioned the company's name change to United Parcel Service. As a selling point to stores already operating in-house delivery groups, UPS would buy the store's vehicles and retain most of its employees when taking over the delivery operation.[55]

In 1929, the company tried a Western regional air delivery service that, unfortunately, fell victim to the stock market crash and the start of the Depression. By 1931, however, with the West Coast territory essentially under his firm's dominance, Casey pressed forward into New York, acquiring the delivery service for Lord & Taylor. Just three years later, UPS had some 250 clients in the city.[56] The now-famous brown trucks of UPS first appeared in this era, and the enterprise expanded after World War II from merchant deliveries into "common carrier" service, delivering to addresses in all forty-eight contiguous states by 1975. Casey died just eight years later, but not before seeing his Western-born enterprise make a national impact.[57]

## Home Not So Sweet in the South . . .

The regional opposite to the West's magnetism was found in the South, as hinted at by figure 2-3. Nearly half of the Southern-born leaders on our list—the highest percentage for any region—went elsewhere to succeed. The economy in the South was still largely agrarian as opposed to industrial, and the Civil War's aftermath affected the region's attractiveness—indeed, the hostilities themselves had driven out families like Elbridge Stuart's. The story is complicated, however, by differences along racial lines. African American leaders, who constituted almost 20 percent of the Southern-born leaders ascending before 1950, faced particular challenges of poverty, prejudice, and segregation (see chapter 7). As a result, nearly 70 percent of Southern-born African Americans departed to find success, despite typically having minimal resources to do so. By contrast, more than half of the whites born in the region stayed, a much higher proportion than African Americans, but noticeably lower than that for all other U.S. regions.

At least as noteworthy as the racial distinction in the South is the divide along socioeconomic lines: among wealthy Southerners, all of whom were white, nearly 70 percent stayed in the region for their successes, while more than half of those with middle-class origins left. On the other hand, the majority of poor whites, who, like African Americans, faced a dearth of means but, unlike them, lacked the race-based stimulation to leave, stayed in the region for success. The singular feature of the South is its production of leaders at both these economic extremes (figure 2-5). Leaders from this region were both rich *and* poor at higher proportions than those from other parts of the United States, with those from other regions being at least 50 percent middle class.

This reduced middle-class presence appears to be a by-product of the lack of industrial activity in the South as well as a legacy of slavery. A stronger dependence on agriculture had concentrated wealth in the hands of landowners, and jobs that might have supported the rise of a wage-earning class had until only a few decades before the turn of the century been filled by slaves. This economic divide diminished the number of likely candidates for local business leadership, leaving the field mostly to the few prosperous and the more numerous disadvantaged, with the latter group finding the road to success much more difficult. As a result of their numbers, however, more than 40 percent of our leaders who succeeded in the South came from poor backgrounds, the highest proportion of any region. In other words, it was the South and not the Northeast that gave birth to the highest percentage, though not the highest number, of Horatio Alger stories.

The closest match to Ragged Dick among white U.S.-born leaders, in fact, grew up in Texas rather than Manhattan. Born in 1899, Cyrus R. Smith, more familiarly known throughout his career as C. R., went to work around age nine after his father walked out on a wife and seven children, of whom Cyrus was the oldest. As the family had hitherto led an itinerant life, moving around Louisiana and Texas wherever their dad could find work, in a roundabout way this departure allowed for more stability. Smith's mother, Minnie, took

FIGURE 2-5

## South missing the middle class as source of leaders

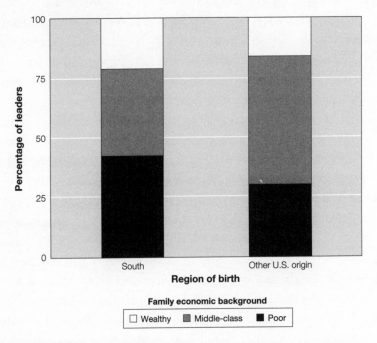

Family economic background
☐ Wealthy ■ Middle-class ■ Poor

*Source*: HBS Leadership Initiative's "Great American Business Leaders of the 20th Century" database.

in boarders and taught school to make ends meet, and all the children supplemented her earnings by working as soon as they were able. The pooled funds ultimately sufficed for all seven to attend at least some college, although Smith had to gain entrance via a special exemption since he had never finished grade school. Minnie also became an active participant in state politics, a venue wide open to volunteers, regardless of their means, and one apt to bring contact with persons of influence. The Texas suffrage movement, in full swing during the 1910s, gained women the right to vote in state primaries by 1918, and Minnie's work acquainted her with Pat Neff, governor of Texas in the early 1920s. Neff made a name for himself as a pioneer in appointing women, Minnie among them, to state boards and staff positions and would prove helpful later in getting her children started in careers.[58] The support of a strong and capable mother thus provided Smith with a significant leg up on forming the kinds of personal networks that could open doors.

Even in his late teens, however, Smith showed every sign of being well equipped to manage his own career. Disgusted by a Christmas bonus of a box of ten-cent cigars after he had spent most of the year working fifteen-hour days to fill in for staffers off serving in World War I, he resigned from his bookkeeping job. He was already cultivating his own Texas political connections and shortly gained an appointment in a tax department under the secretary of state. When he finally enrolled to study business at the University of Texas at age twenty-one, he also had a part-time job as an examiner for the Federal Reserve Bank lined up. By his junior year, he was class president; on the side, he was operating a business that leveraged his state government ties and made him a pioneer in direct-mail-list brokerage. At first, he sold to investment firms the names and addresses of stockholders from Texas corporate listings; then he expanded into compiling lists of new parents from state birth records, which he sold to companies offering products for families with young children. After Smith's death, his son would claim that Smith left the university without graduating because he ran out of money.[59] This may have been a fatherly gloss on the face of a youthful impatience with academia, however. According to an article published during Smith's lifetime, his part-time job and side business during college had been generating twice the monthly income he'd make in his next position as an entry-level accountant with a Dallas firm.[60]

That such a mover and shaker would find his way to the emerging airline industry seems logical, but it happened very much by accident and, initially, against Smith's wishes. After two years with the accounting firm, he joined a power company that had been one of his clients, taking the position of assistant treasurer. His boss, A. P. Barrett, acquired an air transport company in 1928 and designated Smith to run it, despite his protests of a lack of interest in aviation. It was not long, however, before the challenging new field and even flying itself (he trained as a pilot in his spare time) captured Smith. Barrett, with a group of investors, including Fort Worth's master power broker, newspaper publisher Amon Carter, acquired two other small lines and merged them into a regional passenger and transport operation. Carter had, like Smith, risen from quite humble beginnings, quitting school at age eleven.[61] The two would soon be good friends as well as business colleagues. When the regional line was bought by industry consolidator Aviation Corporation (Avco, for short) in 1929, Smith became a vice president in charge of the southern division of Avco's newly christened American Airways, of which Carter remained a large stockholder. Smith was briefly elevated to head of nationwide operations but bounced back to the regional office when an ally lost his struggle for the top corporate post. Competence eventually won out over office politics, however, and Smith returned to the national helm. He assumed the presidency in October 1934—unenviable timing, to be sure. All airmail transportation contracts had been canceled earlier that year by the U.S. Post Office due to a scandal alleging collusion in the bidding process. Since passenger traffic was then a money-losing proposition because of limited plane load capacities, the mail contracts were a crucial source of revenue. As a prerequisite for making new bids, participants also had to reorganize their firms and separate airplane manufacture from airline operations, placing even more pressure on the bottom line for flights.

American, now reconstituted as American Airlines, won its fair share of the rebid contracts, and some suggested perhaps more than its fair share, pointing to the political networks with which Smith was connected. Amon Carter had been a key player in negotiating a compromise at the 1932 Democratic Convention, the terms of which swung the delegates of Texan John Nance Garner to FDR's column in exchange for Garner's vice presidential nomination.[62] In a show of bravado at a time when air travel was viewed as relatively daring, the future president and his family were flown via an American Airways plane into Chicago to accept the nomination. (When a newspaper questioned this favor after the awarding of the mail contracts, tickets signed and paid for by the Roosevelts were produced for inspection.)[63] Smith had also personally accompanied the First Lady, who soon became an inveterate flier, on a flight from Nevada in mid-1933, after she had confirmed to the press the ticklish news of her son Elliott's impending divorce.[64] The "other woman" in that situation, whom Elliott would immediately marry, was a Texas girl he'd met at a Fort Worth rodeo, with Smith himself reportedly making the introduction.[65] Elliott would also be a groomsman in Smith's December 1934 wedding and work for Smith's old boss, A. P. Barrett, in a 1935 broadcasting venture.[66] Smith had obviously learned from his rise in Texas how to make friends in the high places of politics, whether or not those connections made a difference in the mail contracts. In the rebidding of the airmail routes, however, prices had been slashed to the bone, and Smith no less than his competitors was faced with finding a way out of the unprofitable mess.

He headed boldly toward expansion, pushing Douglas Aircraft to develop a new plane (ultimately the DC-3) that would offer 50 percent greater passenger capacity than its previous model, with better fuel performance. The clincher was Smith's commitment to buy the new model in volume (twenty immediately and an option for twenty more) to standardize American's operations on it. The volume commitment was a highly speculative move for a plane without an established track record of safe operation. Cash flow was also so tight that Smith had to borrow the purchase cost from the government's Reconstruction Finance Corporation (RFC), which was headed by Jesse Jones, a fellow Texan of Smith's acquaintance—yet another instance that prompted whispers of influence through his network.[67] Powered by the DC-3s and Smith's aggressive marketing tactics to build awareness and popularity of air travel, American was the only domestic transcontinental airline to avoid red ink in 1938, posting an after-tax profit over $200,000 in a year when United lost nearly $1 million and TWA over $750,000.[68] So convincing was Smith's rise by this time that a 1939 *Fortune* profile mentioned nothing of his Alger-like saga, likening his early career to that of a Texas dandy: "Young Mr. Smith had a wide acquaintance among prominent Texans like Amon Carter and was distinctly a man of parts."[69]

*American Airlines stewardess receives an award in 1941 from C. R. Smith, longtime president of the airline.* (Source: Time Life Pictures/Getty Images)

Smith, however, never seemed to forget his modest origins and maintained the attitude of a man of the people. He typed his own memos, answered his own phone, and swiftly disabused managers in his company of any tendencies toward "executive" airs. Some thirty years before Southwest Airlines honcho Herb Kelleher drew on his folksy, down-to-earth demeanor to differentiate his new airline, C. R. Smith was cut in the same gregarious mold, customarily introducing himself to every American Airlines ticket agent or baggage handler he met (and recalling details of their family histories in the next conversation) and stunning passengers on flights when he wandered up and down the aisle, mingling and introducing himself as "president of this rodeo."[70] In early 1968, Smith finally retired, only to show his political colors again by becoming secretary of commerce for a fellow Texan, President Lyndon Johnson, filling the post for the remainder of Johnson's term. In 1973, Smith, still ornery and active at seventy-four, returned briefly to the helm of American to steady operations and raise the flag of the organization's glory days for several months while a replacement was sought for a deposed CEO. Asked once what his father had done for a living, Smith replied, "As little as possible."[71] Smith made sure that the same could by no means be said of him.

## U.S. Leaders Mainly Build on Home-Field Advantage

The advantages in the Northeast and disadvantages in the South both reinforce the impact that being born in or near an industrialized area had on the likelihood of success for U.S.-born business leaders, particularly early in the twentieth century. Although this is most obvious in the case of inherited leadership, local established industry provided an opportunity for a first job and potential markets for entrepreneurs, either possibility giving the chance for generational upward mobility as wealth was built. These advantages were clearly the greatest in the Northeast and in New York in particular, keeping the vast majority of leaders born there near home for their success.

The Midwest came the closest to sharing the industrialized flavor of the Northeast and thus was more likely to provide good candidates to break into established businesses there. At the same time, the maturing of Midwestern industries, particularly by midcentury, meant that those born in the region found lots of home-grown opportunity in large corporate settings.

At the other extreme, the undeveloped West presented a favorable climate of business opportunity for both locals and newcomers due to the region's rapid growth. Important to those with lesser means, this area was largely unencumbered by the highly structured web of connections and influence that had to be faced when a person was breaking into business in the Northeast.

The South, boasting neither developed industry nor strong growth potential, was the most disadvantaged region. Another handicap was its relative lack of an established middle class, the economic background from which most business successes on our list arose. African Americans and middle-class whites mostly left the region looking for better opportunities, while the wealthy stayed, along with poorer whites. This pattern tended to limit the overall numbers of successful leaders emerging from the South, even as it gave rise to the highest proportion of true rags-to-riches sagas.

As a starting point in our examination of twentieth-century leader backgrounds, we thus come away with the decisive conclusion that even in the United States, the great land of opportunity, not every birthplace was created equal. The fictitious Ragged Dick, for all his disadvantages, should have been glad that he was a New Yorker, and indeed, all his fortuitous connections do materialize from those he meets on the city's streets. While mobility between regions tended to increase later in the century, people with more prosperous family origins—origins that typically stemmed from birth in a similarly prosperous region of the country—retained an advantage when entering business in a new area. The distinguishing features of each of the country's major regions, both as sources of and sites for leaders, will constitute an important backdrop for further discussions about leader characteristics. To appreciate more fully the significance of birthplace in determining access to success, however, we next need to consider the group of true geographic outsiders— newcomers from foreign shores.

# THREE

# Nationality

## From Fiery Melting Pots
## to Mainstream Professionals

*Our expansive territory has enabled the adventurous and energetic of all
nations of the world to come here and make homes for themselves, instead of
remaining in the land of their birth, where many of them were existing in a
modified condition of slavery under other names.*

*The idea of encouraging this large exodus from other lands, and this freedom
of assimilation with our people, has been one of the great bulwarks of our
prosperity.*

—Henry Clews, *Fifty Years in Wall Street*

WHEN HENRY CLEWS waxed passionate in his 1908 memoir about
the ways immigrants had contributed to building American wealth,
he knew whereof he spoke. After all, he himself had come to America from
England in the mid-1800s, expecting to stay, as he later wrote, "for merely a
short visit."[1] Soon enough, though, he became intrigued with "the possibilities that presented themselves for a young man, who had the courage to push,
to compete for a place in the race for wealth and position."[2] Though several
times rebuffed by older, established financiers when he applied for a seat on
the New York Stock Exchange, he forced his way in by buying and selling
stocks at half the going broker commission rate, causing the "old fogies" to let
him into their club rather than face continued loss of customers to the new

competition.³ Fifty years and many financial deals later, Clews was a Wall Street fixture, zealously defending and patriotically upholding the ideals of the country he now called his own.

The same year Clews' book was published, a play called *The Melting Pot*, by Israel Zangwill, also made its debut, lending support to one of the most familiar metaphors for American assimilation of immigrants. Zangwill's play, essentially a love-conquers-all story about romance between a Russian Jewish refugee and a Russian Orthodox Christian aristocrat in New York, celebrated the dissolving of ethnic and class conflicts for immigrants in this brave new land of America. The play opened to wide acclaim, praise that began with none other than President Theodore Roosevelt, who himself attended the Washington, D.C., premiere and boomed his approval from the presidential box. The show later moved to Chicago and Broadway, touring the country for nearly a decade.⁴

The triumphalism of Clews and Zangwill decorated the reality for immigrants with a certain amount of wishful thinking. Clews, of course, came to America already speaking English and was equipped with letters of introduction to "people of culture and refinement" to smooth his way—still, he'd had to battle to get established.⁵ Zangwill spent most of his life in Britain and developed from that rather distant perspective an idealized picture of the American Dream. Ironically enough, Alger's heroic stories championing advancement of the underdog better reflect the real stereotypes and prejudices faced by foreigners. In the New York City world of Ragged Dick, the city's large immigrant population remains invisible except for several rather unflattering cameo appearances—the Irish are represented by the keeper of a low-rent rooming house, a giggly maid thereof, and a bully, Micky Maguire, who acts as the boorish antagonist to up-and-coming Dick. By contrast, Dick's friendly comrades and the successful businessmen who are his benefactors are decidedly unaccented Anglo-Saxon types.

A look at the origins of our identified leaders confirms that the fires under the fabled melting pot did not in fact burn particularly brightly when it came to assimilating immigrants into the country's growing business community during the early twentieth century. As immigration was hitting its high point in 1910, almost 25 percent of white males in the United States twenty-one or older were foreign born.⁶ Moreover, the vast majority of our leaders ascending in the first half of the century were white males in that age group. Foreigners, however, comprised just over 10 percent of our leaders prior to 1950. This leaves foreigners represented among top business leaders at less than half their proportional presence in the United States during the period. Whatever the melting-pot ideals, those born outside the country were outsiders to business circles as well, and their disadvantages are quite apparent.

## Early Welcome Mat in West, Not Northeast

The fable of the melting pot, like the stories of Horatio Alger, focused on New York City, a primary portal for immigration. In 1910, foreigners made up 40 percent or more of the adult white males in New York and the other northeastern coastal states of Massachusetts, Connecticut, New Jersey, and Rhode Island. Together, these states contained over one-third of the foreign-born adult males in the entire United States at that time.[7] In terms of our list, however, this significant presence did not appear to translate into business opportunity for foreigners. Sheer numbers did mean that the majority of our early twentieth-century foreign leaders succeeded in the Northeast, but their representation in business did not approach their proportionate presence in the population (figure 3-1).[8] Instead, it was the frontier territory of the West that yielded the highest percentage of foreign-born leaders, coming closest to achieving proportional representation.

The West, as discussed in the preceding chapter, was a territory essentially made for and by outsiders in the early twentieth century. With almost everyone a newcomer to the region, the rapidly growing cities and economic structures were wide open for development, and even foreigners could find their way in that mélange of activity. As a result, many of those who arrived in the Northeast from abroad and who managed to make their way further across the continent were rewarded with greater opportunity. Dennis Sheedy, for example, was one of the numerous Irish Catholics who arrived in Massachusetts, but his family didn't stay there very long. Sheedy's middle-class farming parents came to New England in 1847, when Dennis was just an infant. He spent his early childhood there, but by 1858, the Sheedys had ventured all the way to Lyons, Iowa, a town on the Mississippi River halfway between Davenport and Dubuque. Somewhere along the way, the family's finances were exhausted, and Dennis's father died, broke and brokenhearted, when the boy was about twelve. Young Sheedy went to work to help support

**FIGURE 3-1**

## Early foreign-born leaders best represented in West

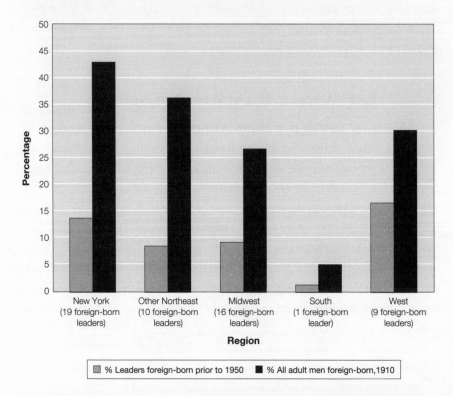

| | % Leaders foreign-born prior to 1950 | % All adult men foreign-born,1910 |

*Sources*: HBS Leadership Initiative's "Great American Business Leaders of the 20th Century" database; U.S. Department of Commerce, *Statistical Abstract of the United States: 1920* (Washington, DC: Government Printing Office, 1921), 45, available at www2.census.gov/prod2/statcomp/documents/1920-01.pdf.

the family. He began as a store clerk, but at age sixteen, he caught the wanderlust that took Elbridge Stuart and so many others further westward for greater opportunities.

After a brief stint in Denver, Sheedy went on to Montana and Utah, working in gold mining and also building a business in supplying groceries and other merchandise to the mining settlements. By age nineteen, he had accumulated a stake of thirty thousand dollars, a figure comparable to more than ten times that amount in today's dollars. He returned eastward for some study at a commercial college in Chicago and brought back with him a sizable cargo of stoves, selling them in Utah to Mormon households for more than five times their purchase price. His enterprising itinerary rambled through Nevada, California, and Arizona to Texas, where he made his entry into the cattle trade. He quickly gained a knack, as it seemed he had in every other endeavor thus far, for sizing up the market and knowing when and where he could buy low and sell high. He established ranches in several western states, including Colorado, and by 1874 a contemporary chronicler of the cattle industry could write of Sheedy, age twenty-eight: "His career stands out high and bold as a beacon light, and it may rightly be regarded as a pleasant oasis amid a limitless, dreary desert of innumerable failures."[9] Ten years later, when Sheedy, by then married and apparently ready to settle into city life in Denver, sold his herd of thirty-two thousand cattle, even *he* might have been surprised to know that he'd barely scratched the surface of his ultimate business success.

Sheedy bought stock in the Colorado National Bank, becoming its vice president by 1886. To help one of the bank's loan recipients recover from financial difficulties, he became involved in the reorganization of a local smelting works. Applying himself to study every available book on the subject and drawing on the assistance of a tutor, he quickly turned himself into a smelting expert. In 1889, the salvaged firm was incorporated as the Globe Smelting and Refining Company, with Sheedy as president. He soon began introducing technological improvements and innovations that, by 1907, had increased the smelter's annual production some eighty-fold, to $16 million.[10] Along the way, he also became president of the Denver Dry Goods Company, which boasted of being the largest department store west of Chicago. In the early 1900s, Sheedy found himself cheek by jowl with the famous Guggenheims, as the family's interests were merged into American Smelting and Refining, of which Globe was a key smelting plant. The merger, controversial with minority stockholders at the time, was apparently orchestrated by the Guggenheims, who controlled the new operation.[11] In 1909, Sheedy resigned from American Smelting's board to help form a competitive trust, the International Smelting and Refining Company.

By then, however, his status as a pillar of business and society was firmly established. In 1911, both daughters of this Irish Catholic immigrant married Protestant scions of Manhattan society, one a Livingston. The linkage of the Sheedys to this august New York family was ironically celebrated in the *New York Times* as a great match for the groom, whom headlines proclaimed to be marrying an "heiress bride"—the "richest girl in Denver."[12] Sheedy's money opened the doors for connections that others of his lineage could never have imagined. As for his younger daughter, whose wedding was several months later, the pope himself cabled blessings to the marriage, over which the bride's uncle, a bishop in Missouri, presided.[13] Wedding gifts, of such value as to require a security detail of three guards, came from Mrs. Cornelius Vanderbilt and the son of Henry Clews, among others. In the end, going west proved the best way (and perhaps the only way, given the times) for Sheedy to make a name for himself back East.[14]

If there's any doubt that Sheedy had an easier time of it as a foreigner in the West, consider the tale of our only foreign-born leader to become CEO of an established Boston-based company. He was not one of Sheedy's fellow Irish-born Catholics, despite their numbers in the Boston area. Instead, he was a Jew named Samuel Zmurri from the region of Bessarabia (now part of Moldova, but then part of Russia). Samuel entered the United States with his aunt in 1892 as a young adolescent, and they left the Northeast even more rapidly than Sheedy's family had. Heading south, the family settled in Alabama, with a surname summarily Americanized to Zemurray. Samuel found his foothold in business at the port of Mobile only a few years later, as he began buying loads of "ripes"—fruit that arrived at the docks too ripe for further transport north—from the banana boats. Locals like Zemurray typically purchased the fruit for resale to vendors and grocers in nearby communities. After about a decade, Zemurray's business was moving hundreds of thousands of bunches of bananas and had expanded to the New Orleans docks. With a local partner, he bought into a foundering steamship company that had been shipping bananas from Honduras. Theirs was a minority stake—more than half the capital to finance the operation came from the era's top fruit importer, Boston-based United Fruit, whose bananas Zemurray had been buying off the docks. United Fruit would sell its share within a few years and, as we will see, would ultimately regret it.

Zemurray ambitiously pressed onward, buying land in Honduras to convert into banana plantations and incurring enough debt to prompt his less daring partner to cash out as well.[15] His most audacious maneuver, however, involved a self-serving intervention in Central American politics. In 1910, the United States was negotiating a treaty to manage the payment of Honduran national debt by putting J. P. Morgan's bank in charge of setting and collecting import and export duties. Zemurray felt certain these Wall Street watchmen wouldn't grant him the concessions he needed to develop his banana plantations and build the necessary railroads for transporting fruit to the coast. He made common cause with a former Honduran president, Manuel Bonilla, who had his own reasons for unhappiness with the country's present leadership. Spiriting Bonilla out of the United States from under the nose of federal surveillance, Zemurray helped bankroll him to obtain a boat, arms, and a mercenary crew to topple the Honduran government.[16] In February 1911, after less than two months of rapid advance by Bonilla's forces, the United States called for an armistice. The peace arrangements provided for new elections that October, and Bonilla won the presidency.[17] Concessions granted by the understandably friendly new regime helped Zemurray's Cuyamel Fruit Company, named for the river that flowed through its plantations, become a thriving enterprise. Though the affair may shock twenty-first-century ears, such were the norms of that time with respect to U.S. involvement in Central America that the saga would two decades later be recounted in *Fortune* as a rollicking adventure, with not a hint of scandal attached. Zemurray, building on his investment by employing innovative techniques for irrigation, drainage, and land reclamation, turned Cuyamel, though it remained much smaller in volume, into a genuine rival to United Fruit in efficiency and product quality.[18]

As a result, by 1929 United Fruit was motivated to reclaim its earlier interest and approached Zemurray with an offer to purchase his business. That December, Cuyamel was merged into United Fruit's operation in exchange for stock that, though only about a 10 percent stake of the company, made Zemurray the single largest shareholder in United Fruit. Now in his early fifties, he intended a quiet retirement in Louisiana, but over the next four years, United Fruit's stock price plummeted by about 90 percent, compelling him to defend his investment interests. In January 1933, Zemurray visited United Fruit's offices in Boston only to be rebuffed, the more colorful version of the story goes, by a jibe that his Russian accent made it impossible to understand his complaints.[19] Zemurray left the room and returned to fling on the table something that needed no translation—a fistful of stock proxies he had obtained from other disgruntled investors, demonstrating that he could take control of the company by force if necessary. This amazing communications breakthrough prompted the Bostonians to appoint him managing director of operations.

Zemurray began to revamp the staid company with the tactics he had used to make Cuyamel successful, emphasizing hands-on management of the Central American operations and pruning deadwood managers who didn't suit his style, replacing Ivy League types with local Hondurans or hard-working immigrants like himself. Within just two weeks of his leadership coup, United Fruit's stock price had nearly doubled. Officially installed as president in 1938, Zemurray was to guide the company until he was in his seventies, achieving an all-time high in profits by 1950. His habits of political meddling apparently died hard, as later years found him helping steer the United States to support another governmental coup for the benefit of United Fruit's interests. This time the country of attention was Guatemala, and the action prompted public outcry when it was discovered. Once Zemurray had learned how hard he had to fight as an immigrant to win his place, though, it's understandable (even if not excusable) that he found it difficult to stop.[20]

## If You Can't Join 'Em, Beat 'Em . . .

As Sheedy's success and Zemurray's hard-won control illustrate, foreigners were decidedly freer to make their way in areas of the country that were frontiers in business terms rather than overgrown with well-developed businesses. It's not surprising, then, that our foreign-born leaders were also decidedly more likely to found businesses than rise to the chief executive post in an existing firm. Almost 73 percent of foreign-born leaders ascending prior to 1950 founded their businesses, as compared with less than 43 percent of U.S.-born leaders in the same period. Immigrant leaders, in fact, founded not only businesses but in some cases whole *industries*, another way of finding frontier territory even under the noses of the business establishment. The early motion picture industry was a field that for various reasons provided such possibilities for success by outsiders. Comparing the industry sectors in which native and foreign-born leaders succeeded early in the century, we see evidence of this openness to outsiders in the large share of foreign-born leaders leading businesses in entertainment and broadcasting (figure 3-2).

Why was this industry such an ideal incubator for immigrant leaders like Louis B. Mayer and Nicholas Schenck from Russia, William Fox and Adolph Zukor from Hungary, Samuel Goldwyn and Harry Warner from Poland, and

FIGURE 3-2

## Foreign-born leaders find niche in entertainment

*Proportions by industry for leaders ascending prior to 1950*

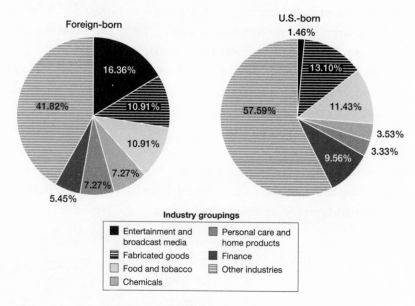

Source: HBS Leadership Initiative's "Great American Business Leaders of the 20th Century" database.

Carl Laemmle from Germany? One reason was that early movie houses flourished in urban settings or factory towns where immigrant populations were already concentrated. Admission at a nickelodeon was the five cents its name suggested, and though the price rose to ten cents in classier venues, movies still constituted a treat within reach of the working class, contrasting with a steep two-dollar ticket for an evening of "legitimate" theater. The industry was also accessible to outsiders because the capital required was low—starting up a nickelodeon was relatively cheap, and producing films was even cheaper. Finally, early moving pictures were the object of suspicion, if not outright scorn, for "respectable" American society, including most businessmen. Subject matter bordered on the titillating and scandalous for its era, and the question of whether stage actors lost prestige by appearing in films warranted a headline in the *New York Times* as late as 1915, even as movie stars like Mary Pickford were becoming household names.[21]

All these factors worked in favor of immigrants being left to find their success in the budding film industry and were particularly important for these leaders who shared, in addition to birth outside the United States, a Jewish faith. While chapter 4 will deal explicitly with the role religion played in leader selection, it is perhaps obvious that immigrant Jews faced a double barrier of prejudice when entering American business. These particular immigrants, largely from Eastern Europe, were even considered outsiders by the Jews of German heritage already established in America. Several of these later arrivals started out in the garment business, which offered an accessible entry point—Laemmle first managed a clothing store, Zukor sold furs, and Goldwyn, back in the days when he was known as Samuel Goldfish, sold gloves. The nascent motion picture industry, however, offered unique potential for greatness. All but Goldwyn began as film exhibitors, owning one or more movie houses. Zukor, Fox, and Schenck (who managed Loew's, the theater chain begun by American-born Jew Marcus Loew) started in the New York area, while

*Adolph Zukor, at age twenty-one, was a successful fur merchant before founding a theater chain and film studio that became Paramount Pictures.* (Source: Bettmann/CORBIS)

Mayer's first theater was north of Boston in Haverhill, Massachusetts. Laemmle's was in Chicago, and Harry Warner's (owned with his brothers) was in New Castle, Pennsylvania. For most of these entrepreneurs, becoming a film distributor was the natural next step, as it offered a way to build revenue by sharing the costs of the films they were already buying as exhibitors.

Unfortunately for these outsiders, the party appeared to be over in 1909, as the U.S. business establishment, in the person of none other than venerated inventor Thomas Alva Edison, tried to establish itself as gatekeeper (and toll collector) at the entry point to the motion picture enterprise. Edison, who had been bickering about patent rights to motion picture camera and projection technology with other early participants in the industry, reached an agreement with the Biograph Company, the leading company in a rival faction, to form the Motion Picture Patents Company.[22] The scope of the new company's combined patents made it essentially impossible for any firm to make motion pictures without licensing the Patents Company's technology. Eastman Kodak Company even pledged to sell its film stock exclusively to licensees. Exhibitors, who needed a steady supply of films, now had only one source for movies and, adding insult to injury, would be charged a license fee for the privilege of showing authorized movies. The days of the independent entrepreneur seemed numbered, as the Patents Company, through its subsidiary, the General Film Company, shortly began gobbling up film distributor exchanges. Warner's Duquesne Film Exchange in Pittsburgh was among those consumed.[23]

Edison's plan, however, did not count on the savvy and ferocious opposition of entrepreneurs like Fox and Laemmle, who helped lead the charge among independents, battling in the courts and in the press. Four months after the Patents Company was launched, Laemmle broke from it, initiating what would be a persistently noisy publicity campaign denouncing its tactics.[24] Initially, he bought films for his distribution company from European producers not under patent restrictions, but even that supply was threatened by actions of the trust. To supplement the quantity of films for his exchange, Laemmle formed the Independent Motion Picture Company (with its apt acronym, IMP) in June 1909 to produce his own films and was soon tweaking the established leaders with such then-revolutionary practices as publicizing actors by name to build their fan base.[25] Fox, too, began producing films and also leveraged politically connected New York acquaintances to press his claims that the Patents Company stood in violation of the Sherman Act.[26] Not all of the immigrant entrepreneurs were confrontational, however. Zukor made an unsuccessful attempt to obtain a filmmaker's license from the trust, but, after selling his theater interests, plunged into production anyway, convinced that high-quality feature films (rather than the short formats favored by the Patents Company) would ultimately be the key to gaining a wider audience for movies.[27]

Independent producers operated with cloak-and-dagger schemes designed to keep them a few steps ahead of the Patents Company "police." One tactic that maverick filmmakers employed was to insert patent-protected internal camera machinery within the outer casing of a brand of camera not under patent protection.[28] The subterfuge also led to increased location shooting, particularly in Southern California, which offered weather favorable to year-round outdoor filming and a site fortuitously far from the East Coast–based Patents Company enforcers. In the extremity, renegade production crews could take a quick trip south of the Mexican border (and out of U.S. jurisdiction).[29] By 1912, however, a federal antitrust suit had been filed against the Patents Company, and a decision in 1915, upheld in 1916, officially broke up the trust, reopening the field. These immigrants then adroitly exploited their regained freedom to build Hollywood's largest and most successful studios—Paramount (Zukor), Metro-Goldwyn-Mayer (Mayer and Schenck), Goldwyn Pictures (Goldwyn), Fox Studios (Fox), Warner Brothers (Warner), and Universal (Laemmle). Yet another of our foreign-born Jewish leaders, David Sarnoff, later helped found RKO Studios while he served as head of RCA.

However much these filmmaking entrepreneurs had in common, though, it would be a mistake to assume that they acted as a team in fostering their new industry. While there were some examples of cooperation, these leaders were also ruthlessly competitive, an attitude that extended to their dealings with each other. Mayer, for instance, never trusted Schenck (head of the Loew's organization, which owned MGM) after learning that Schenck had cut a buyout deal with Fox behind Mayer's back.[30] The deal fell through, but the betrayal stung forever. Harry Warner and his own brother, Jack, fought so viciously that they did not speak for the last two years of Harry's life.[31] Zukor found Goldwyn impossible to work with and forced him out of an early production partnership.[32] In the late 1940s, Goldwyn essentially proved Zukor

*Harry Warner of Warner Brothers Studio and Louis B. Mayer of Metro-Goldwyn-Mayer at a film industry meeting in 1942.* (Source: Bettmann/CORBIS)

right as he headed a coalition of other independent producers in an antitrust battle against Zukor's Paramount, as well as against Warner, Loew's, and others, ultimately forcing these concerns to separate their production companies from their theater holdings.[33] As in Zemurray's case, the difficulty of establishing themselves as outsiders didn't noticeably soften these immigrants. If anything, it seemed to make their hold on their gains more tenacious.

## Higher Grade of Foreigners Makes It in Northeast

The formation of the movie industry illustrates the chilling effect the Northeast region had on the business prospects of outsiders. Although almost all these leaders started out in business there, the industry's move to Southern California was a key step in their escape from the strictures of the Patents Company, which was rooted in the Northeastern establishment. The tight-knit business circles of the Northeast proved relatively impervious to foreigners, requiring some form of extra leverage for penetration. In Zemurray's case, the leverage was accrued from success elsewhere in the country, but many other leaders who made it in the Northeast brought their leverage in the form of connections or wealth from their family origins abroad. Although the majority of foreign-born leaders finding success early in the century in other parts of the United States were poor, those who made it in the Northeast were almost exactly the reverse—nearly two-thirds were wealthy or middle class (figure 3-3).

Among the well-connected nonnatives who rose to business success in the Northeast was the German Jacob H. Schiff. His father, Moses, a prosperous stockbroker in Frankfurt, had fretted about Jacob in a letter to a cousin in America: "My second son, now seventeen—Jacob—is quite a problem because he already feels that Frankfurt is too small for his ambition."[34] In the letter, Moses delicately inquired whether this cousin, who lived in Saint

**FIGURE 3-3**

### Early foreigners who succeeded in Northeast a cut above

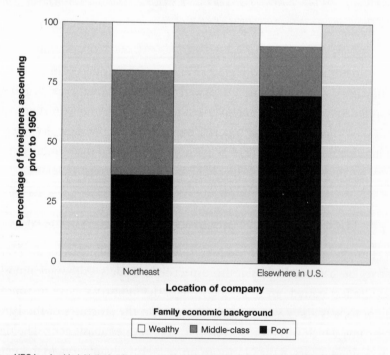

Source: HBS Leadership Initiative's "Great American Business Leaders of the 20th Century" database.

*German immigrant Jacob Henry Schiff, senior partner of the Kuhn, Loeb investment firm, speaking at a groundbreaking ceremony in 1905.* (Source: Getty Images)

Louis, might be willing to host Jacob. The cousin tactfully declined, but it wasn't long before Jacob nevertheless made the journey to America. With his father's blessing, he set off in 1865 at age eighteen, taking five hundred dollars in savings and even leaving behind a series of letters in England to be mailed to his mother during his voyage so she wouldn't worry. Through friends in Frankfurt, he had arranged to meet a fellow countryman with Wall Street connections, and within two years, young Schiff had established his own brokerage firm in New York City with two other German partners. The venture, however, was dissolved in 1872 after a partner's departure, leaving Schiff at loose ends.

Though he'd been naturalized as a U.S. citizen in 1870, Schiff subsequently returned to work in Germany, where, ironically, the connection that would truly launch him to business prominence was made. There he met fellow German Abraham Kuhn, retired founder of the New York banking firm of Kuhn, Loeb and Company. Kuhn, impressed with Schiff, suggested he consider returning to New York and joining the firm now run by partner Solomon Loeb, also a German immigrant. Schiff was torn about leaving Germany now, as his father had died in 1873 and his widowed mother remained. She, on the other hand, purportedly encouraged his departure with words that would prove prophetic: "You are made for America."[35] He came back to New York and joined Kuhn, Loeb in January 1875, becoming a full partner later that year after cementing the relationship by marrying Loeb's daughter, whom he had met during his previous time in New York.

His father-in-law quickly found that Schiff's ambitions not only were too big for Frankfurt but outstripped his own as well. Loeb believed that *no* was the best initial answer to any proposed business deal, since it was always possible to change one's mind later.[36] In keeping with this conservative approach, his firm remained of modest size and scope. Schiff, however, was significantly less risk averse, immersing himself and Kuhn, Loeb in the emerging railroad industry. His efforts yielded such returns that Loeb eventually acquiesced to his young partner's abilities and allowed him to take the lead in setting the firm's direction. At Loeb's retirement in 1885, the transition was official, and Schiff became senior partner of Kuhn, Loeb. He now proceeded full steam into railroad investments, and a partnership with Edward H. Harriman in the 1897 Union Pacific reorganization was one of his most noted ventures. Some ten years later, Schiff and Harriman battled the legendary banker J. P. Morgan and railroad magnate James J. Hill of the Great Northern Railway to a draw in seeking control of the Northern Pacific. (Hill, a Canadian immigrant himself, is discussed later in this chapter.) From his base in New York City, Schiff's influence grew to span the country; by his death in 1920, it was hard to find a spur of railroad track anywhere in America without some financial connection to Jacob H. Schiff.[37]

## Learning the Way to Credibility

Schiff arrived with moderate wealth and connections, but he had only modest attainments in what became another source of leverage for our foreign-born leaders—education. Again, those making their way in the Northeast typically had the edge in this respect over peers succeeding elsewhere. Well over half of the foreigners succeeding there had college degrees or better, versus just 32 percent of those succeeding in other parts of the United States. Overall, however, the educational attainments of the foreigners are lofty enough to suggest that such credentials played a particularly important part in these leaders' access to business roles. The immigrants in our set of leaders came notably close to matching or exceeding the educational profile of comparable native leaders by era, even though the overall population of immigrants had less education than native-born Americans. When education statistics were first tracked in the U.S. Census of 1940, just over 5 percent of foreign-born white men over twenty-five had spent even a year or more in college, though more than twice that percentage of U.S.-born white men had.[38] Meanwhile, over 45 percent of the foreign-born white males on our list falling in that age group in 1940 had college degrees. True, over 56 percent of native white male leaders in the same age bracket were college educated, but the foreign leaders outstripped their peer group educationally by a much higher multiple. The evidence points to education playing a more critical role for foreigners trying to gain business access than it did for U.S.-born leaders. Education, particularly when it conveyed technical expertise, was obviously an important means of overcoming other barriers that stood in the way of outsiders.

One of the best-educated foreign leaders early in the century was Swiss entrepreneur Camille Dreyfus, who earned a PhD in chemistry from the venerable University of Basel in his hometown in 1902, then continued his studies in Paris at the Sorbonne. It wasn't long before Camille and his brother Henri, also a PhD chemist, looked for a way to use their expertise in building a business. Their first effort, appropriate in the context of Basel's thriving dye firms (among them the forerunners of chemical giants Ciba-Geigy and Sandoz), was to produce synthetic indigo dye, a product being marketed then with some success by the German firm BASF. The Dreyfuses, for whatever reason, didn't find sufficient opportunity there and shifted their focus to cellulose acetate. Its chemical cousin, cellulose nitrate, more familiarly known as celluloid, was then widely used not only in photographic film but in hairbrushes, combs, buttons, billiard balls, eyeglass frames, dentures, and more. The compound's popularity was tempered by its extreme flammability—celluloid-related fires occurred with frightening regularity in factories, theaters, and even ladies' hairdos.[39] The Dreyfus brothers reasoned that cellulose acetate, a nonflammable compound, offered a safer substitute if it could be commercially manufactured. After some experimentation, they developed a workable process, and by 1910, their factory in Basel was producing tons of the material weekly for European markets. The Dreyfuses also began exploring ways to produce fibers from the compound.

A more urgent use, however, prompted the British government to extend the Dreyfus brothers an invitation in 1914. At the time, cellulose nitrate solution was applied as "dope" to stiffen and waterproof the fabric of airplane wings, with unfortunate incendiary potential if the planes were struck by gunfire. As air combat became an important factor in World War I, the British wanted a supply of a less flammable doping compound on their own turf. They offered Camille money to build a cellulose acetate plant in England and guaranteed they would purchase its output. In exchange, Britain wanted the Dreyfuses' patent rights. Camille built the plant, but with private financing, as he was convinced there were even more valuable uses of the product ahead.[40] The United States, with motives similar to Great Britain's, helped Camille start American Cellulose & Chemical Manufacturing Company with a plant in Cumberland, Maryland, in 1918, but when the war ended, so did the high demand for cellulose acetate dope, and the half-finished plant in Maryland went into mothballs.

To save their embryonic enterprise, the Dreyfus brothers applied themselves in earnest to the manufacture of fiber from cellulose acetate. They achieved success by extruding the compound from fine nozzles, but there was one *small* setback—the yarn produced from such fibers could not be woven or dyed by any conventional methods. Undaunted, they developed an adapted weaving mechanism and had friends in the dye industry in Basel help create suitable new formulas.[41] By 1920, the brothers began manufacturing their new material, dubbed Celanese, in Great Britain, and the resurrected U.S. plant produced its first fibers on Christmas Day 1924. Feisty Camille fought all attempts to label the product *rayon*, the term already in use for synthetic fabric derived from cellulose. The fibers used in rayon were produced by a process not utilizing acetate, and Dreyfus asserted that Celanese, due to its unique origin, had properties much more like real silk and, of course, warranting a higher price. The company guarded its branded technology aggressively, seeking and receiving hundreds of patents.

In 1927, American Cellulose was renamed Celanese Corporation of America, making the company's new focus crystal clear.[42] That same year, the Dreyfuses wrested control of their British operation from other investors, securing an international empire that included British Celanese and the recently organized Canadian Celanese. While Henri focused on the business in England, Camille became a flamboyant champion for Celanese in the United States, marrying American radio and opera singer Jean Tennyson and always dressing in colorful attire made from his trademarked cloth. Sales began to rise sharply in the late 1930s, and during World War II, American Celanese scored with a new ultrastrong fabric suitable for parachutes and other military uses. The company hit sales or profit records consistently throughout the 1940s.[43] Camille never stopped asserting his invention's uniqueness, and in 1951, just five years before his death, he won a ruling from the Federal Trade Commission. Celanese fiber could officially be termed *acetate*, a name that would distinguish the material from rayon, once and for all.[44]

## Access Advantages to the More Easily Assimilated

Credibility was crucial to outsiders looking for ways to make their mark, and for those not possessed of connections or educational advantages, just fitting in counted for a lot. If we compare our leaders' countries of origin with U.S. immigration patterns, it's obvious that the better a person's speech and religious ties matched those of most Americans, the likelier the person was to find a route to business success. Clear proof is the dominance of English-speaking Canadians, who enjoyed the advantages of common language and, usually, common religion with the U.S. Protestant majority. Most Canadian leaders also grew up in convenient proximity to America's biggest business corridors in the Northeast and Midwest. Such Canadians comprise the greatest number of foreign-born U.S. business leaders in our group, about one-fifth of the total. This overrepresents their proportion of immigrants during 1820–1920, the heyday of U.S. immigration, nearly fourfold (figure 3-4).[45] By contrast, Ireland and Italy, which between them provided about one-quarter of the country's immigrants during that period, are represented by only three Irishmen among our total of ninety-three foreign-born leaders. We will discuss the implications of religious affiliation further in another chapter, but the obvious link between these countries is their majority-Catholic faith. Adding a religious gap to the ethnic and status gaps between these immigrants and the influential majority in U.S. business circles created a chasm too big for most outsiders to cross in one generation.

One of the typical, easily assimilated Canadians was James J. Hill, born to Scotch-Irish Protestant parents in Ontario. However, the early going for Hill was not particularly smooth—his father died suddenly in 1852, when James was fourteen, and he swiftly went to work, despite his mother's protests that he should stay in school.[46] At seventeen, satisfied that his younger brother could adequately care for his mother, he left his home region to seek greater prospects. As he recounted the story, finding a place where he'd fit in was far from his first priority. He dreamed of making his fortune in the Orient and went to Atlantic coast ports to find a position with a vessel headed to the Far East, but without success. Recalling some schoolmates whose families lived in the Canadian west, he next set off in that direction with an idea of making his way from there to the Pacific, which promised more possibilities for reaching

**FIGURE 3-4**

## Canada has biggest access edge

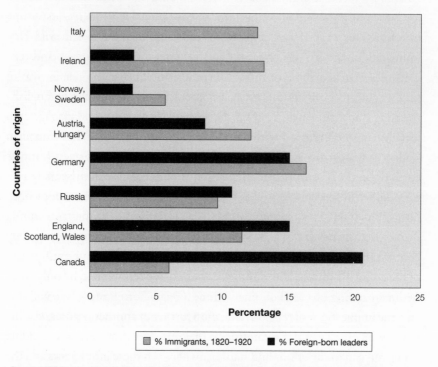

*Source*: HBS Leadership Initiative's "Great American Business Leaders of the 20th Century" database; U.S. Department of Homeland Security, *Yearbook of Immigration Statistics, 2003* (Washington, DC: Government Printing Office, 2004), 12–15.

Statistics for the eight most common countries of origin for U.S. immigrants, 1820–1920.

the Orient. He got as far as Saint Paul, but had missed the departure of that year's final band of migrating trappers and traders by just two weeks, meaning he was left to cool his heels in Saint Paul for nearly a year.[47]

During this forced interlude, the Orient's loss turned into Minnesota's gain, as the enterprising Hill put down roots in local business, working for shipping companies on the docks of the Mississippi and gradually building trading interests of his own. By 1866, he had started his own freight transfer company, landing an exclusive contract with the St. Paul and Pacific Railroad to offload produce from riverboats into railroad cars for points west and north. He also operated a fuel supply business, dealing in firewood and then coal, reportedly bringing the first coal ever to Saint Paul.[48] From his American base of operations, he ventured back into his homeland, buying a river steamer and transporting goods to newly established settlements along the Red River in Manitoba. He found such success on this route that by 1872, the famed Hudson's Bay Company had decided it would rather join him than beat him, and the resulting partnership effectively monopolized the river traffic, to great profit.

Ultimately, though, Hill determined that the region's cold climate, which left rivers frozen for much of the year, required railways, not waterways, to address its future transportation needs. He saw the potential in the struggling St. Paul and Pacific Railroad and in 1878 sold his other businesses to buy it out of receivership with the help of several financial backers, including his Hudson's Bay Company colleagues. That same year, he supervised the completion of the railroad's connection to the Minnesota border, beating a deadline set by the state legislature for retaining the railroad's land grants. Soon after it joined a Canadian rail link up to Winnipeg, the line was renamed the St. Paul, Minneapolis and Manitoba Railway. By 1889, the career of this man popularly known as "the Empire Builder" had really taken flight, as Hill's emerging group of lines had crossed North Dakota and most of Montana and was rechristened the Great Northern Railway. He led the railroad over more than twenty years of successful growth. Alone among the major U.S. transcontinental lines, the Great Northern expanded all the way to the West Coast without government subsidies (apart from the original land grant to the Red River) and without missing a dividend payment to its shareholders.

Hill's consistently profitable operation reached Seattle and Vancouver, thanks to his tight management of construction and operating costs and his commitment to developing rail traffic along carefully selected routes. He promoted agricultural development by sending demonstration trains with expert teachers down his lines, not to mention distributing English-bred bulls to enhance the stock of farmers in the region. He never quite gave up on his visions of the Orient, either, as the prospect of trade to Asia produced one of the few blemishes on his otherwise-successful business record—a steamship venture in the Pacific, which failed in 1905. Hill didn't get to the Far East, but today, nearly ninety years after his death, Amtrak's service from Chicago to Seattle runs on a train named the Empire Builder.[49]

*Canadian James J. Hill (center) in Minnesota inspecting one of his many railroad lines, the St. Paul and Pacific Railroad (circa 1907).* (Source: Minnesota Historical Society/CORBIS)

## New Openings for Foreigners Later in the Century

The percentage of foreign-born leaders dips slightly in the second half of the century (from 10 percent of all leaders in the first half to just over 8 percent in the second half), but this level actually comes much closer to being representative of the foreign presence in the population than was seen earlier in the century. In 1950, just over 10 percent of all individuals in the United States twenty-one or older were foreign-born.[50] Significant restrictions on immigration had been enacted in the early decades of the century, culminating in the quota laws of the 1920s, and the flow of foreigners into America dropped sharply in the 1930s, not reaching 1920s-era totals again until the 1970s. By this time, the country's population overall had nearly doubled, making the proportional impact of immigration much smaller.[51] The improved representation of immigrants among our leaders in the second half of the century suggests changing attitudes toward foreigners in business circles, but a more significant indication of change is the dramatically increased percentage of foreigners who reached success as hired CEOs versus founders (figure 3-5). Clearly, access for these foreign outsiders to what had been an insider path was much improved. Although hired CEO leadership certainly increased throughout U.S. businesses in the second half-century, foreigners participated in this increase as fully as U.S.-born leaders and even more so. Far from a continued dependence on the outsider's path to success through entrepreneurship, foreign-born leaders were now achieving an acceptance that extended to the inner circle of executive leadership.

A key reason for improved business access by foreigners after 1950 was the increasingly multinational orientation of U.S.-based companies. A foreign-born CEO was no longer unthinkable but was instead becoming desirable for companies hoping to sell or produce goods overseas. In this period, foreign-born leaders on our list headed venerable U.S. firms like General Electric,

**FIGURE 3-5**

## Foreigners gain CEO access after midcentury

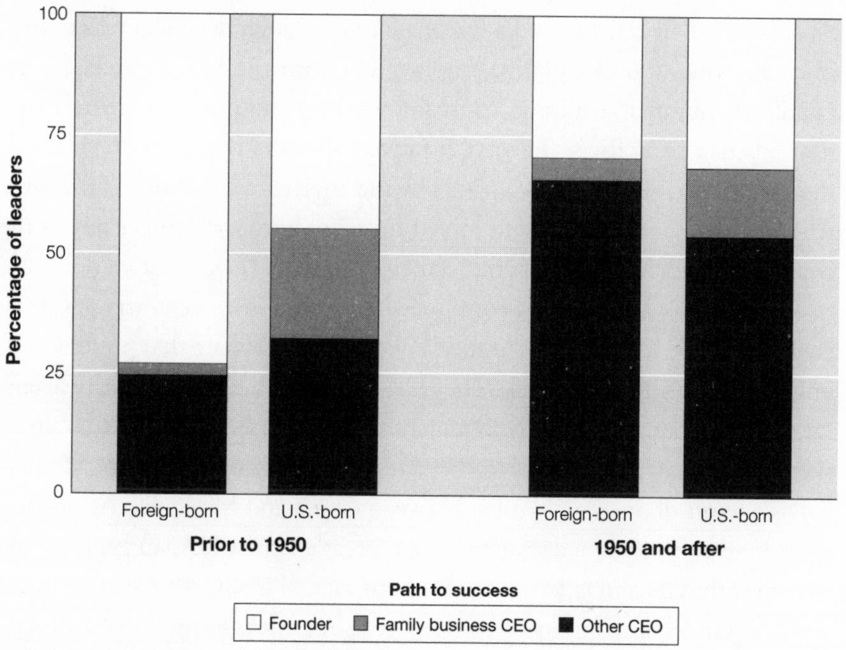

*Source*: HBS Leadership Initiative's "Great American Business Leaders of the 20th Century" database.

DuPont, Coca-Cola, Ford, Campbell Soup Company, Exxon, H. J. Heinz, Revlon, and Warner-Lambert. These hires were also by no means the typical immigrants of earlier generations but often leaders who came from middle-class backgrounds or better. They rose successfully through management ranks in their homelands and were brought to the United States specifically to take leadership roles. As such, they resembled Camille Dreyfus much more than they did Dennis Sheedy. Foreign-born leaders of this period overall had education levels almost identical to U.S.-born leaders, with over 40 percent having graduate degrees. In economic terms as well, foreign leaders from 1950 onward matched or exceeded the status of their U.S. counterparts, with only 30 percent having poor backgrounds in either case. This was a striking change from earlier in the century, when more than half of foreign-born leaders had come from poverty.

Plato Malozemoff was one of those well-heeled CEOs, a leader born to educated, prosperous parents in Saint Petersburg, Russia, in 1909. He reportedly was named after a character in Tolstoy's *War and Peace*, which hints at why his father, Alexander, was regarded as a troublemaker by the czar and was briefly imprisoned for revolutionary activity.[52] The family relocated to Siberia, but their exile offered a fortunate twist. Alexander, who was trained in engineering, found lucrative employment with the British-backed Lena Goldfields Limited, a mining company working the mineral-rich territory near Siberia's Lena River. In 1920, however, after the Bolshevik Revolution, the mining operation was confiscated by the Soviet government. At the time, Alexander was in America. He cabled his wife, Elizabeth, to get out of the country immediately with Plato and their other son. Travel westward in Russia was hazardous because of continued skirmishes in the country's waning civil war, so the Malozemoffs headed toward China, a route that presented an only slightly less daunting trek. They were detained by Soviet security agents for more than a month near the Mongolian border, escaping from that situation only to face further delays in Urga (now Ulaanbaatar, capital of Mongolia) as a result of ongoing conflict between China and Mongolia. Again they escaped, this time just a day ahead of a renegade czarist Russian general who took over the city and killed all the Russians in it.[53] Finally, they were reunited with Alexander in China and proceeded to America, settling in San Francisco. Ironically enough, Lenin, seeking outside capital to develop the new Soviet economy, would invite foreign investment back into the country just four years later, and Plato's father returned to Lena Goldfields at that time with funds from American, British, and German investors. He had restored the Siberian mining group to profitable operation by 1929, only to see it then summarily (and rather ungratefully) seized by Stalin's government.

International mining, with all the political challenges that accompanied it, was thus in the blood of Plato Malozemoff, and as he grew up in the United States, he prepared himself to follow in his father's footsteps. He earned a bachelor's degree in mining engineering at the University of California at Berkeley, then a master's degree in metallurgical engineering from the Montana School of Mines (now Montana Tech of the University of Montana). Upon graduation in 1932, he continued for two years in Montana, working for the State Department of Mines and, later, the Depression-era Works Progress Administration. With job prospects scarce, he even considered taking employment as a violinist, another pursuit in which both he and Alexander excelled. Plato eventually returned to Berkeley and worked for an engineering company for four years. After that, he spent about five years trying to develop mining enterprises in Argentina and Costa Rica with his father.

The Malozemoffs' ventures in South and Central America were stymied by shortages of goods and restrictions on freight movement as World War II began. After a boat carrying the supplies that had offered their last hope for continuing operations fell victim to a German U-boat's torpedo in a Costa Rican harbor, Plato returned to the United States to ride out the war. In 1943 he joined the U.S. Office of Price Administration (OPA), where he analyzed applications from mining companies for premium payouts from the government on the basis of their ability to produce desired quotas of certain metals. Here he met Philip Kraft, a geologist and mining engineer with Newmont Mining Company, whose applications to the OPA Malozemoff was handling.

Newmont, a diversified investment company that had been organized about the same time Plato and his family were making their escape through Mongolia, had a compound name derived from *New York*, where the firm was based, and *Montana*, where the founder grew up. Initially, the company largely ran in a fashion rooted more in Wall Street than the Mountain West, investing primarily in gold and copper mining, but with the aim of quickly developing projects and selling them at an early stage. Newmont generally had little if any involvement in ongoing operations. The firm also maintained a significant stock portfolio to help finance the mining ventures and to hedge those activities against market volatility. The word *Mining* had not even been added to the company's name until 1925. By the early 1940s, however, although it was still structured essentially as an investment holding company, Newmont was starting to pursue more complex mining projects in which success required lengthier commitments and technical expertise. The company's leadership thus included more specialists in prospecting and mineral extraction to complement the financial acumen of earlier principals with legal or banking backgrounds. Kraft was quite impressed with Malozemoff and thought the businessman could be an asset to the team. Newmont's president, Fred Searls, also a geologist, was less enthusiastic, agreeing to hire Malozemoff only after several meetings with him over the course of about a year. The salary Newmont offered was less than what he'd have gotten to stay on at the government office after the war, but Malozemoff accepted, intrigued by the opportunity.

When he started in October 1945 with the job title of *staff mining engineer*, Malozemoff soon learned that he was essentially the *only* staff member, let alone engineer, serving the small, tight-knit group of Newmont executives. He was called upon for assistance by all the principals, including Searls, who shortly began to channel every prospective mining investment through Malozemoff for evaluation, even if the president sometimes ignored his protégé's recommendations. Searls also gave Malozemoff a trial in the Wall Street side of the company's operations, putting him in charge of a $360,000 stock portfolio, the equivalent of several million dollars in twenty-first-century terms. Malozemoff managed this sum to the tune of double-digit annual returns. Searls's confidence in him evidently grew in proportion to such results.

In 1950, Malozemoff got a chance to lead his first mining project for Newmont. A Canadian enterprise, Sherritt Gordon Mines, had been surveying for new mining sites in northern Manitoba near a successful but almost-exhausted copper mine it already operated. The exploration had revealed promising concentrations of nickel and copper a couple hundred miles away from the depleted mine. To make the new mine profitable, however, the team needed a more economical means of extracting the metals than shipping the processed concentrate from the remote location to a traditional smelter. The Sherritt Gordon partners proposed an experimental technique that involved leaching the ore with ammonia. Skeptical at first, Malozemoff gradually became convinced enough to study the problem himself—that other mining companies had rejected the idea as unworkable only seemed to energize him for the endeavor, and he convinced Searls to back the project. A pilot plant was established to validate the metallurgical process, and by May 1952, two test runs had been completed. Although some kinks remained to be worked out, most of the project team members felt they had enough data to start construction of the commercial-scale plant. Malozemoff, however, firmly insisted that another pilot run was necessary and stressed that he needed to be satisfied to present a positive recommendation to lenders.

Eight months later, with the desired proof in hand, he brought in the money. When plant construction costs began running 40 to 50 percent over budget, Malozemoff also negotiated a government advance on anticipated production to make up most of the shortfall, with investments by Newmont and J.P. Morgan Bank supplying the balance.[54] By the end of 1953, with loads of ore concentrate already shipping to the new refinery, Malozemoff's successful management of the project apparently had removed any doubts still harbored by Searls—as of January 1, 1954, Plato Malozemoff, age forty-four, became president of Newmont Mining.[55] Seven months later, the Sherritt Gordon mine was producing its first nickel powder and was on its way to about two decades of profitable operation.

Playing to his strengths, Malozemoff would lead Newmont to deeper involvement in the management of its mines, but he also continuously diversified its holdings, minimizing dependence on returns from politically volatile regions and increasing its North American presence.[56] His father's experience of losing hard-won gains to dictatorial seizure doubtless kept him mindful of the value of governmental stability. Perhaps the company's key triumph was a discovery of gold deposits near Carlin, Nevada. Two Newmont geologists were intrigued by the implications of a 1960 U.S. Geological Survey report on a region in north-central Nevada that had previously been mined for gold. Believing that this new map might provide the guidance necessary to exploit gold reserves missed by earlier prospectors, the staffers persuaded Malozemoff to fund an exploration. In fact, the gold deposits at Carlin were in the form of infinitesimally small particles—invisible to the naked eye and even to microscopes. The accumulated amount, however, was huge, and Newmont gained for its efforts the lion's share of the largest U.S. gold strike of the twentieth century.[57]

One gold mine does not suffice for a Midas touch, and Malozemoff did stumble with an ill-timed investment in the coal industry just before massive strikes of the late 1970s; he also faced continued losses from a failed New York cement company. Still, winners outnumbered and definitely outgained losers during his tenure, and by 1980, he was being hailed for his diversification strategy, which put Newmont in a superior position compared with its industry peers. Malozemoff's attention to detail was also legendary—a dyed-in-the-wool engineer even after over two decades in the executive suite, he was often known to pull out a slide rule to check calculations being presented. "If you plan the wrong diameter pipe, he'll probably find it," quipped one investment analyst, with apparent appreciation for such diligence.[58]

Malozemoff retained his leadership role well beyond retirement age, but analysts didn't fret over the length of his stay, worrying instead that, when he did leave, no successor could possibly lead the company as well as he had. In January 1986, with Newmont's assets now valued at $2.3 billion, over fifteen times its size at his ascension, Malozemoff, seventy-seven, finally retired. Succeeding him as chairman and CEO was a South African mining engineer, reinforcing that a foreigner with the right credentials now faced little or no disadvantage in finding opportunities to lead an American business. Although Plato Malozemoff left Russia around age eleven, only about three years younger than the age of Samuel Zemurray at his immigration, there is no record of Malozemoff's accent being cited as an obstacle to successful business communication.[59]

## A Melting Pot Mellowed

Whether or not early twentieth-century America was indeed a melting pot, we see that knowing how to take the heat was definitely a requirement for foreign-born business leaders successful enough to make our list in that era. Entrepreneurship was the first and most obvious recourse to them as outsiders, but even this route depended on finding the right opening. The old baseball saw to "hit 'em where they ain't" constituted the best advice. The undeveloped but rapidly growing West proved the most porous business environment, with almost everyone a new arrival and few if any constraints therefore introduced on the basis of birthplace. Making the trek there may have been difficult, but the absence of barriers made it worthwhile. An alternative was to find the "frontier" of an emerging industry in which the absence of established competitors enabled an outsider to grab a foothold in spite of prejudice. The Northeast, teeming though it was with immigrants, featured entrenched business leaders harboring a wary if not outright xenophobic attitude toward foreigners. The tools for gaining their trust were money, connections, and education, and the more of those three that an immigrant possessed, the better the chances for such an outsider to penetrate the inner circle of business.

Also, in the early twentieth century, just as all birthplaces within the United States were not created equal, neither were the disadvantages of all foreigners. Those whose language and religious traditions blended easily into the Protestant American majority faced little if any stigma based on their origins. A Canadian like James Hill had no notable disadvantage compared with a newcomer from Iowa or Ohio when he sought work in Minnesota in the 1860s—moreover, as suggested by our exploration of U.S. regional loyalties, he would have had an edge over arrivals from Georgia or Mississippi! On the other hand, Jews, Catholics, and any immigrants who spoke with a strong accent had a much tougher road to acceptance, generally requiring either a heavy dose of entrepreneurial perseverance or a strong package of connections and professional expertise to overcome the challenge. For them in particular, success also required fortifying hard-won gains against attempts, often from the home-grown business community, to reverse these advances. Such leaders learned that the problem wasn't just *finding* a niche in their adopted homeland—they needed to carve it out first, and then be prepared to defend it.

By the second half of the century, the nearly proportional representation of immigrants among this group of leaders signaled both changing attitudes in business and changes in the immigrants themselves. Not so much personal enlightenment as pure pragmatism functioned in prompting large U.S. companies with extensive international operations to include more foreigners in top management, including the CEO role. Overall, preferences for professional and educational qualifications were also beginning to outweigh factors of religion and birthplace, standing many foreigners in good stead to compete with Americans on a much more equal basis than before. That these new immigrants could compete successfully had everything to do with their socioeconomic status, which differed vastly from the backgrounds typical in an earlier era. Those leaders rising later in the century largely no longer represented the "huddled masses yearning to breathe free," but were instead well-educated individuals of the middle and upper classes in their homelands. Ethnic barriers utterly unbreached in the first half of the century began to fall, as foreign-born Latinos and Asians appear on our list starting in the 1950s and make up more than 10 percent of foreign leaders in the second half-century. Although most of them founded businesses, one (Robert Goizueta of Coca-Cola) joined the CEO brigade, heading a large and well-established U.S. firm. These non-native leaders, though, were also atypical individuals who constituted the cream of the crop; they mostly came from well-established families and obtained advanced education in the United States.

Overall, although the impact of foreign birth per se appeared to wane as the century went on, there's no evidence that *poor* immigrants found it easier to succeed in 1980 than they had in 1920. Birthplace may no longer have been determinative, but other related factors continued to sort certain foreigners to the outside of leadership tracks, and the impact of these factors changed more slowly. These observations prepare us for a look at religious affiliation, a dimension that quite commonly amplified the outsider status of foreign-born leaders and perpetuated the barriers against advancement of later generations of their families born within the United States.

# FOUR

# Religion

## Infiltrating the Protestant
## Establishment over Generations

*"You're an honest boy," said Mr. Greyson. "Who taught you to be honest?"*

*"Nobody," said Dick. "But it's mean to cheat and steal. I've always knowed that."*

*"Then you've got ahead of some of our business men. Do you read the Bible?"*

*"No," said Dick. "I've heard it's a good book, but I don't know much about it."*

*"You ought to go to some Sunday School. Would you be willing?"*

*"Yes," said Dick. "I want to grow up 'spectable. But I don't know where to go."*

*"Then I'll tell you. The church I attend is at the corner of Fifth Avenue and Twenty-First Street."*

*"I've seen it," said Dick.*

*"I have a class in the Sunday School there. If you'll come next Sunday, I'll take you into my class and do what I can to help you."*

—Horatio Alger, *Ragged Dick*

YOUNG DICK takes his mentor up on the invitation to church in a chapter entitled "Dick's First Appearance in Society." As the name suggests, the chapter's focus is not on religious conversion but on Dick's acquaintance with a social class for whom churchgoing was part of the routine of respectable living. The prominent role of church attendance in the chronicle of a boy's rise into business signals how important the local church was in the late nineteenth and early twentieth centuries as a place to meet the "right" sorts of people, extend personal networks, and develop access to business opportunities. When Alger wrote the book, the address mentioned by Dick's benefactor Mr. Greyson was in fact the site of the South Reformed Dutch Church, a congregation descended from the earliest established church on Manhattan Island in the seventeenth century. The city's prestigious Union Club, haven to Astors and Vanderbilts, was on the opposite corner, offering a vivid confluence of spiritual and social connections. Indeed, while the Greysons are depicted as compassionate and sincere in their faith, the chapter narrates in great detail not Dick's experiences in Sunday school but his awkwardness during lunch in their elegant home.

The connection between socially acceptable Protestant religious affiliations and business leadership is quite evident in our group during the early part of the century. Equally evident, however, is the vanishing of this pattern by late in the century (figure 4-1).

The proportion of leaders whose religious affiliation could not be identified grows higher with almost every passing decade after 1940, even though we might expect that the characteristics of recent leaders would be more readily known. Instead, the typical sources for this information, such as *Who's Who* listings and press clippings, shift noticeably in the details they provide about leaders, with later materials being much less likely to mention religious affiliation. There is, of course, no way to measure the sincerity of leaders' religious convictions in the earlier decades to discern whether the silence reflects a genuine change in sentiment or just a reduction in the role played by religious affiliation in one's public persona. What is nevertheless clear is that this rising proportion of unknown religious affiliates comes mainly at the expense of the previously influential Protestant denominations, with which it once served a business leader to be publicly identified. Jewish leaders make up a fairly steady proportion of around 10 percent of leaders from 1900 onward, whereas the proportion of Catholic leaders rises to about 10 percent by midcentury and remains there through the century's end.[1]

## Early Access Advantages for Episcopalians and Presbyterians

Leadership traits in the early part of the twentieth century, just a few decades removed from Alger's stories, definitely support Digby Baltzell's classic con-

FIGURE 4-1

## Protestant prominence diminishes over time

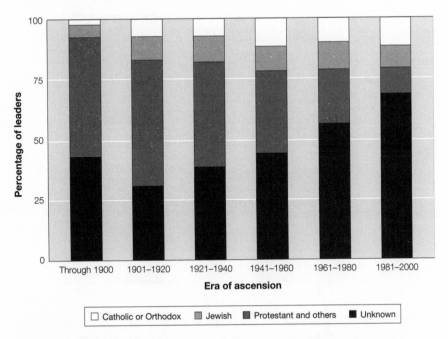

*Source*: HBS Leadership Initiative's "Great American Business Leaders of the 20th Century" database.

For the sake of completeness, in this graph, a very small number (11 of 364 total in the grouping) of "other" religious affiliates not easily categorized as Protestant, Catholic, Jewish, or Orthodox Christian, have been included in the "Protestant and others" category, of whom the greatest number (5) are Mormons.

ception of a "Protestant establishment" in business. For our leaders ascending up through 1949, two-thirds were identified with a religious affiliation, matching very closely with data derived from the 1890 census suggesting that about two-thirds of the U.S. population aged fifteen and over had ties to a church or another religious group.[2] Again, although this comparison fails to meet the standard of a statistical control group, it serves as a basis for understanding how much our leaders reflected a typical sample from the contemporary population. In this way, our group's divergence from the larger population emerges quite clearly, as approximately 30 percent of our leaders were Episcopalian or Presbyterian, denominations together comprising only about 7 percent of the corresponding population (figure 4-2).

**FIGURE 4-2**

## Episcopalians and Presbyterians dominate leadership, not population

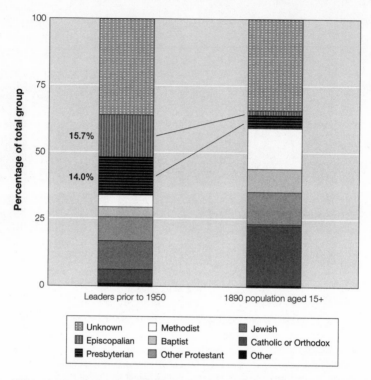

| | | |
|---|---|---|
| ▦ Unknown | ☐ Methodist | ▨ Jewish |
| ▥ Episcopalian | ▨ Baptist | ■ Catholic or Orthodox |
| ▬ Presbyterian | ▨ Other Protestant | ■ Other |

*Sources*: HBS Leadership Initiative's "Great American Business Leaders of the 20th Century" database. Population proportional data estimated by combining statistics from William M. Newman and Peter L. Halvorson, *Atlas of American Religion: The Denominational Era, 1776–1990* (Walnut Creek, CA: AltaMira Press, 2000), 49, with 1890 U.S. Census population totals for persons aged fifteen and over.

These denominations were particularly linked to privileged births: in this earlier period, over 40 percent of leaders who inherited family businesses were identified as Episcopalian or Presbyterian, while less than 20 percent of leaders from poor backgrounds had these religious backgrounds. This strongly suggests the preeminence of the personal networks accessible to members of these denominations. Factors of place amplified the impact of this advantage in personal networks. As previously discussed, nearly 80 percent of U.S.-born leaders of this period came from the business-rich Northeast and Midwest regions of the country. A similar 80 percent of leaders, whether or not born in these regions, found success there. In short, nearly all these leaders either came from or succeeded in places where Protestant faiths were long entrenched, meaning the oldest and best-established families, commonly also those with the most influence, were from such denominations.

An estimate of religious affiliations and data on the concentrations of churches as early as 1776 show that the top four denominations were Congregational, Presbyterian, Episcopal (Anglican at the time), and Baptist.[3] Congregational churches, however, were almost exclusively clustered in New England, while the other three denominations had much more of a Mid-Atlantic presence, including multiple churches in New York City. The Presbyterians and Baptists already spanned into western Pennsylvania (the western frontier of the colonies at that point) and, along with Episcopalian congregations, into the South.[4] In short, these key Protestant groups had, by the year 1900, legacies of a century or more in highly industrialized states such as New York and Pennsylvania. The tightly regionalized Congregational group, once the country's most numerous Protestant denomination but not centered in its industrial core, largely faded from business prominence—only 10 of our 536 leaders ascending before 1950 were so affiliated.

## Business Leaders Voice Protestant Piety

Max Weber's writings were the most famous if not necessarily the first to hypothesize a religious foundation for America's business successes in the so-called Protestant work ethic. By the late nineteenth and early twentieth centuries, however, the hyper-Calvinist Puritan theology of New England that undergirded Weber's arguments was no longer dominant. By then, social prestige was arguably a greater factor in determining which denominations were most prominent among business leaders. Some leaders nevertheless still spoke out about a faith-based outlook on their work, and their proclamations colored public impressions. Among the more notable on our list was none other than John D. Rockefeller, a Baptist who forthrightly stated in a 1915 interview in *Woman's Home Companion*, "God gave me my money."[5] Viewing his business skills, and thus his financial assets, as divinely ordained gifts, he took his responsibilities for church involvement quite seriously and viewed his daily work as an essential part of his charitable obligations. In his memoirs, he argued that the "best philanthropy" was "the investment of effort or time or money . . . to expand and develop the resources at hand, and to give opportunity for progress and healthful labor where it did not exist before."[6] He went on to express "no sympathy" for the viewpoint that one's vocation and one's philanthropy were separate endeavors.

Another distinguished business leader on our list, Presbyterian and department store pioneer John Wanamaker, similarly integrated an ardent faith with his business life. He was a dedicated Sunday school teacher who at age nineteen in the late 1850s founded a mission Sunday school and church in a rough neighborhood of Philadelphia. The mission grew over the years to become the largest Sunday school in America and one of the most prominent Presbyterian churches in its day. As one biographer noted, his success in starting this "new kind of Sunday School" *preceded* the "new kind of store," as Wanamaker christened his flagship retail enterprise, the Grand Depot, by nearly twenty years.[7] Even after his retail business blossomed, he continued to view Bethany Church and its related ministries, including a daughter congregation in the Philadelphia suburbs that survives to the present, as his most significant endeavor. He headed the Pennsylvania Sabbath School Association for twelve years, ceding its leadership in 1907 to his designated successor, interestingly enough also one of our leaders, Presbyterian and ketchup magnate H. J. Heinz. Wanamaker also enjoyed an appointment as postmaster general under President Benjamin Harrison, but nothing reportedly made him prouder than being named in 1920, just two years before his death, president of the World Sunday School Association.[8]

## Episcopal Church Holds Pinnacle of Prestige

Rockefeller and Wanamaker had the benefit of Protestant religious identities placing them comfortably within the established majority culture, but their affiliations by no means provided the greatest possible advantages for a rise in business. Rockefeller's Baptist denomination boasted almost no elites besides him, and Wanamaker's Presbyterians, while solid in the Midwest, lacked prominence in New York's power circles. The Episcopal Church held that pinnacle, as its congregations were estimated to claim as many as half of New York City's seventy-five multimillionaires in 1900.[9] There is a certain irony in the rise of a church from Anglican, and thus largely Tory, roots to a position of social dominance in the post-Revolutionary United States. After all, the titular head of the Church of England is the British monarch! The length of the

*Episcopalian and business tycoon J. P. Morgan Sr. (center) with daughter Louisa Morgan and son J. P. Morgan Jr. in 1910.* (Source: Time Life Pictures/Getty Images)

church's history in America combined with its prominence in the business capital of New York, however, made it a natural haven for well-established business families who formed the new nation's emerging "royalty"—the princes of capitalism.

Perhaps the crown prince of the well-heeled Episcopalians on our list was financier J. P. Morgan, the maker or breaker of deals for decades on Wall Street. His roots in the church were deep and long cultivated. From his youth, Morgan showed a fascination for things ecclesiastical, collecting as a teenager autographs not from athletes, actors, or even bankers but rather bishops, preserving their responses to his letters of solicitation so reverently that the documents remain today in the archives of the New York library established in his name. From his early thirties until his death in 1913, he served on the vestry of Saint George's Episcopal Church in New York City, spending more than two decades as its senior warden.

Saint George's, far from being a social club, was headed from 1883 to 1906 by W. S. Rainsford, an activist rector dedicated to "democratizing" the church's membership and expanding ministries among immigrants and the poor. Among many reforms, Rainsford made Saint George's a "free" church, abolishing the practice of reserved pews paid for by attending members. Morgan occasionally chafed at the changes, but his rector attested to the banker's overall loyalty and support of Saint George's, noting that when Rainsford suffered an extended illness in 1889, Morgan helped sustain the church's energy by posting himself outside the entrance before services and offering vigorous greetings to congregants from all walks of life.

Morgan's passion also was apparent in his hymn singing, which he loudly and freely enjoyed both in services and at home. He was an enthusiastic lay participant in denominational gatherings, once serving on a committee to revise the Book of Common Prayer. His wealth could not fail to set him apart from the mass of delegates, however, and at such events, he entertained bishops and other guests in such luxurious style as to provoke criticism from concerned (and apparently uninvited) clerics.[10] Still, in Morgan's last will and testament, the initial paragraph disposed not of any material assets but his soul, which he committed "into the hands of my Saviour," continuing with a commendation to his children toward the defense of the specifics of the historic Christian faith "at any cost of personal sacrifice."[11]

These pious expressions from a leading businessman and public figure prompted comment in both the press and the pulpit for weeks after his death in 1913.[12] Reactions ran pro and con, but the response shows how extraordinary such statements from a business leader were seen to be, even in that era. While cutthroat competitive tactics and marital infidelities cited by biographers undermine the consistency with which Morgan privately lived out his publicly prominent faith, as a *churchman*, in the plainest sense of the word, he certainly had few peers.[13] His son and namesake would follow in his Episcopalian loyalties and powerful footsteps, also making our list, but even he would find a way to improve on his father's associations. Rather than the relatively populist Saint George's, the son's home parish would be a tonier congregation in the leafy enclave of Lattingtown, Long Island.[14]

## Religious Affiliations Shift "Upward" with Social Status

Indeed, if the elder Morgan is notable for the depth of his convictions, other Protestant business leaders may have capitalized on relatively pliable religious affiliations to migrate into Episcopalian or other higher-status denominations and their associated networks of influence. Mabel Newcomer, a Vassar economics professor whose 1955 study of U.S. executive backgrounds in the early twentieth century offers a still-unmatched milestone of scope and exhaustiveness, observed this pattern of denominational mobility. She noted that five sons of clergymen in the group of executives she studied had departed from the denominational affiliations of their fathers, in each case moving "upward" in the perceived social standing of a hierarchy that placed Episcopalians at the top and Presbyterians second, trailed by Methodists, Baptists, and others.[15] Another example of this trend can be found in the family of John Jacob Astor, an eighteenth-century German immigrant whose business success preceded our list's selection criteria. Astor was born into the Lutheran Church and, in New York, initially attended the Dutch Reformed, but by the twentieth century, his heirs and namesakes were Episcopalians, fixtures at the city's Trinity Church.[16]

One of the most notable cases of fluidity in denominational status among our leaders occurred in an early Gillette executive, Frank Joseph Fahey. Born in Maryland in 1874 to John and Catherine Ryan Fahey, he evidently began life as a Catholic. As he migrated through jobs in Ohio, Illinois, and New York, he made the acquaintance of John J. Joyce, an Irish Catholic immigrant who had penetrated business circles in the Boston area by building success through entrepreneurship, notably with several bottling companies. Joyce used his wealth to become a key early investor in King C. Gillette's fledgling razor enterprise. Fahey apparently made the most of his networking opportunity with this successful fellow Catholic. In 1902, while still working for a commodities broker in New York, he married Joyce's daughter, Genevieve, in a Catholic ceremony before hundreds of guests, including King Gillette himself, at Saint Augustine's Church in Andover, Massachusetts. The local paper breathlessly described the event as "the largest and most fashionable wedding that Andover has had the pleasure of sheltering for some years."[17]

In 1906, Fahey began working for Gillette's sales organization and started his upward climb, receiving a boost when his father-in-law bought out King Gillette and gained a controlling interest in the company. Gillette retained the title of president, but Joyce served as the company's de facto leader. Fahey, who was already a director and an assistant treasurer, became treasurer in 1911, shortly after Joyce's transaction was completed. In 1916, Fahey, by then essentially functioning as Gillette's chief executive, was divorced from

Genevieve, who alleged "cruel and abusive treatment" by Fahey and was by then under a physician's care for emotional distress that the doctor attributed to "continued nervous and mental strain."[18] Remarkably, the breakup did not cost Fahey his erstwhile father-in-law's professional support, although a vocal shareholder with loyalties to King Gillette launched a letter-writing campaign suggesting Fahey's position was shaky. We'll never know, however, if Joyce's goodwill would have survived Fahey's marriage to Florence Meyer in November 1917, as Joyce just happened to have died the previous January.[19]

Interestingly enough, from the viewpoint of Fahey's official biography, his lavish first wedding and Catholic ties, both of which assisted in a rather critical step in his career path, never existed. *The National Cyclopaedia of American Biography* mentions only his second marriage—and identifies Fahey as Episcopalian.[20] At least one of the motives for his "conversion" was probably the desire to remarry after divorce, but the multiple other ways such a change may have helped him blend into Boston's social and business circles cannot be discounted. If nothing else, Fahey appears to have mastered the art of leveraging whatever connections presented themselves. Entering the door opened by his Irish-Catholic roots and his now-invisible first marriage, Fahey successfully led Gillette through almost two decades of worldwide expansion and exponential sales growth until a company scandal involving overstatement of earnings finally prompted his resignation in 1931.[21]

## Regional History Shapes Access

Though Fahey's story shows that a leader's first religious affiliation was not necessarily his last, the birth origins of these individuals do connect to regional religious patterns (figure 4-3). Over 30 percent of leaders from the Northeast or Midwest are Episcopalian or Presbyterian, while those from the South show a notably higher proportion of Methodists and Baptists. Jewish presence is greater among those born on the East and West coasts, but most striking is the markedly higher percentage of Catholics among Western-born leaders. Catholics, as shown previously in figure 4-2, appeared to be decided outsiders to business success in the first half of the century; at around 5 percent, they were significantly underrepresented among leaders, compared with their greater presence (over 20 percent) in the population. The number of Western-born Catholic leaders who found success in this period may be

**FIGURE 4-3**

**Protestant prominence strongest in Midwest and East; Catholic leaders emerge from West**

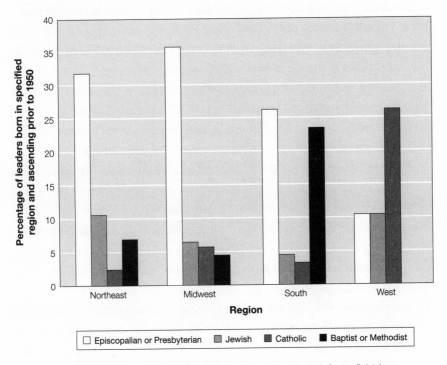

*Source*: HBS Leadership Initiative's "Great American Business Leaders of the 20th Century" database.

small overall (five of only nineteen region-born leaders), but is noteworthy, particularly in contrast to the Northeast, a region that harbored close to half of all U.S. Catholics at the turn of the century.[22] On a percentage basis as well, Catholics made up a significantly greater portion of the population in states like New York and Massachusetts than in California at the time.[23]

Part of the explanation for success by Catholic leaders born in the West seems to be the frontier nature of its developing communities, which, as we have discussed and seen illustrated in the success of foreign-born leaders, presented a higher degree of openness to outsiders. An intriguing secondary element of the story, however, is that this region was one place where Catholics were insiders to some degree, at least by virtue of a long history in the region.

The westward migration of European immigrants in the early part of the nineteenth century helped establish a U.S.-born generation of Catholics, particularly Italians, on the West Coast. This group offered a nucleus of personal networks to support business opportunities there by the early twentieth century. The self-selection of those who had enough resources to make the extra journey from East to West after arriving in the United States biased this group toward families of greater means and education, improving the prospects of the network still further.[24] Perhaps not coincidentally, the West Coast was also one part of the United States where Catholics (mostly Spanish missionaries) preceded the influx of Protestants by several generations, so more recently arriving Catholics found a lengthy and well-established heritage.

After all, when you are born Catholic in a town called San José, in the county of Santa Clara, and the region's largest city is San Francisco, how much of an outsider can you be? Such was the situation for Amadeo Peter Giannini, born in 1870 to two Italian immigrants in California. When he was six, his father, a farmer, was murdered by a disgruntled worker, but the family maintained financial stability thanks to his resourceful mother and his stepfather, Lorenzo Scatena, who joined the family when Amadeo was ten. Scatena's produce-commission business on San Francisco's waterfront offered Giannini his first glimpse of commerce, for which he showed immediate aptitude. At age twelve, he carried out an impromptu direct-mail campaign, soliciting farmers for their crops, to much success and the great surprise of his stepfather. Three years later, Amadeo started working for Scatena full time, and his persistence and prowess in securing contracts quickly became legendary.

In 1901, Giannini, believing his career in the produce business had run its course, turned to exploring real-estate investment. By now he had married, and his wife's family expanded his status and connections from the countryside into the city—her father was one of the prominent business successes of San Francisco's Italian community. About eighteen months after Giannini's departure from the produce industry, his father-in-law died, and the family asked Giannini to assume management of the man's business interests, including a significant real-estate portfolio. Rather than the real estate, however, it was the stock his father-in-law owned in a small Italian-run bank, Columbus Savings and Loan, that would shape Giannini's future.

Giannini took his father-in-law's seat on the bank board and quickly formed strong opinions about its operations. He argued that its conservative lending approach served only the already-prosperous members of the Italian community, missing the tremendous potential market presented by working-class immigrants. Giannini proposed aggressively seeking this group's business by offering basic savings accounts and small installment loans. When nearly two years' worth of his arguments had failed to win over the management, he quit the board in disgust and, a few months later, opened his own bank, Bank of Italy, to operate under the principles he had outlined. On October 15, 1904, he hung out his shingle in a prime corner location, adjacent to Columbus Savings, hiring away one of its most popular employees (at double the salary Columbus Savings had paid the man) as a crowning blow.

Bank of Italy flourished, thanks to its astutely structured credit policies and Giannini's personal salesmanship, which coaxed the nest eggs of many wary Italian immigrants out of mattresses and into the bank's vault. Even so, the San Francisco earthquake of 1906 might have decimated the young enterprise. With the city in chaos, Giannini and key employees stowed the bank's gold, silver, and cash in wagons from his stepfather's business, concealing the valuables under produce crates and thus hauling the load to safety in the face of approaching fires and lurking looters. Within forty-eight hours, a newspaper notice appeared, announcing that Bank of Italy was open for business to help citizens rebuild. Giannini erected a desk on the San Francisco wharf, putting an impressive cache of gold on display. Other banks opened as quickly, but none as noisily and memorably, and the city took notice.

After the calamity, Giannini set his sights on building a branch network, believing that spreading his bank's risk and resources among different communities would enhance its effectiveness and stability. While branch banking was not illegal in California, it was, as in most of America at the time, not typical, either, and state regulations forbade one bank from acquiring another. Giannini, however, exploited a loophole—Bank of Italy executives (not the bank itself) would buy enough stock to gain control of a bank, sell its assets to Bank of Italy, and then merge the stock of the two companies.

Starting on his home turf, Giannini used this strategy first to enter his birthplace of San José, then one California town after another, achieving success by marketing to local immigrant populations—not just Italians but Slavs, Portuguese, Russians, Chinese, Mexicans, and others. While not all these groups shared Giannini's Catholic ties, their most relevant similarity was a common outsider status with respect to the native whites. As fellow outsiders, these foreigners were, like Italian Catholics, underserved consumers receptive to Giannini's grassroots-oriented approach. Bank of Italy employees were encouraged to learn at least one language other than English to help communicate with immigrant populations, and the bank's polyglot capabilities were publicized. As the momentum of acquisitions grew, Giannini set up a nonbank holding company, which was owned by Bank of Italy shareholders, to execute the purchases without requiring officers to extend their personal assets.

By 1913, Bank of Italy had expanded into the Los Angeles market, but the bank's success in this city stimulated efforts by rivals to publicize the outsider aspects of Giannini's background. His marketing tactics were viewed suspiciously and termed "foreign," and at least one opponent alleged that Giannini's enterprise was secretly controlled by the Vatican. To slow the formation of local opposition, he soon learned to send Prentice Hale, a non-Italian bank officer with classic Yankee patrician looks, to negotiate quietly for the bank's entry into a new market. Though Giannini enjoyed support from the state's banking superintendent until 1919, subsequent appointees resisted his plans

*Catholic and founder of Bank of America Amadeo Peter Giannini lifting Jackie Coogan to a teller's window at a branch office in 1923.*
(Source: Bettmann/CORBIS)

for expansion, often at the urging of powerful Southern California bankers. Giannini continuously found ways to circumvent their restrictions, and by 1924, his strategies had paid off in a network of 155 offices spanning the state.

Mastering California, however, was only part of his dream. In 1919, he had established a foothold in New York by using a holding company, Bancitaly Corporation, to acquire East River National Bank. In 1927, a prospective merger with New York City's Bank of America advanced him from curiosity to potential threat in the eyes of Wall Street, bringing him to the attention of J. P. Morgan Jr., son of the famous financier previously discussed. As the West Coast outsider faced down perhaps the definitive East Coast insider, wealth was not enough to win credibility. Morgan *fils* allowed the completion of Giannini's deal, but only with conditions, including his direct approval of all board members. Bank of America's board, quite unlike Bank of Italy's, thus included only five Italians among its thirty-six members. Giannini was also frustrated to see his choice for chairman of the board, Ralph Jonas, a Jewish New Yorker who held 45 percent of the Bank of America's stock, vetoed in a thinly veiled gesture of anti-Semitism by the New York Federal Reserve Board.

Not more than a year after the merger, convinced that Morgan's Wall Street allies were manipulating the stock price of his various companies to destabilize them, Giannini formed a new holding company, Transamerica, to consolidate the businesses. Since Morgan had demanded that the New York banks be kept distinct from Bancitaly Corporation, this constituted a serious betrayal of his wishes, and Morgan-backed appointees resigned from the Bank of America board en masse. To regain some East Coast credibility, Giannini quickly merged Blair Investments, an established Wall Street firm, into Bank of America, naming Blair's president, Elisha Walker, head of Bancamerica, the bank's investment arm. Just a year later, in January 1930, Giannini handed Walker the chairmanship of Transamerica and announced his own retirement.

The retiree would not remain at rest long, because he quickly discovered how deep the current of opposition to him ran. Transamerica's stock price began to deteriorate, as did Giannini's comfort with Walker's leadership. By mid-1931, Walker declared that the company's recovery required a reorganization that would sell off essentially all but the Northern California assets of the company's banking network, gutting the enterprise Giannini had so painstakingly assembled. Furious, Giannini returned from Europe to wage a barnstorming campaign for proxies, and by the company's annual meeting in February 1932, he had secured the votes of enough shareholders to oust Walker by a dramatic margin. The theatrical battle, called "a financial epic" in the *New York Times*, cemented Giannini's image as a populist banker.[25] The confrontation also helped inspire a 1932 film, *American Madness*, in which a decidedly non-Italian but otherwise Gianniniesque banker is saved from a disastrous run on his bank by lots of "little guys" uniting to provide cash. Produced by Columbia Pictures, which had been created with the help of a Bank of Italy loan, the film was directed by Frank Capra, himself an Italian Catholic immigrant.[26] Similar populist ideals in George Bailey, hero of Capra's later, more famous film, *It's a Wonderful Life*, also seem more than a coincidence, as does that film's climactic triumph of the community over the tightfisted, black-suited (and rather Morganesque) Henry Potter.

Of course, there were ironies in Giannini's image as champion of the little guy—the creation of Bank of Italy's network resulted in the closing of many small-town banks, sometimes allegedly through strong-arm tactics. The opposition he encountered also made him quick to perceive conspiracies against him, some rightly so, but others less justifiably. Giannini was not above displaying religious prejudice himself in the heat of battle, despite his attempt to elevate Jonas and his fruitful, long-standing partnerships with Jewish film industry executives. While locked in a struggle in the late 1930s with Henry Morgenthau, Roosevelt's secretary of the treasury, who happened to be Jewish, Giannini blurted out an anti-Semitic sentiment in a board meeting. Jewish board members Louis B. Mayer and Joseph Schenck walked out and shortly resigned, and the incident became public knowledge, sparking customer and shareholder response. Giannini did not deny or apologize for his remarks, but he insisted his anger was directed toward an individual and not a group.

Even though his stepfather and father-in-law helped provide opportunities for business entry, and his compatriot immigrant network supported him through the formation of a large and successful business, Giannini never ceased to experience the struggles of an outsider, and his frustration showed. Despite the turmoil his battles engendered, his success in the face of obstacles preserved his reputation as a hero in the eyes of many, particularly fellow Italian American Catholics. The name Bank of America, although inherited from the acquired New York bank, could also hardly have been better chosen to reflect the transformation of Giannini's enterprise from the immigrant-focused

Bank of Italy to a mass-market concern. At his death in 1949, his banking empire included operations not only in California and New York, but also Italy, the Philippines, Thailand, Japan, and China. Giannini's legacy would receive a blow in the late 1950s, as legislation designed to strip away the bank holdings from Transamerica's grasp finally succeeded, leaving Bank of America a California-only enterprise. Several decades later, however, interstate banking gained legislative favor, allowing today's BankAmerica to undertake successive mergers creating just the kind of national banking network that had fueled Giannini's dreams.[27]

## Religious Prejudice Linked to Prejudice Toward Immigrants

Giannini's business odyssey vividly illustrates not just religious tensions but multiple points of differentiation between insiders and outsiders in early twentieth-century American business: East Coast versus West Coast, Protestants versus Jews versus Catholics, immigrants versus "natives," Anglo-Saxons versus Mediterraneans and other ethnic groups, and so on. As Giannini found when he tangled with Wall Street, becoming an insider in certain respects still failed to ensure that insiders who were more powerful wouldn't try to force you back out. Leaders with the double disadvantage of foreign birth *plus* affiliation with a religious minority typically confronted an even more difficult path. In total, almost 30 percent of non-Protestant leaders on our list in the first half of the century faced this extra challenge of being foreign-born, contrasting with Protestants, nearly 95 percent of whom were U.S.-born. It thus remains something of a chicken-or-the-egg problem to separate out which form of prejudice—religious or ethnic—operated more strongly in the networks that fostered access into American business success. If we narrow the focus to U.S.-born leaders only, however, religion remains a noticeably influential factor. Protestants show a decided advantage in mobility for success, finding business opportunities outside their state of birth in over 60 percent of the cases. By contrast, less than *half* of U.S.-born Jews and Catholic leaders found business success outside their state of birth. Not surprisingly, statistics suggest that the privileged Episcopalians had the greatest edge in mobility—54 of 81, or two-thirds of them, found out-of-state success. The more extensive the personal networks an individual had, the more possibilities might exist for success outside local boundaries. Protestant affiliations, typically a by-product of better-established or more prestigious families, obviously traveled better within the country. Non-Protestants, be they Jewish or Catholic, had not yet overcome an essentially foreign status in their new homeland.

## Limited Options Result in Different Paths for Jewish and Catholic Leaders

Not only in mobility but in their paths to success, minority religious affiliates differed significantly from the Protestant majority in the early part of the twentieth century. Both Catholic and Jewish leaders relied significantly more on the path of perseverance in entrepreneurship compared with Protestants (figure 4-4). Catholic leaders founded their own companies about 50 percent more often than Protestant-affiliated leaders did, while Protestants were more likely than either Jews or Catholics to find a post as CEO of someone else's business. The Jewish group, most limited in its share of such CEO roles, showed the greatest proportion of family business leaders. When foreign-born Jewish leaders are excluded, the distinctions are even more striking— almost half of U.S.-born Jewish leaders joined family businesses, compared with just over a quarter of U.S.-born Protestants.

The significant impact of family business for Jewish leaders shows the benefit of leverage gained through connections and wealth accumulated by their forebears, even in another country (as with Jacob Schiff). It also highlights the head start Jewish leaders had on Catholics, whose largest numbers arrived in later waves of immigration. The Jewish situation as a whole, however, presents a paradox. On the one hand, the group displays characteristics of an advantaged population, as Jews are overrepresented even more dramatically among our leaders in the early twentieth century than Episcopalians relative to their presence in the overall population (almost 11 percent of leaders for the period are Jewish, versus less than 1 percent of comparable population, per figure 4-2). On the other hand, nearly one-quarter of these successes came in classic outsider fashion, via the "frontier" industrial territory of motion pictures, as chronicled in another chapter. The dependence on family business ties for the lion's share of the remaining successes is, at bottom, both good news and bad news: on the positive side, someone inheriting leadership in a

**FIGURE 4-4**

## Catholic founders and Jewish family business leaders contrast with Protestant CEOs in early 1900s

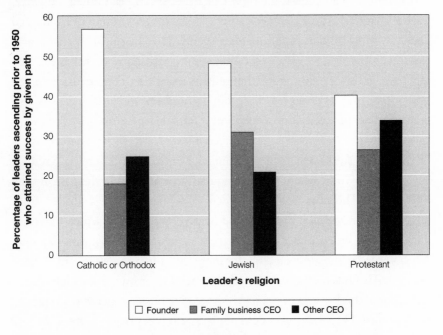

Source: HBS Leadership Initiative's "Great American Business Leaders of the 20th Century" database.

family business enjoyed the advantages of financial stability. The relative dominance of this path, however, suggests that options available beyond the family were limited. Putting it another way, having one good opportunity is better than having none, but neither situation confers the privilege of choice. More evidence of this relative lack of options for Jewish leaders is their concentration by industry. Almost half the Jewish leaders arising prior to 1950 succeeded in entertainment, retailing, or financial services. By comparison, Catholic and Orthodox leaders, though half as many in number as Jewish leaders, spread evenly across a wide sampling of industries, matching up more closely with Protestants.

Jewish business leaders evolved into this category of "outsider insiders" over time. They had played a role in New York City financial circles from the city's earliest days, and this activity had resulted in social acceptance for prominent Jews by the mid-nineteenth century—Jewish leaders such as financier Joseph Seligman, whose children were tutored by Horatio Alger, were among the founding members of several leading clubs, including the Knickerbocker Club and the Union League.[28] As has been noted, however, Jewish characters are essentially absent from the environment of Ragged Dick. A trend of increasing prejudice against Jews began in the late nineteenth century as new waves of immigration, particularly from Eastern Europe, swelled the Jewish population of New York City in particular to a degree prompting wariness of the group's numbers and influence. As this prejudice strengthened, little distinction was made by the majority Protestant culture between the earlier and more recent Jewish arrivals. In a notorious incident of the 1870s, Seligman was denied a booking at a hotel in Saratoga Springs, New York, where he had frequently vacationed in the past. By the early 1890s, Theodore Seligman, Joseph's nephew, was blackballed from membership in the club his uncle had helped found and of which his father then served as vice president. The incident inaugurated new norms of prejudice observed in most similar clubs for more than fifty years afterward.[29] Prosperous Jewish business leaders founded some of their own social clubs in response, but the loss of connections to broader business networks typically made in mixed social settings could not be so easily replaced. In the early part of the twentieth century, in short, while some Jewish leaders enjoyed the benefits of family success, all faced a social insularity that was based on their religion and served to cut them off from access to broader opportunities.

Lehman Brothers, one of Wall Street's most successful and enduring investment banking firms, spans this era with one of the more notable Jewish family business stories—a saga of multigenerational success that gave rise to two leaders on our list. Henry Lehman, coming to America from the German region of Bavaria in 1844, had a head start of about twenty-five years on Amadeo Giannini's parents. Like them, though, Lehman initially settled in a region well removed from the Northeast—he established himself in Montgomery, Alabama, and was joined there by his brothers Emanuel and Mayer. The Lehmans developed into big fish in a small pond, starting off as retail merchants and quickly advancing into wholesaling, particularly the cotton trade. After Henry's death from yellow fever in 1855, next-eldest Emanuel led the business. To get more involved with financial dealings that supported the cotton trade, he relocated to open a New York City office in 1858, leaving

Mayer in charge of the Montgomery operations. In New York, Emanuel married, and in 1861, his son Philip was born. The Civil War's onset effectively severed business ties between Montgomery and New York, and although Mayer formed a new partnership in Alabama and expanded his dealings in cotton, Emanuel could now do little more than wait out the conflict.

Within a year after Lee's surrender at Appomattox, the brothers had reopened their New York office. Its work expanded so rapidly that Mayer joined Emanuel in New York City in 1868. The Lehmans became significant players in the cotton market and were among the founding firms of the New York Cotton Exchange in 1870, with Mayer a member of the inaugural Board of Governors. As the decade went on, the brothers leveraged Southern contacts to their advantage, facilitating investment deals in redeveloping industry and infrastructure in Alabama and other former Confederate states. Prosperity derived from their position in the South also translated to credibility in New York society. At the 1884 wedding of Emanuel's daughter Harriet to her cousin Sigmund, the proud father of the bride presented a generous wedding gift of fifty thousand dollars, nearly equaled by a thirty-thousand-dollar gift by Mayer, father of the groom; the occasion (complete with gift amounts) was chronicled in the *New York Times*.[30] By 1887, the Lehman Brothers had acquired a seat on the New York Stock Exchange.

Philip, the first of the Lehman leaders on our list, joined the already solidly established family business in 1882, becoming a partner three years later at age twenty-four. He would lead Lehman Brothers to still greater heights, expanding its investment banking activities in ways that largely drew on connections within the network of Jewish business leaders. His good friend Henry Goldman of Goldman Sachs partnered with Philip in stock offerings for the Studebaker Corporation, F. W. Woolworth, and Sears, Roebuck and Co., initiating what for the Lehman Brothers became a successful niche of working with consumer businesses rather than traditional industrial firms. In developing the retail market, the company benefited from other family and religious ties: a member of the Sachs family had married Julius Rosenwald, an early CEO of Sears. Philip Lehman's cousin Irving married the cousin of Jesse Isidor Straus, whose family had bought out and operated R. H. Macy's, another business that later figured prominently on the client list of Lehman Brothers. Indeed, family ties bound tightly and exclusively—it was not until August 1924 that the Lehman Brothers added a partner who did not share the family name.

*Lehman Brothers' first outside partner John M. Hancock (left) sitting with Robert Lehman, grandson of one of the founders of the firm, in 1945.* (Source: Time Life Pictures/Getty Images)

The first outside partner's name, John Hancock, betokened a dramatically different heritage from that of the Lehman family, though he seems to have had no affiliation with the historic Massachusetts family or Declaration signer, having been born in North Dakota to a family recently immigrated from Canada. Hancock's connection to the Lehmans had come as an officer in the U.S. Navy Supply Corps during World War I, when he became friendly with Philip's cousin Herbert Lehman, who served on the War Industries Board.[31] It may be overstating the case to suggest that Hancock was the Lehmans' "Prentice Hale" (the patrician-looking envoy employed by Giannini to be his advance man into new markets), but his inclusion did signal the emergence at Lehman Brothers of a new generation of leaders who would build bridges beyond the family networks.

Philip's son, Robert, a graduate of Yale (an institution we will discuss in chapter 5 as a bastion of the mostly Protestant established business families), was the driving force behind the changes. By 1925 he, the second Lehman to make our list, had essentially taken over from his father as head of the firm. Just four years later, Lehman Brothers' most notable stock offering involved not Goldman Sachs but W. Averell Harriman. This son of Wall Street legend

E. H. Harriman and grandson of an Episcopal clergyman would later serve as ambassador to Russia and England and, after that, governor of New York. With Harriman, the Lehmans underwrote a stock offering for Avco, a significant new conglomerate of aviation interests that incubated the success of C.R. Smith, as previously discussed. The Lehmans were also advancing in politics: Herbert Lehman was elected lieutenant governor under Franklin Roosevelt in 1928 and succeeded FDR as governor from 1932 to 1942, later serving in the U.S. Senate.[32] Meanwhile, Robert Lehman continued to expand the firm's financing activities, adding clients like American Airlines, PanAm, RCA, and television pioneer Dumont Laboratories. By 1967, Lehman Brothers reigned in the mainstream as one of Wall Street's top four investment banks.[33]

## Jewish Leaders Still Outsiders Later in the Century

From the broadening influence of the Lehmans and the diminishing proportion of identified Protestants among leaders in the latter half of the twentieth century, it's tempting to conclude that religious affiliation ceased to play a role in leader selection by that time. In marked contrast to those of Catholics and Protestants, however, the paths to success for Jewish leaders in the latter half of the century largely continued to depend on the outsider's typical means of prospering—that is, founding a new business (figure 4-5).

Jewish leaders remained at a disadvantage in accessing roles as hired CEOs, the path that dominated the Protestant and Catholic leader groups later in the century. In fact, only from 1980 on, when nearly two-thirds of the ascending Jewish leaders succeeded in this manner, did they approach the proportion of Protestants or Catholics attaining CEO roles in established firms. A prominent forerunner of this group was Irving Shapiro, who rose in the 1970s to the head of DuPont. His early career provides examples of the persistence of anti-Semitism, but his ultimate success became a noted landmark in the dissipation of anti-Semitism's influence on corporate hiring.

Shapiro, a Minneapolis native and son of Lithuanian immigrant parents, graduated fourth in his class from Minnesota's law school in 1941 and was encouraged at the time by professors and friends, including some fellow Jewish attorneys, to change his last name to one less strongly associated with his Jewish heritage.[34] He declined to do so and got no offers from Minneapolis law

**FIGURE 4-5**

**Jewish leaders still largely founders after 1950, while Catholics make significant progress as CEOs**

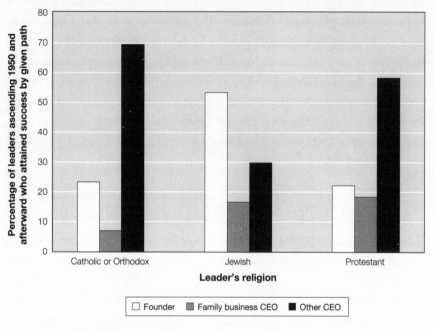

Source: HBS Leadership Initiative's "Great American Business Leaders of the 20th Century" database.

firms. He began a private practice, but with the onset of World War II, he went to Washington, D.C., answering a call for lawyers to help the Office of Price Administration (OPA) establish agreements controlling wartime prices and the production of goods. As previously discussed, this agency provided Plato Malozemoff, an outsider by virtue of his birthplace, a similar entry point to opportunity. After a few years with OPA, Shapiro transferred to the Department of Justice. He became a noted writer of briefs, even though he worked at a time when one departmental supervisor was known to remove the names of Jewish attorneys from documents that they had authored.[35]

Shapiro's skills eventually won him a lead prosecution role in a widely covered trial of several Communist Party members on charges of promoting the overthrow of the U.S. government. A *New York Times* article chronicling a June 1950 appeal of their convictions quoted Shapiro's arguments at some length.[36] Oscar Provost, a former supervisor of Shapiro's at the Department of Justice and at that time a senior member of the legal department at DuPont, saw the piece and decided to recruit Shapiro for the company's legal team to help fight a massive government antitrust suit. DuPont had some reputation of anti-Semitism, and at least one account suggests there was opposition to Shapiro's hiring on that basis.[37] His prominent role in the prosecution of the Communists, however, might have offered some ammunition to counter the xenophobic arguments that often sustained anti-Semitic attitudes. Whatever the reason, Provost's advocacy won the day, and Shapiro was offered a job. He wound up not only serving on the antitrust team but also drawing the assignment—somewhat unusual for a new employee—of acting as ongoing liaison between the legal team and DuPont's top management regarding the case. Shapiro endeared himself to company leaders still more when he was instrumental in shepherding through Congress a bill that saved DuPont shareholders (including du Pont family members, who naturally held some of the largest stakes) millions of dollars. Had this bill not been enacted, the shareholders would have been obliged to pay taxes on the portion of their stock related to control of General Motors, which they were forced to divest after the antitrust ruling.[38]

Shapiro's capabilities, in short, won him the confidence of top managers, who whatever their private prejudices may have been, saw firsthand that the barrier that might have kept him out of their ranks didn't make him hard to work with. Shapiro was promoted in 1965 to assistant general counsel, and in 1970, he gained a seat on Dupont's executive committee and was appointed a senior vice president and director, a promotion that placed him in the inner circle of top management. By July 1973, his prominence rose as he assumed the newly created role of vice chairman, a post the company explicitly identified as "the No. 2 spot."[39] Perhaps the move was a testing of the waters, an exploration of whether negative reaction inside or outside the company to Shapiro's promotion would be too strong. Or perhaps the company, already having settled on a succession plan, simply intended for the market to get comfortable with the idea. Whatever the case, the preparatory step did little to quell a sense of genuine astonishment in media coverage of Shapiro's appointment as chairman and CEO less than six months later. More than one article invoked Horatio Alger's name in recounting Shapiro's upbringing as the eldest son in a family living hand-to-mouth on the limited income from a pants-pressing business started by his father. Beyond noting his poverty, however, the articles explicitly catalogued the ways that Shapiro stood out from the DuPont management team and his CEO predecessors in being unconnected to the family, a lawyer (all previous company heads had science backgrounds), a Democrat, and, last but by no means least, a Jew.

Shapiro had never soft-pedaled those differences. He had invited his superiors to his son's bar mitzvah not long after he joined DuPont—reportedly it occasioned the first visit any of them had made to a synagogue.[40] Still, he downplayed his role as a barrier breaker. At the time of his appointment as chairman and CEO, he said, "Once you are on the payroll you are part of the team. You are accepted for what you achieve and judged by your performance, regardless of how you pray."[41] Upon his ascension, Shapiro's acceptance within DuPont was quickly translated to the wider business community. He was elected in June 1976 to head the Business Roundtable, a high-powered enclave of some 160 executives to sponsor public-policy research and advocate views on legislation. Shapiro was a loyal supporter of Jimmy Carter, so that fall's election results only solidified the CEO's influence. Reportedly, Carter made overtures to him regarding a cabinet post, but Shapiro withdrew his name from consideration so as to continue his role at DuPont. In any case, he continued to be recognized as a corporate leader who had Carter's ear, and Shapiro's was the name most frequently cited as a business opinion leader in a 1980 survey of over one thousand executives.[42] His original status as outsider to the business fraternity had now reversed to that of an insider among insiders. In 1981, turning sixty-five, he retired from DuPont and returned to practicing law, joining the Wilmington, Delaware, office of the prominent New York law firm, Skadden, Arps, where his son, obviously not facing the limitations his father had when graduating from law school, already was a partner.[43]

## Catholic Progress As CEOs Contrasts with Jewish Experience

The more rapid rate of Catholic versus Jewish assimilation into mainstream U.S. society and business in the later twentieth century, as suggested by Catholics' greater access to CEO roles in figure 4-5, is highlighted by the fact that John F. Kennedy, a Catholic, was elected U.S. president in 1960. While

Kennedy's religion provoked significant conversation during the presidential campaign, JFK's election still predated Shapiro's noisily noted rise to DuPont's head by more than a decade (and, of course, over forty-five years have since elapsed without any such election of a Jewish presidential candidate).

Apparently, the multigenerational success that served Jewish leaders well in family businesses earlier in the century failed, due to its insularity, to spark later business success in wider circles. By contrast, although somewhat behind as a group economically at the century's start, Catholics experienced a more rapid and thorough assimilation into the Protestant establishment. Indeed, Catholics had penetrated the business culture significantly enough later in the century to approach and even outstrip those with known Protestant affiliations on the increasingly prevalent leadership path of the professional CEO. Moreover, though the typical path during this era required a leader to serve a long company tenure before becoming CEO, the time it took for these Catholic leaders to reach the top averaged slightly less than that for known Protestant counterparts. The kinds of connections and acceptance required to be trusted as a hired manager seem fully as prevalent in Catholics as Protestants in this later generation. Place was still a factor in Catholic leadership, but Catholics now displayed an advantage in the Northeast, the very region that had dramatically spurned Amadeo Giannini. Almost 60 percent of Catholic CEOs in the second half of the century led businesses in the Northeast, while Protestant CEOs were split differently, with only about a third in the Northeast and close to half serving in the Midwest.

These factors appear to confirm that Catholics in the Northeast (including, of course, Kennedy) were now reaping the rewards from their critical mass of immigrant population in that region earlier in the century. For a contrast to Shapiro's story, consider the well-paved path to success for Thomas Murphy, one of the well-assimilated Catholic leaders who built on the advancement of his father's generation. Murphy's father, Charles, from a working-class home, had forged ahead by attending urban colleges in New Jersey and New York, earning a law degree at night. Although a practicing attorney, Charles Murphy held an early job in advertising and in 1930 became president of the Advertising Club of New York, an influential city business group. Just thirty-five at the time, he was claimed to be the club's youngest president to date. At the club, he became friendly with prominent figures like Lowell Thomas, a well-known radio and television commentator, who presided over the association shortly after Murphy.[44] Thomas bought some property near Pawling, New York, during the Depression and recruited friends to build summer homes there.[45] Charles Murphy became part of that vacation crowd.

Murphy also got involved in politics, managing the 1941 campaign for the city Democratic ticket headed by William O'Dwyer. Although that run was unsuccessful, O'Dwyer was elected mayor a few years later and appointed Murphy to the city's top legal office of Corporation Counsel. Murphy rubbed shoulders with elite Republicans during summers in Pawling, becoming a regular in the golfing foursome of governor and erstwhile presidential candidate, Thomas Dewey. With such connections, it's not surprising that Murphy was a candidate palatable to the endorsement of the Republican, Democratic, *and* Liberal parties in a 1947 compromise slate and was elected to a seat on the State Supreme Court.[46] He received an additional appointment by Dewey to an appellate post in 1954; Governor Nelson Rockefeller, also a Republican, renewed it five years later.[47]

Charles Murphy's rise in business and politics thus offered his son Thomas a very different start from his own. Thomas "Tom" Murphy enjoyed an Ivy League education: a college degree from Cornell and then, after service in World War II, an MBA from Harvard. Upon graduation from Harvard Business School in 1949, the young Murphy took a marketing post with Lever Brothers, following his father's early path into advertising. His family connections, however, soon produced a more exciting option. During the Labor Day weekend of 1954, he attended a cocktail party at Lowell Thomas's home in Pawling. Like his father, Tom Murphy had become friendly with the broadcaster and his family, and he had served as usher in the wedding of Lowell Thomas's son in 1950.[48] Frank Smith, business manager for Lowell Thomas and an occasional golf partner of Charles Murphy's, not to mention a Harvard Business School alumnus himself, approached Tom at the party with a business proposal. Smith had assembled an investment group, led by Lowell Thomas, to purchase an ultrahigh-frequency (UHF) television station in Albany, New York. Seeking someone to run the station, he asked the young Murphy for suggestions. Tom at first took Smith's request literally, but soon recognized it as a thinly veiled job offer and decided to accept the challenge.

In fact, the prospects were speculative at best—UHF broadcasting looked like a losing proposition in the early 1950s. These higher-frequency bands (associated with channels numbered fourteen and above) were considered a necessary means for expanding television coverage nationally, but the majority of television sets in use lacked the capability to receive their signals. Installation of an adapter costing an additional 15 to 25 percent of the price of a typical television was necessary to receive UHF broadcasts, and if VHF (very high frequency) channels were available, there was little motivation to spend the extra money. With a diminished potential viewership, UHF channels had difficulty attracting advertisers or getting commitments from networks for programming; the dearth of programming increased the difficulty of attracting viewers, completing the vicious cycle. UHF stations were folding right and left, and those that weren't were barely holding on. The *Wall Street Journal* noted that only thirteen of the eighty-seven UHF stations reporting results to the Federal Communications Commission (FCC) for the first three months of 1954 were making money in that period.[49]

The prize envisioned by Smith and company, however, was not Albany's UHF broadcasting, but a path into VHF broadcasting. Thomas Dewey, the former governor of New York, and Frank Stanton, president of CBS, had alerted Smith that a VHF license was authorized in a sparsely populated region on the fringes of the Albany broadcast area. The owner of the UHF station would have the right to petition to exchange that license for the VHF license in order to serve more effectively the larger Albany market. After purchasing the UHF station, Smith wasted no time filing a request for the exchange. Political connections represented among Smith's investors, who included at least five U.S. congressmen (four Democrats and one Republican) and former campaign managers for both Republican and Democratic New York governors, would come in handy in cutting regulatory red tape. Moreover, as a leading broadcast personality for CBS, Lowell Thomas had clout to offer over and above his funds.

Within a month of FCC approval of the purchase in November 1954, CBS had transferred its network affiliation in Albany from a rival UHF station to the one purchased by Smith, Thomas and company. The spurned station lodged a protest with the FCC, charging that Thomas had negotiated behind the scenes to secure the programming contract prior to purchasing the station. The protest made the even more serious accusation that the station now owned by Thomas and friends was under the effective control of CBS, a possible violation of antitrust provisions.[50] The claim about Thomas's role rang true, but it failed to engender redress, and the other station, voicing continued protests, ceased operation as of the following February.[51]

In 1956, an FCC proposal to make the whole Albany broadcast area UHF-only was reversed, and in June 1957, the station transfer was finally approved, with a VHF license granted to Smith's consortium. The high-influence quotient of the players involved continued to attract scrutiny, however. Two years later, a New York University law professor who had served as counsel to a legislative subcommittee investigating the FCC claimed that improper influence had been exerted in the Albany situation by James Hagerty, a former press secretary to Dewey and White House press secretary under Eisenhower at the time of the deliberations. Hagerty, not an investor in the station, denied the charges.[52] In 1960, crusading senator William Proxmire raised allegations of preferential treatment again, this time regarding the congressional stockholders, but no further action ensued.[53]

Without a doubt, young Thomas Murphy, a bystander to the regulatory battles, reaped the benefits of political pull exerted by a high-powered network. Running the Albany station while the fighting continued in Washington, however, was no picnic. The station was housed in a somewhat dilapidated building that formerly served as a home for retired nuns. With funds scarce, Murphy only painted the two sides visible from the road, but even such frugality did not prevent the station from running some seven hundred thousand dollars in the red during its first few years of operation. Fortunately, Smith's investors had cash to match their clout and kept the money coming. After the path to VHF operation was cleared in 1957, the company, then known as Hudson Valley Broadcasting, laid out more dollars for the first in a long line of acquisitions, purchasing a VHF station in Raleigh. As it now served North Carolina's capital along with New York's, the enterprise chose an apt new name—Capital Cities Television. By December 1957, Capital Cities announced its first public stock offering. The next acquisition, in 1959, of a VHF station in Providence, continued the theme of state capitals and significantly boosted the company's earnings, particularly since it was the first station among Capital Cities' purchases that was already profitable. Other television and radio station acquisitions followed, and the more generally suitable Capital Cities Broadcasting became the company name by 1960, when the stock began trading on the American Stock Exchange. Smith, now managing an expanded empire, rewarded Murphy's toil in Albany with a promotion to executive vice president and relocation to the company's New York City headquarters. After another significant round of acquisitions, Smith ceded his role as president to Murphy in October 1964, continuing as chairman and CEO.

By July 1965, Capital Cities' stock was trading on the New York Stock Exchange, and before the end of that year, a two-for-one stock split was announced. Earnings per share for 1965, even after adjustment for the split, had grown some tenfold since 1958, the first year the company reported positive earnings. Murphy's next promotion came for regrettable reasons, however, when Smith, aged fifty-six, died of a heart attack in August 1966. At forty-one, Murphy lost the security of Smith's mentoring but continued unintimidated, acquiring yet another VHF television station in Houston by mid-1967 and simultaneously selling a Providence station to a friendly former colleague. The transaction raised eyebrows yet again at the FCC, as a commissioner dissenting in the approval of the station swap noted that the deal ignored guidelines adopted by the FCC to limit ownership by a single entity to no more than two VHF television stations within the nation's fifty largest markets.[54] Capital Cities, grandfathered in to its current situation, already owned stations in four of the markets and was still allowed to swap one for another. Whatever his somewhat privileged position, Murphy realized that limits in broadcasting could only be stretched so far, and in January 1968, he led Capital Cities in a crossover to print media, acquiring Fairchild Publications, producers of *Women's Wear Daily* and several trade publications. The merger effectively doubled Capital Cities in size yet again. More acquisitions in both print and broadcasting followed, and by 1973, still another company name change, to Capital Cities Communications, was warranted.

Though he largely owed his start in business to personal networks created by his father, by the early 1970s, Thomas Murphy's own network was now filled with increasingly powerful players. A former Capital Cities executive, James Quello, was appointed an FCC commissioner in 1974, supplying the company with yet another likely friend in Washington. Even more important, however, were some of Murphy's Harvard Business School classmates, who were coming of age and into prominence. John Shad, a Wall Street heavy hitter at E. F. Hutton, had helped facilitate newspaper and radio station purchases for Capital Cities. Good friend Jim Burke was on the rise in consumer goods, soon to make his mark as head of Johnson & Johnson, and Burke's younger brother Dan was second in command at Capital Cities. William Ruane, who founded the Sequoia Fund in 1970, introduced Murphy to a fellow value-investor on the rise, Warren Buffet, who would play a key role in the coup of Murphy's career. In March 1985, Capital Cities, with assets topping just $1.2 billion, announced it was paying in excess of $3.5 billion to purchase the ABC television network and its own set of significant broadcasting outlets. Buffet committed to purchasing over $500 million in Capital Cities stock, a holding of more than 18 percent of the company, to help facilitate the deal. In at least as significant a vote of confidence, he gave voting control of his shares for the next ten years to the company as long as either Murphy or Dan Burke ran it. The deal, characterized as "the minnow swallowing the whale" in many circles, put the formerly anonymous Murphy and Capital Cities in the bright lights reserved for the country's major broadcast networks. In 1995, Murphy negotiated a merger of ABC/Capital Cities and Walt Disney Company, bringing to a triumphant close his four-decade adventure that started with a cocktail party conversation.[55]

*ABC/Capital Cities CEO Thomas Murphy (right) and Michael Eisner, CEO of Disney, at a press conference announcing the firm's buyout by Walt Disney Company in 1995.* (Source: Najlah Feanny/CORBIS SABA)

## Timing Is Everything in Religion's Influence on Access

The overall picture presented by our leaders leaves little doubt that religious affiliation played an important role at the start of the twentieth century in facilitating the personal networking that opened doors to business success. The primary advantage enjoyed by Protestants appears not so much to be a fabled work ethic but rather a long head start in establishing such networks, beginning effectively with the *Mayflower*. That these networks centered on the country's most well-developed business regions made them all the more powerful in helping determine the makeup of this mostly Protestant group of leaders. The importance of timing is also evident in distinctions between the Jewish and Catholic minority communities, as Jewish families with longer roots in the country had already developed dynasties to hand down to later generations by the early 1900s. Catholic nineteenth-century immigrants, primarily from Italy and Ireland, largely did not possess the experience with business in urbanized settings that some European Jews did. Still, the longer presence of Catholics on the West Coast, combined with the pioneering openness of the region, helped create networks conducive to their business success.

To emphasize the role of timing is not to deny the ugly reality that prejudice explicitly worked against the development of business networks by non-Protestants and affected the relationships that members of minority religious groups had with each other. The truth is that a network, whoever dominated it in a certain industry or region, could function so as to cut off access to outsiders. Though this arrangement normally operated to the benefit of the Protestant majority, there were pockets where outsider groups gained ground and could hold it. This enabled later arrivals to leverage the gains of their community and, in cases like Giannini's with the Bank of Italy, eventually to generalize such successes into mainstream businesses. Similarly, the firm of Lehman Brothers is one of several Jewish family businesses that were developed significantly through partnership with those of common religious background but then expanded into the wider business community. With both Bank of America and Lehman Brothers, the leadership of the companies became sufficiently diverse that distinctions in business operations based on the religious affiliation of their founders had almost vanished by the middle of the twentieth century.

At that point, religious factors were weakening in importance as a means of access to opportunity, and the Protestant elite was being superseded by a crowd of leaders with unspecified religious convictions. The gains in openness to minority religious affiliates came most rapidly for Catholics, who now began to benefit from generational advancement in the business corridors of the Northeast, where sons like Thomas Murphy built on the networks their fathers started in business and politics and began to operate as true insiders. Jewish leaders, on the other hand, faced a lengthier isolation from the typical corporate paths to leadership, continuing to depend on entrepreneurship as relative outsiders. By the last two decades of the century, however, even this trend seemed to break down, and Jewish leaders very much blended into mainstream business leadership. By the time Sandy Weill took leadership of Citigroup, articles that happened to mention his religion did so with none of the marked astonishment reserved for the ascension of Irving Shapiro. Although the majority of leaders at the end of the century were probably nominal Protestants, the increasing silence regarding religious affiliation among business leaders overall reflected a sea change from the century's beginnings. Religious affiliation undoubtedly still constituted a foundation for personal networks, but it no longer served as a public and widely appreciated signal of legitimacy (e.g., with Episcopalians) or stigma (e.g., with Jews and Catholics) as it had in the early 1900s. If religion and birthplace were waning in significance over the century as tokens of qualification for business leadership, however, something else was naturally rising to fill in the vacuum. As we will see, this something was advanced education.

# FIVE

# Education

## Degrees Go from
## Ornamental to Essential

*"Can you read and write well?" [Dick] asked, as a sudden thought came to him.*

*"Yes," said Fosdick. "Father always kept me at school when he was alive, and I stood pretty well in my classes. I was expecting to enter at the Free Academy next year."*

*"Then I'll tell you what," said Dick; "I'll make a bargain with you. I can't read much more'n a pig; and my writin' looks like hens' tracks. I don't want to grow up knowin' no more'n a four-year-old boy. If you'll teach me readin' and writin' evenin's, you shall sleep in my room every night. That'll be better'n door-steps or old boxes, where I've slept many a time."*

*"Are you in earnest?" said Fosdick, his face lighting up hopefully.*

*"In course I am," said Dick. "It's fashionable for young gentlemen to have private tootors to introduce 'em into the flower-beds of literatoor and sciences, and why shouldn't I follow the fashion?"*

—Horatio Alger, *Ragged Dick*

DICK'S COLORFUL LANGUAGE notwithstanding, his assessment of the "fashionable" form of education in his day was not far off. Fewer than half our business leaders in the early part of the century had college degrees. Ironically, many of those whose names we now associate with great schools, libraries, and university buildings created through their bequests did not themselves have the benefit of higher education. At the time, there was no particular sentiment that they should. Our Wall Street friend Henry Clews wrote in 1908: "As the college curriculum and training stand at present, the ordinary course is not in general calculated to make a good business man." Moreover, he believed there could be "no greater mistake in the beginning of a business career" than to assume that time spent in college made any kind of adequate substitute for on-the-job business experience.[1] Business education pioneer Henry Babson also argued against college, though of course with the interest of encouraging would-be businessmen to enter the one-year business training program he had established. He asserted that achieving success in business required the early formation of fundamental habits such as "integrity, industry, thrift, promptness, [and] initiative." His argument concluded with this pointed punch line: "The chances are strong that, unless intensely inter-ested, [the student] is most likely to acquire the *very opposite* habits during four years of college work."[2]

The leader on our list whose name is perhaps most associated with educa-tion, James Buchanan Duke, had this to say in late 1924, just after he formu-lated the Duke Endowment: "I don't believe that a college education does a man much good in business, except for the personal satisfaction it gives him."[3] He identified instead ministers, teachers, lawyers, chemists, engineers, and doctors as the kinds of leaders he hoped his bequest would help train, to the benefit of the Carolinas. Duke himself spent only about six months studying at the Eastman College of Business in Poughkeepsie before starting the career that amassed his sizable fortune with the American Tobacco Company and supported the development of Duke Power, a dominant hydroelectric utility company in the Carolinas. It was Duke Power that provided the steady in-come stream to fund his endowment in perpetuity. Duke's $40 million origi-nal grant, later supplemented by about $69 million in residual funds from his estate, not only financed the formation of Duke University (an expansion of the already-existing Trinity College) in Durham, North Carolina, but also provided ongoing support to Davidson College near Charlotte, the histori-cally black Johnson C. Smith University in Charlotte, and Furman Univer-sity in Greenville, South Carolina.[4] Financial support to all four institutions from the endowment has now continued for over eighty years, totaling more than $38 million in grants in the year 2004 alone.[5]

Despite early skepticism about the value of a college education in business, bequests like Duke's contributed to rising overall educational levels in the

*James Buchanan Duke (left), head of the powerful American Tobacco Company, provided the financial support for the expansion of Trinity College in North Carolina into Duke University. Main entrance of Duke University (above) pictured in 1917.* (Sources: Left, Bettmann/CORBIS; Right, Lake County Museum/CORBIS)

United States, and the levels among our leaders rose accordingly. By the last decades of the twentieth century, about 90 percent of the ascending leaders had graduated from college. As undereducated as the leaders in earlier decades seem by today's standards, as a group they had quite high academic qualifications for their day. Formal education statistics were first gathered in the census of 1940, when less than 6 percent of U.S. native white males over twenty-five had attended four or more years of college.[6] Obviously, rates earlier in the century were even lower, as were those for women, immigrants, and racial minorities. Most of the leaders on our list ascending from 1921 through 1940 possessed bachelor's degrees, however. This gap in education between the leaders and the general population closed slightly as the century went on, but even in the century's final decades, the leaders were more than three times as likely to have college degrees as were other U.S. adults (figure 5-1).

## Education Primarily an Ornament for Early Insiders

The disparity in education levels mainly points to a status gap between the bulk of these leaders and the American public. Particularly early in the century, college education was not so much a route to the top as it was a mark of those who already belonged to a certain social class. This is perhaps best illustrated by the fact that family business leaders, whose bloodlines offered them

**FIGURE 5-1**

## Business leaders far outpace population education

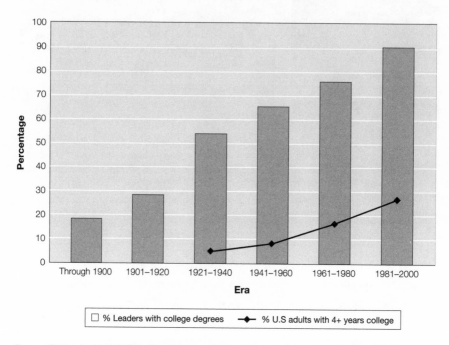

*Source*: HBS Leadership Initiative's "Great American Business Leaders of the 20th Century" database.

Census data reflects statistics for U.S. adults twenty-five and over in census for last year of era. The 1940 statistics are from U.S. Department of Commerce, Bureau of the Census, "Population: Nativity and Parentage of the White Population, General Characteristics," in *Sixteenth Census of the United States: 1940* (Washington, DC: Government Printing Office, 1943), 194. The 1960, 1980, and 2000 statistics are from U.S. Bureau of the Census, *Statistical Abstract of the United States: 2001* (Washington, DC: Government Printing Office, 2001), 139, available at www.census.gov/prod/2002pubs/01statab/educ.pdf.

all the connections they needed for business success, were also the most likely to have college degrees among leaders prior to 1950. Nearly 55 percent of family business leaders had graduated from college during that era. The next most educated group were those being hired as CEOs, of whom 48 percent had degrees, though these leaders, too, were often the offspring of successful businessmen.

The prestige factor in education was evident in the dominance of East Coast Ivy League colleges.[7] As was the case for the proud German immigrant father of Princeton graduates Gordon and Frederick Rentschler, those who found business success anywhere in the country were still inclined to send their offspring back East for school, presumably as much to build the family's reputation as to gain education or connections. Half of the college-educated family business leaders on our list prior to 1950 attended Harvard or Yale, and nearly 70 percent attended Ivy League colleges overall, although just 28 percent of other collegian leaders of that era did. Together, leaders of family businesses, who constituted less than a quarter of the leaders before 1950, made up more than half of all Ivy-educated leaders for the period, including about two-thirds of the graduates from Yale, Princeton, or the University of Pennsylvania. Individuals who had themselves founded flourishing enterprises without college educations spared no expense to give their progeny the best, establishing family dynasties at the premier institutions.

Frederick Weyerhaeuser, for example, had left formal schooling behind at age fourteen, stepping up to run his family's farm in Germany when his father died. A few years later, the lure of potential success in America was too strong, and he and other family members emigrated in 1852. His first job was in a brewery, where he observed, as he later put it, that many brewers seem to become their own best customers, and he decided to seek a different profession.[8] By 1856, Weyerhaeuser was employed at a sawmill in Rock Island, Illinois, where the enterprising young man made his first connection with lumber, the business that would produce his fortune. His oldest child and the first leader from the family on our list, John "J. P." Philip, was born just two years later, in 1858. Frederick formed a partnership with his brother-in-law in the lumber business and, by 1870, had negotiated the formation of a logging and sawmill cooperative, of which he became president in 1872. This business was the foundation from which the far-reaching Weyerhaeuser timber empire grew, extending over the coming decades through numerous associations and partnerships to reach from the Mississippi to the Pacific Northwest. While the Weyerhaeuser family always shared ownership with many partners and did not maintain a controlling interest, theirs was the name that would dominate the company's management.

J. P. Weyerhaeuser, being oldest, had the disadvantage of undertaking his education early in his father's career, meaning his options were correspondingly modest. He attended a private academy in Aurora, Illinois, less than 150 miles from his birthplace in humble Coal Valley. As it happened, he may well have been the last Weyerhaeuser man for several generations to receive advanced education west of the Hudson River, excepting those who prepped at the respected Hill School in southeastern Pennsylvania. His brother Charles went to Phillips Andover Academy, as did the youngest brother, Frederick, who, along with brother Rudolph, also collected a diploma from Yale. Yale did establish one of the nation's earliest forestry schools, in which the Weyerhaeusers understandably took a supportive interest, but their association with Yale started before the forestry school's inception, and most of the Weyerhaeuser men majored in other disciplines.

The tie to Yale seems to have arisen instead from the Weyerhaeuser patriarch's conviction that, as soon as his means permitted, he must educate his children in the East and with the best. The conviction apparently passed down through generations in much the same way as the family business did, and the list of Yale alumni in the Weyerhaeuser clan includes both the company's other representatives on our list of leaders: J. P.'s son, John Philip Weyerhaeuser Jr. ("Phil"), and J. P.'s grandson, George. Frederick, J. P.'s older son, was also a Yalie, as was another grandson (John P. III), a great-grandson (George Jr.), and other nephews and extended family into the present day. A couple of J. P.'s nephews attended Harvard (one was the son of his sister Margaret, whose husband became a Harvard professor), but these apparent black sheep stand out from the dominant family legacy. Nearly every decade from the 1890s onward has seen the graduation of one or more Weyerhaeuser descendants from Yale. For fewer than eight of the fifty-four years from 1934 to 1988 was the presidency of the Weyerhaeuser Company out of the family. The balance of time was served by four different Weyerhaeusers, all of them Yale alumni.[9]

## Yale Prime Turf for the Protestant Establishment

Yale's popularity among family business leaders like the Weyerhaeusers vaulted it to a preeminent position in the early part of the century: it was the most popular school for all our leaders prior to 1950, educating thirty-two of them (about 15 percent of all that era's college graduates). With twenty-seven leaders, Harvard came next, and Massachusetts Institute of Technology (MIT) ranked a distant third with fourteen graduates. Yale was a perfect fit for the era of the dominant Protestant establishment, to which the Weyerhaeusers, steadfast Presbyterians, belonged. Yale was seen as a bastion of conservative, faith-oriented values during this period, in contrast to the more intellectual and individualistic attitudes at Harvard. Not until 1899 did Yale appoint a college president who was not a clergyman, and daily chapel attendance was required until 1926.[10] In 1898, 70 percent of the students in its incoming class were listed as church members, and two out of three undergraduates were active in the Young Men's Christian Association (YMCA), with Yale's reputedly the largest of all the college chapters of that organization.[11] The great evangelist and YMCA missionary D. L. Moody sent his sons to Yale in the late 1800s, a ringing endorsement of the school's continuing Christian ethos.[12] In 1914, a college official and alumnus from the class of 1896 declared: "The typical graduate has the believing attitude of mind . . . A Yale atheist, or a Yale cynic, or a Yale pessimist, is rarely found."[13]

The distinctions between Yale and Harvard also appeared in the origins of the Connecticut school's student body: while Harvard in the early twentieth century drew almost 60 percent of its students from New England, nearly 60 percent of Yale's came from outside that region, with over 30 percent (versus Harvard's 20 percent) coming from a region including business-rich Mid-Atlantic states such as New York, Pennsylvania, and New Jersey.[14] Even Yale's relative dominance of the old football rivalry, winning eleven of eighteen championships awarded from 1876 to 1898 in an early "pre-Ivy" League including Harvard, was cited as evidence of the superior teamwork inspired among Yale's more regionally diverse students.[15] Finally, and perhaps what was most important, as a commentator wrote in 1910, "Yale men have the very useful reputation for 'getting there.'" As proof, he added this statement, purportedly from a Harvard alum who sent his son to Yale: "I used to think that Harvard gave the better training, but at my time of life I find that all the Harvard men are working for Yale men."[16] The consistent production of successful corporate achievers anchored Yale's favored position in the education of budding business leaders.

Protestants, however, were not the only college graduates of this era among our leaders, nor did they have a monopoly on Ivy League attendance. With a high percentage of Jewish business leaders prior to 1950 arising in successful family businesses, as discussed earlier, they likewise had the means to enjoy high-prestige educations. Of seventeen college-educated Jewish leaders, ten attended Ivy League institutions, a proportion over twice as high as that among Protestants or Catholics. Walter Sachs of the Goldman Sachs banking firm was a Harvard man, as were Jesse Straus and his son Jack, successful leaders of Macy's who made our list. Robert Lehman, discussed earlier,

*Yale University (left, pictured in 1925) and Harvard University (pictured in 1930) were the alma maters of many early-twentieth-century business leaders.* (Sources: left, E. O. Hoppé/CORBIS; right, courtesy of Harvard University archives)

graduated from Yale in 1913 and was the only Jewish leader on our list from the first half-century to attend that school. The five-to-one ratio for Harvard versus Yale among Jewish leaders in this era suggests, as might be anticipated, that their preference between the two schools went in the opposite direction from Midwestern Protestants. Interestingly enough, as mentioned earlier, Yalie Robert Lehman was a key figure in opening his company's leadership to nonfamily (and non-Jewish) partners, a posture consistent with the greater assimilation required by his choice in schooling. By the late 1910s and early 1920s, however, Ivy League schools were discussing ways to limit Jewish enrollment, concerned that this group's influx (about 20 percent Jewish at Columbia, 14 percent at Penn, and 12 percent at Harvard in 1918 and rising to over 20 percent for Harvard's entering class in 1922) was diminishing the desirability of the schools to other (i.e., Protestant establishment) applicants.[17] Several of these schools established quotas to stabilize or reduce Jewish enrollment in the late 1920s and 1930s, but this move largely came too late to affect our leaders rising before 1950.[18]

In contrast to Jewish leaders, Catholic leaders were decidedly disadvantaged in terms of Ivy representation early in the century, another indication of how much less well established their families were, especially in the East, where these prestigious schools were situated. There were only two Ivy-educated Catholic leaders in the period—both attended Yale, and both had behind them the advantage of a strong family business, which they achieved success in leading. One was J. Peter Grace, a scion of a well-established New York City businessman. The other was Louis Hill, son of the previously discussed Great Northern founder James, who, though Protestant himself, deferred to his Catholic wife in their children's religious upbringing. Louis thus enjoyed an enviable entry point into both business and education—a position that his father's more socially accepted religious background helped make possible.

## Legal Eagles Work Their Way Up

Even as college educations played mainly a prestige-oriented role early in the century, more advanced, specialized education was functioning as a tool to facilitate penetration into business circles. Though fewer than one in every ten leaders arising prior to 1950 had graduate degrees, this extra level of education was a factor in helping foreigners like Camille Dreyfus and African Americans, as we will see in a later chapter, gain access to opportunities that would probably not have been available otherwise. Law, by far the most popular field of graduate study in the first half of the century, was pursued by about 45 percent of those with advanced degrees. Given that graduate business education was in its infancy when most leaders of the period were educated, law constituted the likeliest substitute as preparation for a business career. This makes even more sense in light of the thicket of legal issues, from antitrust suits to increasing levels of industry-specific regulation, being faced by firms in the early twentieth century. It was not uncommon for an attorney to become acquainted with a firm as its counsel and then move into management.

One such able lawyer-leader was Earl D. Babst. Born in Ohio, he began his formal schooling there at Kenyon College and continued at the University of Michigan, where he completed his bachelor's and law degrees. Upon graduation in 1894, he started practicing law in Detroit with Otto Kirchner, a former Michigan attorney general. As legend has it, Babst got his big break on a train trip from Chicago to New York in 1898, when he encountered attorneys representing the newly formed National Biscuit Company, a combination of the country's three major cracker and biscuit companies, spanning from the Rocky Mountains to the East Coast. The attorneys asked Babst's opinion on a case, and his insights turned out to be so accurate that he was quickly retained as a consultant.[19] In 1902, he moved to Chicago to become a partner in the law firm of Adolphus W. Green, who was the mastermind behind the creation of the company more familiarly known as Nabisco.

Legal advice was critical to corporations developing nationwide markets in the early 1900s, as protecting valuable trademarks like Nabisco's Uneeda Biscuit from regional imitators with names such as Uwanta and Ulika required constant vigilance. Also, laws in some states prohibited sales by "foreign" (i.e., out-of-state) corporations. In negotiating Nabisco's entry into his home state of Ohio, Babst obtained agreement on a formula for an entrance fee weighted by the in-state proportion of the firm's overall assets, an arrangement that became a model for other interstate commerce agreements. Getting permission to sell products in a state was only the first hurdle, however. Food packaging regulations varied widely from state to state, and it was impossible to satisfy them all while maintaining large-scale production efficiencies. Babst visited state legislators, bringing samples of some eight hundred grocery items to one such presentation to illustrate how Nabisco's products already exceeded the quality of those from local and regional producers. His state-by-state appeals for regulatory relief fell on deaf ears, but lobbying by him and others in Washington, D.C., paid off in the passage of the Federal Pure Food and Drug Act in 1906, which introduced national standards. That same year, Babst moved to New York to become Nabisco's corporate counsel when Green ascended to the presidency. Babst's involvement in the firm was by no means restricted to legal matters, however. He was an important player in marketing decisions, championing the development of and suggesting the name for the well-known Lorna Doone shortbread cookies. Colleagues and observers generally expected him to succeed Green as president, but Babst shocked all of them, and Green in particular, by leaving to join the American Sugar Refining Company in March 1915, becoming its president just four months later.[20]

Whatever Babst's motives for moving on, he stepped into a company with as much if not more immediate need for his legal talents. American Sugar, also known in its day as the Sugar Trust, was in the process of recovering credibility after a lengthy era of family management that had been characterized, especially toward its end, by suspect pricing practices and adamant refusals to divulge company financials and ownership data.[21] The New York–based company faced federal antitrust litigation and an immediate crisis in Louisiana, where the state legislature was attempting to bar American Sugar from operating, claiming it had artificially depressed the price of raw sugar for local planters. Nearly two hundred civil suits lodged by planters, seeking total damages of about $170 million, were pending. The plaintiffs' grievances hinged on the discrepancy in raw sugar pricing between the Louisiana and New York markets. The price paid for raw sugar in Louisiana was New York's market price *ex freight*, that is, less the cost for shipping to New York (where most refineries were located). In-state Louisiana refiners also observed this pricing convention, but a new state law decreed that any firm paying more for raw sugar out of state than in Louisiana would be deemed a monopoly, a penalty applying only to American Sugar, as it alone made both in-state and out-of-state purchases. American Sugar's refinery in Chalmette, Louisiana, its largest, had been forced to cease operations in December 1914 rather than buy sugar in the open market and expose itself to the state's punitive claims.[22] In May 1915, Louisiana's Supreme Court upheld a lower-court ruling against the state in its lawsuit to oust the firm, but the legislature retaliated the following month with a law declaring sugar refining to be a public utility subject to state regulation—including, of course, the provision that refiners could not pay less for raw sugar in Louisiana than elsewhere.[23]

As Babst assumed the presidency in July, he addressed this thorny situation with a two-pronged attack. A challenge to the new law was launched in federal court, but he also began personal communications with Louisiana businessmen and planters, culminating his interactions with a visit to the state in November. The locals surely had incentive to compromise, given the lost income for a thousand or more unemployed refinery workers, a backlog of unsold raw-sugar stocks, and low supplies of refined sugar in the state. They were, however, unwilling or unable to offer Babst assurances of immunity from prosecution if the factory resumed operation. Before returning to New York, Babst made an announcement that demonstrated his possession of skills in public relations to match those in law. The Chalmette refinery would reopen, he said, as a result of his "confidence and reliance in the sincerity of the good-will and spirit of fairness universally manifested in the conferences of the past few days."[24] In early January, however, the plant closed again with a statement that the higher raw-sugar prices mandated by Louisiana made it fiscally impossible to continue operations.[25] Babst then enjoyed the validation of the U.S. District Court, which struck down the state law just a week later, and the U.S. Supreme Court, which upheld the decision in April.[26] By

September 1916, American Sugar was dangling $100,000 in guaranteed purchase contracts for Louisiana sugar as an incentive for reaching settlement on the planters' lawsuits.[27] In April 1917, 189 of the suits were successfully settled for an estimated $600,000 to $700,000, less than 0.5 percent of the damages initially sought.[28] "Probably never in the history of American corporations has so complicated or so apparently hopeless a legal tangle been adjusted outside of court," wrote the *Wall Street Journal*, crediting the "tact and patience of President Babst."[29] Only a handful of Louisiana lawsuits remained, the last resolved in July 1918, and a final victory came with dismissal of the federal antitrust action in December 1921.[30]

Babst successfully guided the company not only through this legal minefield but through sugar shortages in World War I, a postwar price collapse, and the familiar marketing challenges of an industry that, like that of Nabisco's crackers and cookies, was moving from bulk goods to packaged products. The promotion of the Domino Sugar brand, introduced in 1900 but expanded in the decade following Babst's arrival to deliver an estimated 33 percent of sales by the early 1920s, would prove a catalyst for stabilizing and growing the firm. As a trademark, Domino endures into the twenty-first century.[31]

## Educational Norms Shift As MBA Emerges

It was not long before law lost its monopoly as the graduate degree of choice among business leaders. By 1955, author and researcher Mabel Newcomer saw evidence of changing educational patterns among the business executives she studied. She remained cautious in her conclusions, however: "The graduate school of business administration is too recent a phenomenon for its graduates to have played any important role among the executives at mid-century, but in another generation it should be possible to judge better whether graduate degrees in this field are to become increasingly important as a way of getting to the top."[32]

The first MBA among our leaders ascended in 1931, and with only 7 more appearing in our group of more than 200 leaders rising between then and the mid-1950s, the trend was, understandably, hard for Newcomer to assess in 1955. Given the advantage of the passage of not one but more than two generations, however, we have the perspective she lacked, and the pattern becomes crystal clear. Going generation by generation, it's relatively astonishing how quickly the MBA degree penetrated this group of leaders. While the inaugural linkage of business schools with universities is typically dated to the 1880s, when the Wharton School was established at the University of Pennsylvania, the scope of such graduate programs remained small through the 1920s. Only 1 of our 473 leaders born before 1900 had an MBA. For those born in the first two decades of the century, however, the percentage pops up to over 6 percent—more than 1 in 20 (figure 5-2). These leaders were in their midthirties to early fifties at the time of Newcomer's writing, when she observed the start of a possible trend. In the next decade, the percentage of MBAs among leaders more than *tripled*, and the upward trend continued. More leaders ascending to top posts in the 1990s had MBAs than lacked them. In other words, the

**FIGURE 5-2**

## The rising tide of MBAs

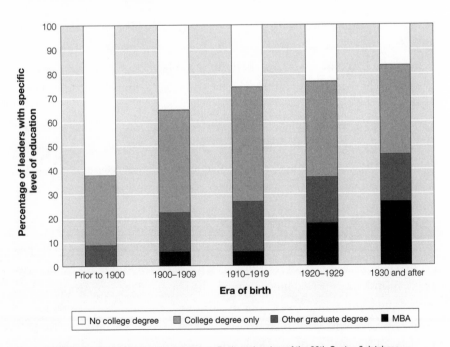

*Source*: HBS Leadership Initiative's "Great American Business Leaders of the 20th Century" database.

The MBA group includes any with an MBA, regardless of other degrees earned (seven of the ninety-two MBAs had other degrees).

degree went from nonexistent to standard equipment in top business leadership circles within a span of about fifty years.

These percentages hint at changes even more startling in U.S. industry as a whole, because our group is less well educated than Newcomer's in the periods she studied. Her sample groups of leaders from the turn of the century and midcentury were nearly 60 percent and nearly 15 percent more likely, respectively, to have college degrees than leaders on our list from the comparable period.[33] This discrepancy most likely results from Newcomer's exclusive focus on officers in large industrial corporations, railroads, and public utilities. Our leaders were drawn from a much wider range of institution sizes and industries. The implication, of course, is that if ascending 1990s leaders of organizations in sectors and sizes comparable to Newcomer's were sampled, their proportion of MBAs might be even *higher* than the 52 percent seen in our group.

## "Early Bird" MBAs Set the Trend . . .

The future prominence of the MBA would probably have shocked leaders in that first generation, who were relatively unlikely to be lauded for their decision to enroll in business school. Marvin Bower learned this firsthand in 1928, when, finishing his degree at Harvard Law School, he innocently shared with that school's dean his intent to attend the university's business school, whose campus had been completed two years earlier, across the Charles River. Pointing in the general direction of the Charles, the dean took a book in his hand and threw it the length of the table in his office, exclaiming, "You are about to graduate from the greatest educational institution in the world, and now you're going to *that* place?"[34]

Ironically enough, Bower's reason for going to Harvard Business School was not to enter business, but to improve his standing with a law firm. His desired employer, Jones Day, the most highly regarded firm in his hometown of Cleveland, had rejected him because he hadn't made the *Law Review* at Harvard. If he went to business school, he reasoned, perhaps he could make the *Business Review* (which was then student-edited) and raise his stock enough to get Jones Day to reconsider. Indeed, so lukewarm was his commitment to business school that he considered withdrawing after the first year, but he was convinced to stay by a J.P. Morgan partner who told him he'd spend the rest of his life insisting that he hadn't flunked out. Bower's summer job during business school, just as it has been during law school, was with a law firm, and he happily accepted the hoped-for offer from Jones Day upon graduation, seemingly never giving a career in industry so much as a passing glance.

His MBA did play a part, however, in helping him wind up on our list rather than a list of accomplished attorneys. When he worked for Jones Day as an associate during the early 1930s, with the Depression at its height, the law firm was becoming increasingly involved with bondholder committees formed to run companies that had defaulted on bonds but were still viable. Because of Bower's business training, he was designated, despite his junior standing with the firm, as a lead participant in these efforts and served as secretary of eleven such committees.[35] Quickly he found that even his limited business knowledge was held in high regard. Bower also saw how an outside party interviewing workers about problems could bring to light solutions that their CEOs wouldn't have seen otherwise. He began to believe that independent management advisers able to collect and analyze such information could become as valuable to companies as their legal counsel.

One of the papers he wrote for these distressed clients came to the attention of James O. McKinsey, a professor of management at the University of Chicago and principal in a small firm of practitioners in the field of management engineering, a discipline largely focused on operational efficiency evaluations and motion studies of the kind pioneered by Frederick Taylor. Impressed, McKinsey tracked down Bower through Harvard Business School Dean Wallace Donham and wrote to offer him a job interview. Bower discussed the offer with his wife, who was wary of Chicago's reputed gangsters and reluctant to move from Cleveland, so they shelved the matter for two years.[36] In 1933, Bower finally took up McKinsey's invitation. In his discussions with the professor, Bower shared his vision for developing a business consulting practice that used professional and ethical standards modeled after those of the best law firms. The notion resonated with McKinsey, and Bower made the leap from the security of Jones Day to land not in "gangster-ridden" Chicago but in the tiny, new New York office of McKinsey's firm.

In two years, the firm actually became even tinier, as one of its largest clients, the Marshall Field & Co. department store, invited McKinsey to become CEO and implement a restructuring plan his firm had developed for the retailer. His absence was expected to be only temporary, but in 1937, the forty-eight-year-old McKinsey died quite suddenly of pneumonia, leaving his firm at loose ends. By then, fortunately enough, Bower had found an ally in Guy Crockett, a principal in the consulting group of a slightly larger New York–based firm, Scovell Wellington, which had formed a partnership with McKinsey's firm when McKinsey had left for Marshall Field. Bower, short on money but long on vision, convinced Crockett that it was worth investing to try to keep the business together.[37] They formed a partnership separate from Wellington and ultimately also separate from the former Chicago office of McKinsey, which would later take the name of principal A. T. Kearney and become a prominent firm in its own right. The split with Chicago arose because, even then, Bower aspired to build a nationwide practice with multiple offices, employing smart, young college or business school graduates and training them to deliver professional consulting services. Kearney felt quite content with a Chicago-based firm, wanted to hire people who were more experienced, and had little interest then in the concept of professionalization for consulting. Prominently, Bower's vision also included the ironclad principle of separating the consulting firm from the ac-

counting business (a departure from the McKinsey firm's prior inclusion of both).[38] The wisdom of this guideline would be ratified through legislation more than a half-century and at least one notable corporate scandal later.

Although Bower would not assume the role of managing partner until 1950, his was the influence that shaped the McKinsey firm, starting from its rebirth in 1939. He retained his mentor's name on the company both out of respect and because, as he later said, he didn't want to be subject to demands by petulant clients for service from the "name" partner of the firm.[39] In the interest of his own time management, the firm never became even McKinsey-Bower, no matter how much his personality and principles defined its identity. That identity, from the start, emphasized professionalism and independence—the

*Marvin Bower propelled McKinsey into becoming one of the largest and most successful management consulting firms in the world. He was a pioneer in hiring recent MBA graduates to build a pipeline of management consulting generalists.* (Source: Portrait Photograph Collection, Baker Library, Harvard Business School)

freedom, as well as the responsibility, always to tell clients the truth about their businesses rather than what would please them, and to walk away from clients where such candor was not valued. More remarkable to many, the company's identity also included an obligation to such candor within the firm, where a nonhierarchical leadership style was emphasized and even Bower would calmly submit opinions to review or correction by junior associates. This didn't mean, however, that Bower shied away from dictating to employees specific requirements for behavior that betokened professionalism. He claimed to have softened his approach early on, on the basis of advice from other partners, shifting from sharp criticism to positive reinforcement by noting and praising instances where associates were doing things the right way.[40] In years to come, though, Bower effectively codified strict standards. Through the mid-1960s, hats were to be worn by all consultants, and socks (no argyles, please!) were to extend above the calf, with garters to prevent sagging. The preferred, if not exclusive, choice for lunchtime companionship should be previous or potential clients. Bower was even known to issue directives about punctuation for project write-ups, at one stage reportedly forbidding the use of dashes or ellipses.[41]

Carrying forward the legal profession's tradition of molding young associates to the firm's specifications, by 1953 Bower formalized his conviction that freshly minted MBAs were the employees of choice, even though this was an era when most such graduates had no meaningful work experience.[42] McKinsey became one of the first recruiters to grab the best and the brightest from Harvard Business School and other key institutions year-in and year-out, offering top-dollar salaries even after investment banking firms joined the fray and upped the ante. McKinsey could afford it, too, as the firm established a cachet as the premier firm in management consulting, with a price premium to match. By the late 1950s, this reputation was spreading worldwide as McKinsey opened its London office, the first outside the United States. Though some accounting-affiliated consulting firms would outsize it and boutique firms like Boston Consulting Group would "outbuzz" it in the 1970s, McKinsey would grow into an international giant, the largest in its management consulting niche. Throughout this success, however, Bower consistently resisted suggestions to take the firm public. In the 1960s, in a notably unselfish gesture, he returned his partnership shares to the firm at book value, eschewing negotiations for a higher payout even as he complied with his own decision that

McKinsey's continuity would be best served if no partner owned more than 5 percent of the shares (he owned half or more at the time).

Bower created not just a firm but also standards for a new industry that would play an increasingly important role in American, and eventually global, business circles. In 1967, he stepped down as managing partner, resolute in his conviction that passing on a legacy was as important as building it. The ultimate testimony to his vision is that it lived on even as he limited his involvement in McKinsey, though he continued to work there until formally retiring in 1992. The firm's "up or out" philosophy, forcing continuous evaluations and demanding excellence from consultants on the track to partnership, became part of McKinsey's legend, as did the network of former McKinseyites who rapidly populated corporate America, becoming a rich source for client referrals and the outplacement of associates who didn't make the cut for the next promotion level. Said one alumnus, himself a corporate president at the time: "You got your BS, your MBA, and your McK."[43] Prominent leaders on our list, such as Lou Gerstner of IBM and John Malone of TCI, put in time as consultants at McKinsey. Devotion to the firm's culture and, along with it, appreciation for the MBA credential, were thus solidified more and more in top corporations. Long an involved alumnus, Bower also played a key role in reframing Harvard Business School's mission when it came under fire from Harvard University President Derek Bok in 1979. The analysis Bower helped prepare in response to Bok's criticisms solidified the school's commitment to the case method of learning while also paving the way for changes, such as the creation of a formal PhD program. In retrospect, his old law school dean might have been even more exasperated had he foreseen the many ways in which Bower's choice for continued schooling would help cement the credibility of business schools and their graduates over decades to come.

## Leaders Rapidly Disperse for MBA Offerings

More than half our leaders who obtained their MBAs did so, like Bower, at Harvard Business School. The next-largest school, Stanford, was represented by less than one-fifth as many graduates. Because both our database source and we the authors are associated with Harvard Business School, we may be liable to the suggestion that the findings privilege our institution's position, but the conclusions are not unique to our study. Dominance by Harvard was also suggested in Newcomer's data, as thirteen of her 1950s-era executives had MBAs from Harvard, the only school with any significant representation. While this constituted less than 2 percent of her overall group, she pointed out that the school was established after most of these executives had completed their educations, so the presence was noteworthy.[44] Indeed, in the early decades, the school held a unique position—all but one of the twenty-one MBAs on our list who ascended to leadership prior to 1970 received their degrees from Harvard Business School. Granted, volume alone might be credited for this preeminence: Harvard's program, at approximately nine hundred in current class size, is over four times the size of most similarly prestigious schools. Although the ratio has not always been the same through the decades, Harvard Business School has typically been the largest in sheer numbers among comparable programs. Its dominance in our leader set, however, dispersed significantly after these early decades (figure 5-3).

Although Harvard still dwarfed most other single institutions, and 80 percent of MBA leaders ascending after 1970 did obtain their degrees at moderately prestigious schools, the degree now conferred credibility even without a brand name. Among leaders ascending in the 1990s, almost as many received their MBAs at "other public" universities (as categorized in the figure) as had graduated from Harvard Business School.

Richard Rosenberg, for instance, showed that a pedigreed MBA and prestigious family tree were not required to climb the CEO ladder in his era. Growing up in working-class Fall River, Massachusetts, Rosenberg was the son of a clothing salesman. The young man earned his undergraduate degree (in journalism) at Suffolk University, a private institution located in downtown Boston and at the time primarily a night school for working students—it boasted a respected law school, but was overall a decidedly lesser light in the constellation of prominent area colleges. After Suffolk, Rosenberg enlisted in the navy, which helped propel him to a port on the opposite coast. When he left active duty in 1959, he and his wife settled in San Francisco, where he took a job as a publicity assistant with Crocker-Anglo Bank, a temporarily hyphenated incarnation of the city's historic Crocker National Bank. The somewhat awkward name had resulted from a 1956 merger with Anglo-California Bank, another long-standing San Francisco bank with founding ties to the Seligman banking family and British and French investors. Both

**FIGURE 5-3**

## Harvard's MBA dominance rapidly diluted

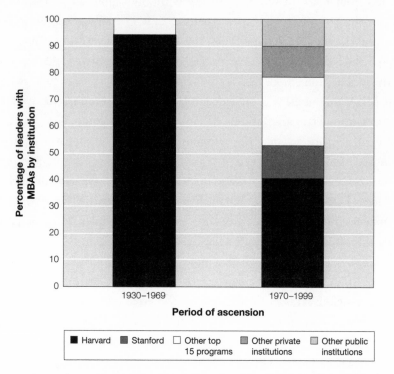

**Period of ascension**

■ Harvard ■ Stanford □ Other top    ▨ Other private    ▢ Other public
                                      15 programs      institutions      institutions

*Sources*: HBS Leadership Initiative's "Great American Business Leaders of the 20th Century" database; *U.S. News and World Report* business school rankings for 2004, available at http://www.usnews.com/usnews/ edu/grad/rankings/mba/brief/mbarank_brief.php.

The "Other top 15 programs" category represents the schools besides Stanford and Harvard that *U.S. News and World Report* ranked as the top fifteen in 2004.

banks had faded significantly from their former glory and, even when combined, took a backseat to Wells Fargo and BankAmerica in prominence. Still,
the position offered a modest foothold in West Coast banking from which
Rosenberg would climb.

He began that process by applying himself to business and law studies in
the evenings at Golden Gate University, a private urban institution that was
not dissimilar to Suffolk and that focused on part-time professional studies for
working adults. As he finished his MBA (he would add his LLB—a law degree—a few years later), he was also taking his next step up the career ladder,
joining Wells Fargo Bank as an officer in banking services. Wells Fargo was

his professional incubator, providing opportunities to move upward, rung by rung, over a twenty-year career. He particularly excelled in the marketing arena and held successively greater authority over those functions. Colleagues later credited Rosenberg as the "father of packaged accounts," pioneering the now-pervasive practice of bundling products like checking, savings, and credit cards. He also introduced the first scenic check designs and, perhaps most material to the consumer, urged Wells Fargo to move quickly in raising deposit interest rates following bank deregulation in the early 1970s.[45]

At the same time, Rosenberg developed a high profile in industry associations, participating in the American Banking Association and particularly the Bank Marketing Association, for which he served in several offices, including president, and as an instructor in its school. By 1980, he was promoted to vice chairman at Wells Fargo, essentially becoming the third-highest company leader behind CEO Richard Cooley, Rosenberg's mentor, and chief operating officer Carl Reichardt. However, when Cooley departed suddenly at the end of 1982 and was replaced by Reichardt, Rosenberg's rise at Wells stalled. By mid-1984, the Fall River native elected to return to his earlier employer, now known just as Crocker National Bank, to take another vice chairman position, probably with his eye on a higher prize. He participated in a significant turnaround of Crocker, helping it regain profitability. Being roughly the same age as Crocker's CEO, however, Rosenberg found himself amid a logjam of recent top management hires with no clear path to the top. He spent only eighteen months there before reuniting with Cooley at Seafirst Corporation, the Seattle-based bank Cooley had left Wells Fargo to lead, which was now owned by BankAmerica's holding company.

At Seafirst, it seemed clear that Rosenberg was in line to be the next CEO, but too quickly he received a better offer; the parent company, BankAmerica, wanted him to run its California operation and apparently wanted him badly enough to promise him a shot at the top corporate post. By 1987, he was back in San Francisco leading the California bank, with a vice chairman's title to boot. He excelled again in marketing and was credited for reversing the bank's decline in local market share, in large part because of a branch sales rewards program that included bonuses not just for the branch manager but for key subordinates who contributed to the success.[46] In 1990, BankAmerica's CEO stepped down, and Rosenberg gained the promotion ahead of a younger rival, becoming, an industry publication noted at the time, the first Jewish CEO of a U.S. money-center bank.[47] With the history of activity by Jewish families in other parts of the U.S. financial sector dating well over a century, the time taken to reach this milestone seems rather startling. The significance of the move was amplified in the eyes of industry watchers because there had been whispers that a bid by Sandy Weill to lead BankAmerica just five years earlier had failed at least in part because Weill was Jewish. (Weill, undaunted, shortly gained control of several East Coast financial businesses, paving the way for his ultimate leadership of Citigroup.)

Whatever the reason for Rosenberg's getting his chance, not only his religious affiliation but his alma maters were less than typical of his peers at similarly sized banks. Appropriately enough, he stood in the legacy of the hardworking and self-made Amadeo Giannini, and like Giannini, he made a name for himself in lifting up the underdog, winning praise for lending in low-income communities and for advancing the interests of women and minority employees at his bank. Rosenberg could also display Giannini-like flashes of temper when things weren't going his way, however, and he didn't hesitate to battle, shooting off an accusatory missive to the Federal Deposit Insurance Corporation about a "marginally capitalized" rival in bidding for a bank acquisition.[48]

Giannini's legacy was most fully realized in Rosenberg's efforts to restore BankAmerica to a nationwide entity that once again suited its name. Interstate banking laws had now legalized what the bank's founder had concocted schemes to achieve, only to have his efforts largely dismantled in the decade after his death. Rosenberg's ambitious expansion efforts began with a 1991 merger with Security Pacific, the largest such transaction completed to that date. He followed it with acquisitions of smaller banks and thrifts in Nevada, Texas, and Hawaii, plus a failed bid for Bank of New England. The inheritance of a significant portfolio of bad loans from Security Pacific made that merger a disastrous write-off in the near term, and absorbing the other acquisitions took time. A slumping California economy made the bank's recovery more difficult, but Rosenberg's final acquisition, of Chicago-based Continental Bank in 1994, was viewed as a great success. By then, BankAmerica was starting a run of nine straight quarters of increased earnings per share to close out Rosenberg's term. When he stepped down at the end of 1995, BankAmerica had advanced from the nation's third-largest bank to its second-largest, with branches in ten states and assets more than doubled in size since

Rosenberg took over.[49] He had even started the ball rolling by discussing with Nationsbank a potential merger that would ultimately occur in 1998, making BankAmerica bicoastal again. It may seem ironic given Giannini's angrily anti-Semitic comments about Treasury Secretary Morgenthau, but Rosenberg helped relight the fire at BankAmerica in a way that its founder would undoubtedly have appreciated.[50]

## What You Know, Not Who You Are

Even as the MBA was emerging in prominence and rapidly shifting from a Harvard-only phenomenon to a qualification available around the country, a similar shift away from prestige educations was happening for all college-educated leaders. Admittedly, Princeton's jump from fourth place in the first half of the century to edge out Harvard as the top undergraduate school among leaders from 1950 onward may not signal a dramatic difference in the schooling of business leaders. Yale, the top choice for college in the first half-century, comes in a very close third, with Cornell fourth. Still, quite a lot was different about the educational patterns of our leaders in the second half of the century. The number of leaders graduating from the University of Nebraska equaled the number graduating from Columbia University—by itself, this fact speaks volumes about the changes under way. The proportion of college-educated leaders who had attended Ivy League undergraduate colleges was cut almost in half (figure 5-4). This drop correlated directly with a doubling of the proportion attending less prestigious "other public" institutions and a fivefold increase in the percentage attending "other private" schools (more than a quarter of those schools were Catholic, most of which were attended by Catholic leaders).

At least part of the broadening in the spectrum of educational institutions among later leaders may be attributable to the post–World War II GI Bill, which supported the reintegration of veterans by paying for college or vocational training, among other benefits. The bill is often pointed to for its role in raising educational levels across a broad class spectrum—according to some studies, 20 percent or even 30 percent of those completing college through its provisions probably would not have done so otherwise.[51] Among our leaders, it's hard to say for sure how many benefited in this way, but among those who definitely obtained college degrees with GI Bill assistance was pharmaceutical

FIGURE 5-4

## Ivy league dominance drops; number of leaders educated at less-prestigious schools grows

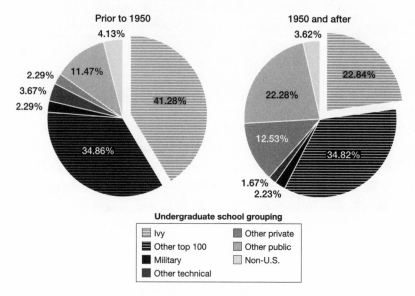

Sources: HBS Leadership Initiative's "Great American Business Leaders of the 20th Century" database; U.S. News and World Report college rankings for 2003, available at http://www.usnews.com/usnews/edu/college/rankings/rankindex_brief.php.

To recognize prestigious schools outside the Ivy League, a grouping of "Other top 100" institutions was created. This group incorporated those ranked among the top fifty colleges or top fifty universities in 2003 by U.S. News and World Report. Although a 2003 listing is obviously not a perfect reflection of the school's status in the early 1900s, the vast majority of these schools are reasonable possibilities for leaders throughout the century to have attended. After eliminating (1) the schools founded after 1900 (meaning they were not open or well established when most early-twentieth-century leaders were educated), (2) all the Ivy League schools (which were grouped separately), and (3) women's colleges (all the college-educated leaders ascending before 1950 were male), seventy-two schools remain.

executive Edmund Pratt of Pfizer. William Ruane, founder of the value-investing Sequoia Fund, received his Harvard MBA with help from the benefits, and there are doubtless others whose graduate educations were similarly subsidized.

Although founders of companies remained the least likely and those in family businesses the most likely to possess prestigious educations, the broadening in educational backgrounds was most apparent among hired CEOs. A third of them had been Ivy graduates earlier in the century, but only a fifth were such from 1950 on, a smaller percentage than attended "other public" institutions. Regional loyalties were also diminishing in importance; among established companies based in the Northeast, where nearly half the hired leaders with college degrees in the first half-century had been Ivy graduates, the percentage of Ivy Leaguers dropped to under 30 percent, and more than 15 percent had graduated from "other public" colleges. The reduced importance of elite undergraduate education and the phenomenon of the MBA are, moreover, not unconnected. Nearly half of those "other public" college graduates who ascended to leadership from 1950 on had augmented their college studies with at least one graduate degree, and 45 percent of those degrees were MBAs. Education appeared to be shifting from a largely ceremonial function of ratifying status for leaders from well-established families to a more substantive one, in which it was perceived to build competencies rather than just connections. The school where a degree was earned was becoming less important even as higher education itself was increasingly viewed as pertinent to business success.

Consider, for example, the coast-hopping career of John Chambers, whose rearing and college education in West Virginia would have certainly placed him on the outside track for top business leadership early in the century. However, after supplementing his undergraduate business degree from West Virginia University with a law degree there, plus getting an MBA from Indiana University, Chambers was actually inclined to think the IBM sales job he was offered was beneath him.[52] His parents were both physicians, and his father dabbled in real estate and politics on the side. Chambers expected to be running his own company, not toiling in sales, but he was persuaded to accept the offer by the compensation package and the profile of the company, which was, in 1976, at very much its "Big Blue" height as the dominant mainframe computing player. Chambers was a rainmaker at IBM, getting steady promotions, but something about that steadiness ultimately disquieted him: the organization seemed geared to reward mediocrity rather than excellence, an observation confirmed when a manager suggested to Chambers that setting three goals and meeting all of them rather than setting ten and missing one was a better practice if he wanted to reach the top there.[53]

As a result, Chambers left for Massachusetts-based Wang Laboratories in 1982, working in regional sales and eventually running the company's Asian sales group at a time when, like IBM, this firm that became synonymous with corporate word processing was riding high. His numbers zoomed and he enjoyed working closely with the company's founder, An Wang, another leader who made our list. Chambers and Wang, however, got a rude awakening when the office automation market was overrun with PCs in the late 1980s. Wang's closed minicomputer systems were superseded virtually overnight by versatile, networked desktop PCs running multiple software applications. In 1989, Chambers was shifted abruptly from overseas sales management to running U.S. operations and was shocked to find himself presiding over the layoffs of thousands of workers. Inwardly, he vowed he'd never do the same in a business he ran and would avoid the trap of sentimental allegiance to a particular technology—the kind of allegiance that he perceived to have been Wang's undoing. In December 1990, he left Wang after a brief, quiet job search. A call from a former Wang colleague enticed him to a small technology start-up in the midst of Silicon Valley, where he began work in early 1991. The cash Wang Laboratories had been bleeding in any one of several recent quarters equaled or exceeded the fiscal 1990 total revenues for Chambers' new employer, but unlike Wang in 1982 or IBM in 1976, little Cisco Systems was anticipating rather than already enjoying its glory days.

Cisco had been founded by Stanford University computer technicians to market the networking technology they'd developed on campus—devices called "routers" that enabled communication between computers regardless of the architecture, operating systems, or network protocols in use. The multitalented boxes facilitated support for a little thing called the Internet. In early 1990, the company had gone public at eighteen dollars a share and, while Chambers was slogging out his final months at desperate Wang, had more than doubled in value. The tech-focused founders had departed by the fall of that year, and the company was being led by John Morgridge, an MBA and "old tech" veteran (he had spent twenty years at Honeywell before two stints with computer start-ups) who had been brought in by venture capital investors in 1988 to add experience and stability to Cisco's management.

The high level of venture capital financing in such technology companies indeed appears to have contributed to strong MBA representation in the sector (over 16 percent of our MBA leaders succeeded in high technology versus about 7 percent of a sample of non-MBA leaders matched proportionately by time period). Venture capitalists largely had MBAs themselves and for reassurance looked to someone with similar credentials, brought in from the outside if necessary, to guard their investment interests. In this case, Morgridge, himself an MBA hired by venture capitalists, in turn hired Chambers with a view to making Chambers his successor.

Though the two men had serious professional differences over a proposed merger deal in 1993, Morgridge still endorsed Chambers to succeed him as CEO when he was ready to retire to the chairman's seat. A salesperson was not a popular choice to head a start-up in Silicon Valley, however, and Cisco's board was skeptical that the Wang refugee with the West Virginia twang in his voice had the right stuff to lead a cutting-edge technology company. Morgridge, however, nurtured the candidacy of Chambers, giving him opportunities to make presentations to the board and to help persuade board members that skilled management of sales and customer relations was as vital as technical excellence to the success of the burgeoning enterprise.[34] In January 1995, Chambers became president and CEO at Cisco, finally finding himself in the kind of position he'd rather precociously considered his destiny at his business school graduation some twenty years earlier.

For the next five years, Chambers and Cisco rode the wave of the World Wide Web through five stock splits, multiplying the value of a single share held at the beginning of Chambers's tenure some fortyfold by March 2000. By that point, the company's market capitalization had briefly surpassed both General Electric and Microsoft, making Cisco, by that measurement, the most highly valued business on earth. At its peak, the stock traded at a price-to-earnings multiple approaching 200. The stock's increasing value made it ideal currency for use in a steady stream of acquisitions that delivered a wealth of adjunct technologies and engineering talent to Cisco's doors, and the company's goal was to retain the people as well as the product lines. Spiffy new customer-friendly networking elements developed by start-ups were thus rapidly transformed from competitive threats to Cisco selling points. Articles about Chambers regularly likened him to a preacher or an evangelist, as his sales-driven persona prompted him to spout glowing predictions about Cisco and its impact, not only on technology, but on the world. He hobnobbed with heads of state, serving on a Trade Policy Committee under President Bill Clinton and on the Transition Team for President George W. Bush. Also, he made himself almost continuously available to customers, speaking engagements, and the press, never varying from his upbeat gospel.

In 2001, however, the bubble burst, as corporate information technology (IT) spending was slashed across the board. Cisco missed its first earnings

*A native of West Virginia educated at state universities (West Virginia and Indiana), John Chambers led Cisco Systems through the phenomenal growth of the Internet boom of the 1990s and through the turbulent technology downturn in the early twenty-first century.* (Source: JAGADEESH NV/Reuters/CORBIS)

projection in eleven years as of the quarter ending that January. For critics ready to pounce on Chambers for being all style and no substance, a field day was at hand. In March, only a year after the company's peak valuation, Chambers reluctantly presided over just what his experiences at Wang had made him swear he'd avoid, laying off nearly eight thousand workers, close to 20 percent of Cisco's payroll. The cuts were a particularly humbling move for a company that had hired some two thousand only the month before, still basking in "go-go" sentiments.

A second blow came quickly with the write-off of $2.2 billion in obsolete inventory. The vultures were circling, the stock was tanking, and Chambers's ebullience of just a few months prior seemed vacuous and ill-informed at best, even though industry analysts and publications had been singing much the same tune. His often-cited comment that his company might be the first to reach $1 trillion in market capitalization, for example, was nothing more than what analysts from Credit Suisse First Boston and other investment firms had said in February 2000.[55] For Chambers, the fall was hard, but he minimized the mea culpas in favor of picking himself and his company up off the ground. Some saw the layoffs as excessive, but he saw them as being the one deep cut that would remove the need for more.[56] Quickly he began to change the company's business practices in directions that would improve efficiency, streamlining product lines, tightening purchasing procedures, trimming reseller programs, and dramatically slowing the acquisition pace. He reduced his own salary to one dollar a year, taking compensation in stock options only.

By 2004, although its stock still traded at only about 25 percent of its 2000 peak value, Cisco was posting profits higher than any seen since those glory days.[57] Those who underestimated Chambers on the basis of his accent or origins hadn't counted on the determination of the boy who, diagnosed with dyslexia, overcame it to rank second in his high school class. His MBA may not have endeared him to the techies of Silicon Valley in the first place, but applying some typical business school principles helped his company regain its footing in a slippery and dynamic environment.[58]

## Education Shifts from the Mark of an Old Club to the Definition of a New One

In the early twentieth century, higher education remained almost as uncommon among our leaders as it was in the general U.S. populace. For leaders arising through 1920, the majority reached the pinnacle of success without a college degree, and those who did possess one seemed to have realized primarily symbolic value from it in their careers. It reflected a certain social standing for the graduate's family and operated as a badge of credibility for those traveling in similar circles. Just as one's religious denomination at the time was often related more to status than to distinctive faith convictions, so a college diploma indicated something other than knowledge. It offered evidence of respectability and standing that even successful self-made men, whose prestige could readily be ascertained by the size of their pocketbooks, wanted for their children and grandchildren. Connections formed through the college experience made one part of the insider club, figuratively if not literally. With money no object for most college graduates among our leaders at this time, Yale dominated the degrees, with Harvard close behind. In no case, however, were college studies viewed as relevant for building competence in business management. Only the technical or professional skills gained in disciplines like engineering or law offered recognizable value in America's developing economy, and in these fields, a less well-connected but bright individual with a reputable degree might realize some advantages in business access.

In fact, although higher education initially reinforced status and class consciousness, college admissions at even prestigious institutions operated in a relatively more egalitarian way than society in general (at least until the late 1920s and 1930s, when certain discriminatory quotas based on religion were introduced, as discussed earlier in the chapter). Lower-cost or even free educations were also becoming available at public institutions. As such, educational attainment became a potential wedge opening leadership to outsiders who capitalized on their chance and who, in the process, began the transformation to insiders. Even if they couldn't hold the door open to admit everyone of their nationality, race, or religion, getting inside allowed outsiders to begin the slow process of adjusting the balance of opportunity to offset its dramatic tilt in favor of the well-established descendants of white, native-born Northeastern Protestants.

By the middle of the century, the impact of these transformations began to be seen in a diversifying array of colleges attended among leaders. The GI Bill was, of course, an important factor then, opening college and graduate studies to veterans from a wide variety of backgrounds. Elite institutions no longer completely dominated the picture, and having a diploma from the "right" school ceased to matter as much. At the same time, the diploma itself was largely becoming a requirement rather than a luxury in business. The good news was that college educations were more widespread, among the population as well as among leaders, but the bad news was that the degrees were no longer optional. Graduate degrees, most notably MBAs, were also rapidly extending the educational prerequisites for top business leadership. Here opened yet another potential path for outsiders, however, since excelling at a less prestigious undergraduate school might pave the way to a more elite graduate program. Several well-regarded business schools developed as part of large public universities, adding to their accessibility. The increased diversity of undergraduate schools in theory provided a wider group of individuals with the chance to take an important first step toward opportunity. There were signs, though, that the true insider's track may have simply been bumped to the next educational level. Getting additional credentials (and access to a more influential alumni network) through graduate education showed signs of becoming a proxy for the previous generation's pattern of undergraduate prestige.

By the latter part of the twentieth century, a new kind of club was undeniably emerging among American business leaders—one to which admission depended not so much on social factors such as birthplace or religious affiliation as on educational credentials. The rise of college educations and particularly the MBA degree blurred the previous markers of distinction. Because becoming an insider by this means required access to an educational opportunity, family resources still played a role, but government subsidies, student loans, scholarships, and public universities bridged the gap to allow bright outsiders a chance for diplomas. Granted, women and racial minorities at first remained among the missing in this brave new world of graduate schools of business administration, but this also began to change in the 1960s and 1970s. Regarding this new means of access to the top, Newcomer again appears prescient in her 1955 comments:

> In the past, starting a new enterprise has been one important channel through which the poor boy with only a grammar school or at best a high school education could reach the top. But the virtual disappearance of this channel appears to have been more than compensated for by the increasing opportunity of getting the necessary college education in the first place, and then working up in the big corporation. A college degree has become more important than great wealth, and easier to obtain. The sons of families in the low-income groups will not reach the top as quickly as the sons of the wealthy, but the chance of arriving eventually is improving. This is important because it means that *the chance of those from low-income families reaching high position is, if anything, better than earlier, and social mobility has to that extent increased.* (emphasis added)[59]

Given her focus on the leaders of large corporations, Newcomer may have overstated the "virtual disappearance" of entrepreneurship. Nonetheless, her expectation that this new means of access to business leadership through education would break down social barriers more rapidly than the former means of starting a new business appears justified. After all, creating businesses from scratch required outsiders to devote most of their lives to building companies, with real insider benefits accruing only to their offspring and later genera-tions. A graduate was a graduate, however. Whether the name on the diploma was Bower or Rosenberg or Chambers, its recipient could begin real-izing the benefits of that credential right away. To test Newcomer's predic-tions, however, we need to turn to consider the impact of yet another set of criteria over the century—the economic backgrounds of leaders.

# SIX

# Class

## Advantages That Persist

*"I wish you'd tell me a little about yourself. Have you got any father or mother?"*

*"I ain't got no mother. She died when I wasn't but three years old. My father went to sea; but he went off before mother died, and nothin' was ever heard of him. I expect he got wrecked, or died at sea."*

*"And what became of you when your mother died?"*

*"The folks she boarded with took care of me, but they was poor, and they couldn't do much. When I was seven the woman died, and her husband went out West, and then I had to scratch for myself."*

*"At seven years old!" exclaimed Frank, in amazement.*

*"Yes," said Dick. "I was a little feller to take care of myself, but," he continued with pardonable pride, "I did it."*

—Horatio Alger, *Ragged Dick*

WITH RESPECT to his parental status, it must be said, Dick's story departs most significantly from the norm for leaders on our list. Only thirty-five of our thousand leaders can be identified as even coming close to poor Dick's situation—their fathers died or were seriously ill or entirely absent while the leaders were young, and no stepfather entered the child's life to offer alternative support. It's perhaps evidence of people's fascination for Alger-like tales that three members of this small group (C. R. Smith, James J. Hill, and, in this chapter, Kemmons Wilson) are included among the lives we recount in detail in this book. All three, however, as well as the thirty-two similarly bereft leaders on our list, had mothers or other guardians who took active roles in supporting them well beyond age seven. In the respect of chronicling successful orphans, Alger's fiction appears to be at its most far-fetched, romantic extreme. The youngest age at which any of our leaders is recorded to have gone to work is eight, but fewer than a hundred are known to have worked before age sixteen.

Of course, the presence of *any* such individuals among those reaching a high degree of business success is proof of a society open enough to allow advancement from such circumstances. By the early twentieth century, there was a growing awareness, however, that such rags-to-riches tales celebrated the rare exceptions, not the rule. Moreover, there was a sense that such stories were becoming progressively scarcer as the decades passed. Pitirim Sorokin, then a professor at the University of Minnesota and soon to be the first head of the Sociology Department at Harvard, spoke the opinion of increasingly many in 1925:

> The period of the de facto "open door" for social circulation of the individuals in the United States is passing and the stage of class-differentiation with the wealthy class is becoming more and more hereditary and is more and more closing its door to newcomers. *American society is being transformed—at least in its upper stratum—into a society with rigid classes and well outlined class divisions.* (emphasis in original)[1]

This heresy to the cult of Alger was rapidly spreading in the 1920s, a brushfire fanned into flame by the recent Bolshevik Revolution and its inspiration in the class-based rhetoric of Marx and Engels. Sorokin himself was as ardently anti-Communist as he was anti-czarist, a combination of sentiments that predictably led to numerous imprisonments and finally exile from Russia after a hair's-breadth escape from execution in 1923.[2] The strife he had left behind, however, left him in no way timid about applying a keen eye to the societal dynamics of the country where he had been welcomed. He pronounced his conclusions in a quotable sound bite that would be echoed throughout the period: "The wealthy class of the United States is becoming less and less open, more and more closed, and is tending to be transformed into a caste-like group."[3]

The pointing finger of a Russian émigré doubtless presented a particularly strong motivation for an American response, and F. W. Taussig and C. S.

Joslyn, Harvard faculty members in economics and sociology, respectively, wasted no time undertaking a study that confronted Sorokin's claim. They surveyed over fifteen thousand top American business leaders of 1928, of whom nearly half provided the requested information about their family backgrounds. On the basis of this data, the researchers rejected Sorokin's assertion that American business leaders were "a caste-like group."[4] This rejection, however, was based on the strict interpretation that a group must get a substantial majority of its members via direct descent in order to be described as caste-like. Since "probably not more than half" of the executives or owners in the largest class of businesses Taussig and Joslyn evaluated had directly inherited those roles from their fathers, the researchers dismissed Sorokin's claim.[5] They nevertheless acknowledged that the offspring of top executives were quite disproportionately represented among the group, and indeed, 10 percent of the population (businessmen and professionals) appeared to be supplying 70 percent of the leaders.[6]

Mindful perhaps of the narrow definition on which their denial rested, Taussig and Joslyn did note a not-so-congenial trend apparent when the younger leaders serving in 1928 were compared with the older ones: "There is clear evidence that the representation of the well-to-do classes among American business leaders is increasing at a rapid rate, and is likely to become preponderant if the present rate of increase is maintained during the next few decades."[7] In short, while they rejected the idea that American business leadership in 1928 was caste-like, they all but predicted it would become so shortly. In a development that may have disappointed the authors, this somewhat oblique prediction, rather than their repeated denials of Sorokin's claim, became the portion of their study most commonly cited by later writers.

An examination of our leaders through the 1920s strongly supports Sorokin's initial claim and Taussig and Joslyn's predictions. Compared with previous periods, that decade continued an ominous decline in two proportions: leaders coming from poor backgrounds and leaders who were business founders (the route to success for over 70 percent of poor leaders up to that time). At the same time, the decade saw a sinister-looking rise in the proportion of leaders whose fathers were owners or executives of big businesses (figure 6-1).

**FIGURE 6-1**

## Rise of the "caste-like group" of 1920s leaders?

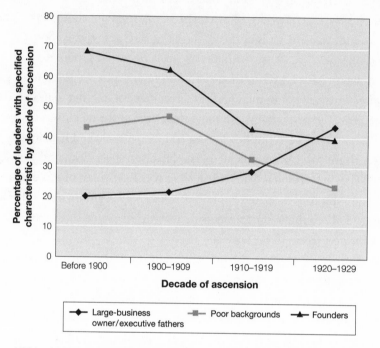

*Source*: HBS Leadership Initiative's "Great American Business Leaders of the 20th Century" database.

Proportions of leaders by economic background and father's occupation are based on the total number of leaders who could be coded for that variable (approximately 80 percent of all leaders in either case, but not identical sets).

More than 70 percent of the owner or executive fathers of our leaders arising in the 1920s had headed up the very companies in which their progeny achieved success. With this number representing just over 40 percent of all ascending leaders in the decade, the group might indeed have fallen short of being caste-like, by Taussig and Joslyn's definition, but it showed no indication of heading in a different direction. All signs suggested that the time for fresh faces was ending and that the inbreeding and calcification of a business aristocracy was inexorably under way. The early "up by the bootstraps" entrepreneurs were producing silver-spoon scions into the second and third generation—scions who seemed quite likely to multiply until they eclipsed all entrants not sharing their advantages.

## Members of the Club Advance

A typical member of the 1920s-era group of rising executives was Carle C. Conway. Born in a Chicago suburb in 1877, Conway had no shortage of business connections. His father, Edwin, a Canadian immigrant, had advanced from salesperson to vice president of W. W. Kimball, where he was one of two top lieutenants to the founder of the successful piano and organ manufacturing enterprise. Desiring his own children to be blessed with Kimball's good fortune, Edwin Conway made sure each of them (Carle C., Earle E., and Sylvia S.) had matching first and middle initials, like his boss.[8] Active in Republican politics, the self-made Edwin Conway counted Presidents McKinley, Taft, and Theodore Roosevelt among his friendly acquaintances, and he reportedly turned down several entreaties to stand as a candidate for the U.S. Senate. Given Edwin's success at Kimball, son Carle quite understandably became a piano salesman there after graduating from Yale in 1899. The following year, Carle also extended his network into a very different business arena by marrying the daughter of Edwin Norton.

Norton was an inventor who over his lifetime held numerous patents for devices and processes related to canning foods and manufacturing cans. One account credits him with five thousand patents.[9] Thomas Edison, commonly cited as the leading patent-holder, had just over a thousand, however, making this claim seem a bit overexuberant. Whatever the actual number of Norton's inventions, his mechanical ingenuity helped the business that he and his brother operated become a market leader in the canning industry. Their firm became the core of the Chicago-based American Can Company, a combination of over one hundred can-making companies. Together, the firms constituting American Can represented about 90 percent of U.S. can production when they were united in 1901.[10] Norton was the combination's first president, but remained in the role only a year. In November 1904, he backed his son and other family members in organizing the rival Continental Can Company, a New Jersey corporation that combined a different, much smaller set of can-manufacturing interests under the leadership of several former American Can executives. They brought with them to Continental the lucrative account of Campbell Soup Company, a client that quickly put the start-up on solid ground.[11]

By 1905, Carle Conway, already a top sales producer for Kimball, had decided to build a "combination" of his own. With his brother and one of the

Kimballs, he created a holding company in New Jersey to acquire a Boston-based piano manufacturer and some other regional musical instrument companies. In 1908, Conway also bought a stake in Continental Can, perhaps noticing, as piano sales started to slip with the rise of the phonograph, that his father-in-law's area of business might hold more promise than his father's. Four years later, Continental Can undertook significant expansion and re-capitalization.[12] The following year, Conway joined the firm as vice president and secretary of its executive committee. In 1921, Conway, his friends, and other Norton family interests gained voting control of Continental's stock, and Carle became more active in operations, assuming the presidency in 1926. He knew much more about pianos than cans, but he placed his trust in company experts regarding the technical issues and focused on an expansion strategy. Over the next three years, Continental merged with the third-largest U.S. can maker and acquired additional operations in the South and West, doubling its plant assets and positioning itself to compete with American Can nationwide. Conway became chairman in 1930 and continued in this role for twenty years. During that time, Continental continued to grow and hold its own as a strong second to American Can in what proved to be an enduringly profitable industry.[13]

## How the Rich Get Richer

Conway's access to a choice corporate post emerged through business connections in both his and his wife's families—the kinds of advantages only an insider would have. Even more discouraging to business aspirants from poor backgrounds, however, the descendants of wealth in the early twentieth century were also now drawing on such advantages in entrepreneurship. From 1900 to 1920, almost 45 percent of the wealthy leaders on our database gained their success by that method, more than double their proportion prior to 1900. Wealth obviously gave them an edge in starting companies just as it did in finding executive positions. Even geography put no restraint on these well-heeled entrepreneurs.

For example, there are quite a few theories floated to explain the concentration of automobile manufacturers in Detroit—ready access to raw materials via its port on the Great Lakes, availability of skilled machinists and laborers from its sizable railroad car manufacturing industry, and so on.[14] One could also cite Henry Ford, a leader on our list, who is undoubtedly the most famous Michigander in the automotive field. At least part of the credit for making sure the industry thrived there, however, should go to Henry B. Joy, a rich Detroit native who found a car he loved and brought the company home with him as well.

Joy was born in 1864, the son of a very wealthy attorney and businessman, James Frederick Joy, who made his fortune in the country's early incarnations of the transportation industry, leading the construction of a canal in Michigan's Upper Peninsula as well as heading multiple railroad organizations in the Midwest.[15] Henry enjoyed the privileges of an education at Phillips-Andover Academy and then Yale's Sheffield Scientific School, where he dropped out a year short of his degree. He began work at the Peninsular Car Company, a maker of wooden railroad cars. His beginning as a lowly $15-dollar-a-month office boy is noted in biographical write-ups, but his rapid rise (to assistant treasurer within two years) was equally notable and suggestive of his not-so-lowly origins. In 1890, he joined one of his father's railroad-related ventures, the Fort Union Depot Company, and became its president six years later, upon his father's death. In the interim, Joy had also married well, taking as his bride the daughter of John Stoughton Newberry. His new father-in-law, in addition to riches, sported a Northeastern family lineage traced back to within five years of the landing of the *Mayflower*.[16] An attorney and businessman like Joy's own father, Newberry held numerous lucrative interests in railroads and manufacturing, including the Michigan Car Company, a railroad-car enterprise that had, around the time Joy was off at prep school, employed teenager Henry Ford.

In November 1901, Joy, by then also a veteran entrepreneur after organizing a successful Michigan sugar refining company, traveled to New York City with his similarly well-to-do brother-in-law, Truman Newberry, during the second annual New York Automobile Show. Accounts differ as to whether they were searching for a reliable boat engine, a new car, or an investment opportunity, but they found at least the latter two. While they were watching a demonstration of a steam-powered car, a glass gauge on its boiler exploded in Newberry's face, leaving the two men fortunately uninjured but understandably wary of steam-powered vehicles. Later that day, Joy and Newberry were admiring a pair of automobiles (with gasoline motors) developed by James W. Packard. A fire engine then passed by, prompting two other men to hop into the Packard cars, start them up, and race off in search of the fire. Intrigued by the quick and apparently reliable start of the cars—not a thing to be taken for granted in the early days of automotive development—Joy bought a Packard-made automobile from the local sales agency on the spot. He quickly set his sights on a still larger acquisition, purchasing one hundred shares in the Ohio Automobile Company, which was based in Warren, Ohio, and which Packard and his brother had incorporated with a few other investors. Knowing the value of publicity, Joy shrewdly followed up his stock investment with a notice to the press about his vehicle purchase (then a newsworthy event), his satisfaction with his new automobile, and his pending order for the next model.[17]

At the time, Packard's vehicles were sound but the company's success modest; the 165 cars it had built by the November show reflected a significant ramp-up from the 33 built before 1901, but Ohio Automobile was just one of many similar-sized fledgling automakers dotted across the Midwest and Northeast from Missouri to New England. Names long lost to history such as the Winton Company in Cleveland and the Locomobile Company in Bridgeport, Connecticut, had already produced many times more automobiles than Packard had.[18] Joy, however, recognized the singular value of a well-made, reliable car—within a few months, he had more than doubled his stock holding and had begun a steady correspondence with Packard, visiting the company in Warren as early as January 1902.

Ohio Automobile was well positioned: a new state-of-the-art factory building had just been added and production now averaged one car a day, with sales rising accordingly. Still, the Packards and their small investment group were realizing the need for more capital, which must have been music to Joy's ears. In October 1902, the company was reconstituted as Packard Motor Car Company, a name that emphasized its founder but conveniently deemphasized its Ohio location. A new stock offering at a cost of $250,000 was subscribed in total by Joy, Newberry, and other wealthy Detroiters of their acquaintance, constituting a stake that, with Joy's earlier stock purchases, more than doubled the investment of the original partners and the Packard family. The capital influx was expected to increase the company's production capacity tenfold. Although James Packard denied to local media that a move from Warren was part of the deal, the alacrity with which Joy began making plans for the firm's new plant in Detroit suggests otherwise.[19]

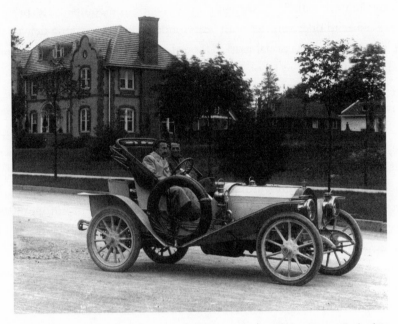

*Henry B. Joy, president of Packard Motor Car Company, taking a test drive in his 1904 Packard.* (Source: Bettmann/CORBIS)

In April 1903, Joy was telling the editor of a local paper, "We hope to make Detroit as prominent a manufacturing town for automobiles as it is for stoves."[20] Indeed, he did his part to ensure that Detroit would be known as the "Motor City" long after the Michigan Stove Company and Detroit Stove Works, which had made the city the "Stove Capital of the World" in the late nineteenth century, were forgotten.[21]

By October 1903, the Packard firm had moved to Detroit lock, stock, and camshaft, with control solidly in the hands of Joy and his investor friends. James Packard retained the title of president for several more years, but he also retained his Ohio residence, leaving little doubt about who was really in charge. Indeed, from the time the company came to Detroit and even a bit earlier, Joy was heavily involved in discussing specifications for all of Packard's models, testing them personally and pressing for high quality along with a design that could be mass-produced. By 1909, when he officially assumed

Packard's presidency, his position only confirmed the leadership role Joy had been performing for at least six years.

Joy showed a marketer's insight, encouraging the company to produce trucks so as to offer vehicles with year-round utility for making deliveries.[22] This overcame the seasonal market for ordinary automobiles, which were at the time considered to be of use primarily for fair-weather pleasure outings. Recognizing also that good roads were necessary to encourage more motorists, Joy championed the development of the Lincoln Highway, a project to cross the continent from New York to San Francisco with a paved roadway. For all his pragmatism, however, it is perhaps appropriate that Packard became a car most associated with wealthy owners like Joy and his peers. Packards were the only automobiles used in the 1913 inaugural parade for President Woodrow Wilson, and the make was a favorite of European royalty. Joy stepped down as president in 1916, resigning from the board and selling his company stock the following year, reportedly disappointed that the leadership would not consider merging with another automaker as he proposed. If the company leaders had followed Joy's advice, perhaps Packard would have fared better in later days. Ultimately unable to compete with the multiline offerings of Ford, General Motors, and Chrysler, the company slunk meekly into the sunset in the 1950s after a "too little, too late" merger with Studebaker. For most of its first half-century, however, Packard prospered, a legacy of one of Detroit's prosperous favorite sons who did his part in forming the city's automaking reputation.[23]

## Climbing Career Ladder Assists Outsiders

A funny thing happened, though, on the way to the "caste-like" domination of insiders like Conway and Joy in business leadership. In the mid-1950s, social scientists W. Lloyd Warner and James Abegglen attempted a study to answer Taussig and Joslyn much in the way the earlier authors had attempted to answer Sorokin. Sensibilities in the early Cold War era had rekindled the eagerness by Americans to examine the structure of their own society, some transparently eager to prove, others to disprove, its conformity to a class system. Warner and Abegglen drew data from the lives and careers of 8,562 business leaders in top executive positions across a range of industries, collecting their information in categories that corresponded with the earlier study. By

now, however, their observations suggested that over the intervening decades, mobility from lower social classes into their defined "business elite" had
*increased* rather than decreased. For instance, the proportion of 1952 leaders
whose fathers had been laborers, clerks, or salesmen was about 50 percent
higher than that for leaders studied in 1928. This increase directly corresponded to a *decrease* in the percentage of leaders whose fathers were "major
executives" or business owners.[24] Warner and Abegglen then compared these
percentages to the occupational distribution of Americans in the preceding
(i.e., the father's) generation. The researchers found that categories considered "disadvantaged" for business advancement—categories such as laborers,
farmers, and clerks—had all improved their proportional representation relative to 1928. In contrast, businessmen and professional fathers, while still proportionately overrepresented, had diminished significantly in this respect.[25]
The authors likewise found a dropoff of more than a third from 1928 to 1952 in
the percentage of leaders who inherited the same leadership role as their father's within a family business.[26] On the basis of what they saw as slow but
steady progress over multiple generations since 1900, Warner and Abegglen
proudly (and rather patriotically) pronounced: "Rather than closing in on
men of low birth, holding them to the positions into which they were born,
our social system continues to make it possible for men from all levels to move
into elite positions in commerce and industry."[27]

What Warner and Abegglen discovered is largely mirrored in our leader
set. The less-than-one-quarter proportion of leaders arising from poor backgrounds in the 1920s was a low never again reached in the century's subsequent decades. By the same token, the large percentage (more than 40 percent) of leaders coming from top executive fathers was a peak never exceeded;
in the 1990s, fewer than 20 percent of rising leaders would have such backgrounds. What helped flatten the curve was the new phenomenon of *managerial capitalism*, whereby business leaders were developed from within the ranks
of workers rather than exclusively drawn from the ranks of ownership. Although the percentage of such opportunities being obtained by those from
poor backgrounds remained essentially constant through the century, the
multiplication of the number of hired management posts presented openings
for more and more aspiring outsiders willing to bide their time. Climbing the
career ladder wasn't a shortcut to riches, but it did present a situation, as with
the tortoise and the hare, where slow and steady could win the race.

One such climber was Joseph Martino, a Catholic of Italian descent born in 1900 in Long Island. A cobbler's son, Martino was poised to take his family a significant step forward in a multigenerational path to prosperity. At age sixteen, he went to work in the offices of United Lead Company, a subsidiary of National Lead Company that was eventually absorbed by and took the name of its parent firm. During World War I, Martino, too young to serve in the military, was instead enlisted with the other office boys to run billing and monthly accounting functions in place of those who had left for war duties.[28] He worked full-time from then on, taking only some night classes in accounting to supplement his on-the-job trial by fire. Bit by bit, he learned the intricacies of his company's business, which centered on the manufacture of lead-based products like paints, pipe, and solder, with the Dutch Boy paint brand being National Lead's most well-known consumer offering. By the early 1930s, as he was gaining on two decades of service, Martino had made it all the way up to assistant controller.[29] Obviously, the willingness to keep on plugging went with the territory for someone of Martino's background. He would not complete the further leap to controller until 1945, but thereafter, the moves began in rapid succession—vice president in April 1946, executive vice president in November of that year, and president in April 1947.[30] A decade after his arrival, a colleague noted, "Those closest to the business couldn't say exactly *how* he got to the top. He has always been so capable a guy that it just couldn't be otherwise."[31]

By the time Martino took over, National Lead's products were beginning to be much more diversified, a direction he had helped promote during his succession of higher posts in the company. The market for lead-based paint products was shrinking, due in part to increasing awareness of the dangers of lead poisoning, and Martino, probably driven not so much by virtue as by pragmatism, pointed the company toward rapid expansion in a Dutch Boy line of premixed, titanium-based paints. He made this move despite its side effect of bringing the firm into competition with other manufacturers of premixed paint—manufacturers that were purchasing the bulk of their titanium dioxide from National Lead. Fortunately for him, the company's position in the component material was dominant enough and the ready-mixed paint market large enough that clients were disinclined to show resentment. The early years of Martino's presidency were marked by acquisitions and other initiatives that broadened the company's markets while satisfying the former accountant's nose for profit margins—Martino steered clear of businesses that would dilute his target return of 10 percent on sales. Moreover, the acquisitions were all made through stock exchanges, never cash, a happy privilege occasioned by a stock price that continued to soar. Over the first ten years of Martino's presidency, sales doubled while earnings increased a breathtaking fourfold.[32]

At the same time, the cobbler's son was traveling in increasingly rarefied air, gaining seats on company boards in rapid succession. The top prize was Martino's appointment in 1952 to the board of Chase National Bank, then chaired by Winthrop W. Aldrich, another on our list of leaders, but one whose father had the rather more prominent occupation of U.S. senator.[33] The next year, Martino was joined on the Chase board by none other than C. R. Smith (see chapter 2), and both self-made men would continue on the Chase Manhattan board after Chase's 1955 merger with the Bank of Manhattan.[34] In 1958, Martino was appointed by Governor Averell Harriman to the New York Port Authority, more familiar territory, perhaps, for the son of a tradesman, but no less prestigious. He was also appointed a lay trustee of Fordham University; this Catholic institution in the Bronx named its business school after him for a time.

Growth of National Lead slowed in the late 1950s as the market for titanium, which was heavily dependent on U.S. military spending, flattened, and the overall economy cooled. The toll of managing widely diversified operations seemed to be catching up with the company, and profit margins had fallen. Martino ceded the presidency of National Lead in 1965, when he ascended to chairman, but he hung on to the latter position stubbornly for three more years, violating the compulsory retirement age of sixty-five that he himself had introduced to the company. Reportedly, he had expressed in 1967 his intention to stay "as long as I can walk."[35] Not surprisingly, Martino clung quite tenaciously to the role he had devoted his life to attaining.[36]

## Trip to the Top Lengthening for All, but Advantages Are Narrowing

The journey of leaders like Martino affected the findings of Mabel Newcomer, whose 1955 research also noted a shift away from family leadership in large corporations compared with earlier in the century and an increased representation of leaders from poor and middle-class backgrounds in the largest corporations. She observed that the gap between the time it took poorer candidates and wealthier ones to reach the top was narrowing to a year or less, suggesting more of a level playing field. Moreover, Newcomer noticed that the "younger" generation of 1950s-era managers (appointed in 1944 or later) had a higher percentage of working-class fathers than did their counterparts appointed just a few years earlier. Overall, she concluded: "The evidence points to the fact that the advantage of the wealthy group has diminished as compared to fifty years ago."[37]

Among our leaders, professional managers from poor backgrounds did appear to rise more slowly to CEO posts than the rich or middle class, although, as with Newcomer's data, the gap was closing as the century went along (figure 6-2).

**FIGURE 6-2**

### Time to the top for hired CEOs increasingly equalized by status

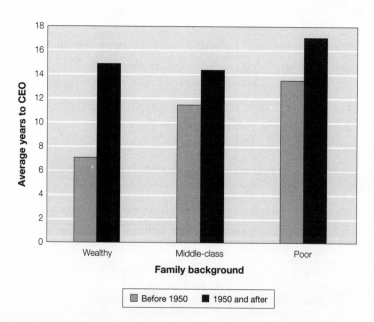

**Family background**

Before 1950 ■ 1950 and after

*Source*: HBS Leadership Initiative's "Great American Business Leaders of the 20th Century" database.
Years to CEO role calculated only for leaders hired from the outside and rising in a firm; entrepreneurs and family business leaders are excluded.

Although the gap between wealthy and poor narrowed, the average time to the top had lengthened significantly for all groups. As Alexis de Tocqueville wrote, "Equality, while it allows any man to reach any height, prevents his doing so fast."[38] Consider, for example, John Culligan, CEO of American Home Products in the mid-1980s. Culligan had risen to his role from the mailroom, where he started in 1937, making his pre-CEO tenure of over forty years the longest of any leader on our list. A Catholic born in Newark, he joined New Jersey–based American Home Products at age twenty-one without a college degree or any other trappings of advantage. Patience and loyalty seemed rather to be the primary qualities prerequisite to his opportunity. His service to the company was interrupted only by service to his country in World War II, after which he returned to American Home and continued his steady, if slow-paced, ascent. "There is only one top job, and only one person can fill it at a time, so you just have to wait," he said with all apparent sincerity after attaining the post.[39] Although he was sixty-four when he reached the top spot and was viewed by the press as a likely "interim" placeholder, he served five full years and ushered in the company's new focus on pharmaceuticals.[40]

Over 30 percent of the CEOs in our sample ascending from the 1940s through the 1980s were "lifers" who, like Martino and Culligan, had worked since they were age twenty-five or younger for the firm that they eventually headed. Of CEO leaders from poor backgrounds during this period, more than 40 percent met that lifer description, versus a little over a quarter of leaders from middle-class or wealthy backgrounds. Climbing the corporate ladder may not have entailed the kind of risk involved for outsiders in starting businesses of their own, but clearly it was a path that required as much or more investment of time to reap rewards.

## Wartime Opportunities Also Open Doors

Another factor that helped moderate the advance of those well-heeled business leadership candidates from the early twentieth century was the impact of World War II. As discussed briefly earlier in the book, the GI Bill is one example of a postwar initiative that leveled at least some educational advantages among classes. Of our U.S. leaders from poor backgrounds born in the 1920s (and thus of typical age to serve in World War II), 75 percent of those with military service had college degrees or better, while less than 60 percent with similar backgrounds but no record of military service had degrees. Of all leaders from this age bracket and poorer economic background, 65 percent were college graduates. This level was also a significant advance over some 47 percent of those of similar economic status born in the 1910s, hinting at the GI Bill's role. By comparison, middle-class and wealthy leaders born in the 1920s who did not serve in the military were actually *more* likely to be college educated than those who served: their combined college graduation rate of better than 80 percent was also actually slightly *lower* than the rate for peers born in the preceding decade. With educational expectations rapidly rising in corporate hiring, helping the less-advantaged catch up in access to schooling offered a critical boost.

There was more to the war's impact than the GI Bill, however. Wartime needs drew together capable individuals across the country from a wide variety of backgrounds, breaking down geographic and class boundaries and widening spheres of acquaintance. We've already seen how Irving Shapiro went from a low-profile law practice in Minneapolis to arguing cases for the Department of Justice as a result of wartime service, and how Plato Malozemoff met a Newmont Mining Company executive while working for the Office of Price Administration. World War II also pushed the country forward in technological development and presented leaders with business ideas they might otherwise never have imagined. This definitely was the case for William Norris, a Midwesterner whose wartime journey propelled him from cattle to computers.

Norris grew up on his family's farm in Inavale, Nebraska, and had nearly completed a major in engineering at the University of Nebraska in 1932 when his studies were curtailed by his father's death. Bill was granted his degree even as he rushed home to take over the farm amid the challenging conditions of the early 1930s. Bitter winters, droughts, and pestilence bombarded the Midwest in veritable plague-like succession, killing cattle and devastating most crops in 1932.[41] Late that year, with cattle feed scarce, many farmers were desperately selling their herds before winter, causing prices to plummet. Norris, however, made the radical decision to gather and store a common weed known as Russian thistle to use as cattle fodder through the winter—he'd noticed that his cattle often favored it as they grazed, even when alfalfa was available. Local farmers believed that the plant, a variety of tumbleweed, was harmful to cattle in large quantities, but Norris, having admittedly few options, took the chance. His cattle survived and bred successfully in the spring, rewarding his daring choice.[42]

Norris hadn't completely abandoned hope for a career outside farming, but jobs were hardly plentiful at the time. He did some civil engineering work and assisted with administering Agricultural Adjustment Act (AAA) relief locally. In 1934, he got word from his university dean that Westinghouse was hiring engineers. Norris took a job selling X-ray equipment, since he was offered a full-time position in sales but only a part-time one in engineering.[43] By 1941, he was happy to accept an electrical engineering job with the U.S. Navy in Washington, D.C. In the wake of Pearl Harbor, the job was converted to a commissioned reserve post, and Norris served with top scientists and engineers in highly intensive code-breaking efforts during the war. In the urgency to decrypt enemy communications, members of the team began inventing electronic calculating devices as a faster substitute for the use of slide rules or pencil and paper. The inventions represented the precursors of digital computing technology.

As the war's end neared, Norris and some coworkers wanted to convert their team into a private company and continue providing technology and services to the navy. Finding financing was difficult because the classified nature of their endeavors precluded open discussions with investors, who were themselves scarce enough in the days before the blossoming of venture capital funds. In late 1945, Norris and his team connected with John Parker. An investment banker, entrepreneur, and U.S. Naval Academy graduate, Parker had run a business constructing gliders for troop transport in wartime and was now seeking to divert his capital to a new enterprise. He had a glider production facility standing empty in Saint Paul, ready to house the business.[44] He mustered a group of investors willing to put up half the equity in the new business and to guarantee a line of bank credit. The other half of the equity came from Norris and his colleagues. By early 1946, Engineering Research Associates (ERA) had started operations with Parker, who was still based in Washington, D.C., serving as president. Norris relocated with his colleagues to Saint Paul and became a vice president in charge of marketing. Within a year, Norris was heading the Minnesota operation, running essentially all but the financial aspects of the company.

ERA's early projects usually involved the creation of a unique, single-purpose computing device, built to solve the same algorithm repeatedly. In 1950, the company produced for the navy a breakthrough system that could receive instructions—the device was essentially its first programmable computer. Though cash flow was tight, ERA was making money, and its work-force numbered some fifteen hundred. All of this amplified Norris's shock when Parker decided in late 1951 to sell ERA to Remington-Rand Corporation. Norris had no stomach for life in a big company, especially one that was mostly known for making typewriters and razors and that had only recently bought its way into the computer business. Despite his discontent, he was tabbed to head up the Univac division in 1955, when the computer operations were reorganized in a merger yielding the Sperry-Rand Corporation. Norris, however, found the new leaders no more willing than the old ones to invest at a level needed to compete with IBM, which had established a little-challenged dominance in the budding computer market.

By 1957, when a consultant and a few colleagues began talking with Norris about the possibility of forging out on their own again, he wasn't hard to persuade. His main stipulation, given his experience with Parker, was that the venture be financed in such a way that no single stockholder held enough control to sell out without the consent of the others. The obstacles to getting financing, though not quite so high as when ERA was launched, were still significant in the fledgling computer industry. The group's solution was to sell shares of stock directly to the public, something that the puzzled securities commissioner for the state of Minnesota had never seen done without a bank or securities firm as intermediary. Still, he could find no rules against it, so the sales mission was assigned to the new company's first employee, Willis Drake. Drake hosted potential investors in coffee shops, restaurants, and even his home, flooding the streets of his neighborhood with parked cars.[45] Norris was one of the roughly three hundred to buy a stake, putting in his $75,000 for a little over 12 percent of what was called Control Data Corporation (CDC).

Seymour Cray, a brilliant engineer who had also been part of ERA, joined CDC from Sperry that fall, quickly sharpening the new enterprise's focus with his vision to build the world's most powerful computer. In other hands, the mission would have sounded outrageous, but given the credibility Norris, Cray, and others had already built developing cutting-edge computer systems, it wasn't hard finding a buyer for their as-yet nonexistent device. The first order for what would be the CDC 1604 model was placed by the U.S. Navy Bureau of Ships in 1958, and delivery was made less than two years later.[46] By the time a second system was purchased by the British government, the firm was well on its way to an international reputation as the leader in its niche, offering machines with higher performance and versatility at a lower cost than competitors. The emerging company's sales hit $100 million in 1963, a year when it was the only other firm besides IBM (which, by way of comparison, reported 1963 sales in excess of $2 billion) to make a profit in the computer business.[47]

The difference in size did not mean IBM suffered this competitor gladly, and in fact, the giant firm worked hard to undercut CDC's position. Norris watched his company pushed to the brink of bankruptcy twice by IBM's marketing tactics, and by December 1968, he had seen enough. Although some of his top officers objected that the effort would be quixotic and too costly, Norris sued Big Blue, charging monopolistic practices such as intimidation of customers and interference with competitive sales activities. The allegations were substantiated with several years' worth of specific incidents documented by CDC's salespeople under Norris's direction.[48] Knowledge of this trove of smoking-gun material seemed to open the floodgates, as Justice Department officials, who had been investigating IBM for nearly two years, filed charges the following month, and lawsuits against IBM by other small competitors quickly multiplied.[49] The suit was timed to coincide with CDC's release of its latest computer, which found miraculously clear sailing in the market, given the spotlight now trained on IBM. For taking the lead, Norris garnered a plum settlement from IBM in early 1973. Valued at $100 million, the settlement included the chance to purchase IBM's Service Bureau business on advantageous terms, providing Norris with a prize he had coveted—to diversify CDC from dependence on mainframe sales.

An even more critical event shaping Norris's legacy as a leader also occurred in the late 1960s, as riots hit the predominantly African American North Side neighborhood of Minneapolis in the summer of 1967. Norris met with Whitney M. Young Jr., leader of the National Urban League, whom he had heard speak earlier in the year, to get suggestions on what could be done to alleviate the tensions. Young responded that job creation was the most critical need. Norris asked associates at CDC for recommendations and swiftly approved plans for a company plant in the North Side. He stipulated that the plant's manufacturing be focused on a component critical to the core business so that its successful operation would be a top priority for managers. Rather than screening potential workers by traditional means, CDC adopted an aggressive first-come, first-served approach, giving new employees at least three chances to succeed in different functions before they could be fired.[50] As managers became aware of the daily struggles that contributed to worker tardiness or absences, CDC also began to offer employees support such as local day care, legal assistance, counseling for substance abuse issues, and even bail-bond assurance. North Side operations were scarcely under way before Norris authorized even more plants in depressed inner-city and rural locations.

By the late 1970s, with CDC's sales exceeding $2 billion and its technical reputation still strong, the company was nonetheless becoming best known for how Norris directed resources toward solving social problems, though he always touted the initiatives as having strong profit potential as well.[51] The most costly of his pet projects was PLATO, a computer-based learning system guilty of being perhaps too farsighted in an era when computer prices remained beyond the reach of most public school systems. Other smaller projects supported family farming, inner-city community development, and alternative energy providers such as wind farms. Unfortunately, the 1980s brought rough sailing for mainframe computer makers, which began to founder on the rising competitive outcroppings formed by minicomputers and PCs. CDC suffered not only in the sales of its own mainframes but in the peripherals market, where it had built a profitable business. Layoffs and plant closings became necessary in 1982, and Norris's noisy public persona invited observers to fasten blame on the company's social ventures. Financial maneuvering, including the sale of several subsidiaries, staved off disaster for CDC in late 1985, but by now, Norris, seventy-four, had become the scapegoat for all that investors perceived was wrong with the company. He stepped down with little fanfare in January 1986, leaving the board as well in 1991.[52]

In May 1992, the company Norris had built was broken up. A spin-off called Control Data Systems was created in the image of the firm's initial incarnation as a small computer start-up, but the new entity failed to reprise CDC's early success and was bought out seven years later.[53] Ironically enough, the more radical ideas of Norris would survive even longer. Ceridian Corporation, the renamed core of Control Data as constituted in 1992, grew into a thriving business by marketing later versions of employment assistance services such as those that had been pioneered in the North Side plant. Ceridian was a profitable $1.3 billion company as of fiscal 2004.[54] The North Side plant itself had closed in 1988, but CDC sold the facility on favorable terms to a buyer committed to keeping technology jobs in the community. Although that business closed in 2000, it was survived by several other firms in a neighborhood business park that employed hundreds of workers.[55] PLATO Learning, sold in 1989, generated over $140 million revenue in 2004 and was the second-largest education technology provider in the United States for grades K through 12.[56] Norris never forgot about family farms, the preservation of which was the focus of one of CDC's many ventures. Overall, however, his transition from farm boy to businessman, facilitated by technology, was a significant example of mobility and development stimulated through World War II activities.[57]

## Revival of Entrepreneurship in the Postwar Boom

After the war, a reversal of the trend away from entrepreneurship that Mabel Newcomer had noted was also at work to thwart earlier predictions of class rigidity. Though the proportion of founders among leaders on our list declined as the country's larger industries crystallized in the 1920s and the percentage dropped still further during the Depression-era 1930s, entrepreneurship rebounded in the strengthening postwar economy. A key factor in the revival of entrepreneurship, and particularly the participation of poorer individuals in it, was the emergence of business formats allowing start-ups to grow with even lower capital requirements than before. The increasing importance of service businesses in the economy, combined with the franchise approach to expansion, resulted in a particularly attractive model. Although Howard Johnson had made our list for the restaurant chain he started in 1925, the real boom in franchising began after World War II. A local idea could now turn national with much less needed in the way of resources—good news to poorer leaders and all outside the business establishment. This cost-effective avenue for entrepreneurship, in combination with the previously discussed trend toward managerial capitalism, helped to improve representation of poor leaders on our list overall by the 1970s (figure 6-3).

Perhaps the quintessential entrepreneur of this era, who excelled both in franchising and in figuring out how to get something from nothing, was an

**FIGURE 6-3**

## Poor leader presence and entrepreneurship renewed postwar

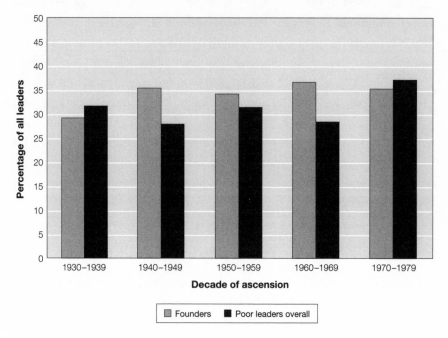

_Source_: HBS Leadership Initiative's "Great American Business Leaders of the 20th Century" database.

Proportion of founders calculated for all leaders; proportion of poor leaders calculated only for those with known economic status—approximately 75–80 percent for all decades shown, except the 1970s, when 64 percent were known.

Alger-worthy hero—Kemmons Wilson. Wilson was born in Osceola, Arkansas, son of Kemmons Wilson Sr. and his wife, Ruby, better known as "Doll," an affectionate nickname owed to her tiny four-feet-eleven stature. The senior Wilson, an insurance agent who had transferred from Memphis to open a company office in Osceola, died suddenly just nine months after Kemmons was born, in 1913. Doll, penniless after a funeral director coaxed her into a lavish service that exhausted her husband's life insurance payout, headed back to Memphis.[58] She moved in with her mother, who ran a boardinghouse, and worked multiple jobs to provide for herself and her son.

Young Wilson pitched in, too. He posed for a local bread company advertisement when he was just a toddler and sold the _Saturday Evening Post_ door-to-door at age six. In his earliest "franchising" effort, he recruited neighborhood children as salespeople to fan out all over the district, giving them two-thirds of the three-cent commission on each magazine. As he grew older, Wilson built rocking chairs for sale and bagged groceries at a Piggly Wiggly store owned by Clarence Saunders, a Memphis-based grocery pioneer also on our list. By age fourteen, Wilson was working as soda jerk and delivery boy for a local druggist. While making deliveries on his bicycle, he was run over by a car; his legs were so severely injured that doctors initially doubted he would walk again. In yet another Alger-like turn, however, a determined surgeon took on Wilson's case. After a year-long recovery that included nearly eleven months in a body cast, during which time Doll took a leave from work to provide round-the-clock nursing and tutoring, Kemmons returned to school. He regained full mobility, and a left leg two inches shorter than the right was the only external evidence of his ordeal.

Within a few years, he would be the one supporting Doll when she, in poor health, lost her job as the Depression was cresting in 1930. Wilson quit school and went to work in a brokerage firm, but, discouraged with low pay and limited prospects, decided that it was time to strike out on his own. Noting that the Memphian Theater, where he had worked odd jobs in the past, offered no snacks for moviegoers, he approached the manager about starting a popcorn concession. Once Wilson got the OK, all he needed was to obtain a popcorn machine—seemingly a tall order for a seventeen-year-old with empty pockets. Wilson took the credit-driven approach he would put to work in many future transactions, negotiating a no-down-payment, $1-a-week payout for a machine costing $50. Happily, popcorn sales more than met expectations, but unhappily, the theater owner decided to buy out the concession when he saw that its weekly receipts often doubled those from ticket sales. Undaunted, Wilson spun the money from the popcorn machine sale into five pinball machines, which he positioned in high-traffic locations, splitting the take with proprietors. He branched out into cigarette machines, eking out another creative financing plan when he paid for $8,000 worth of cigarettes with ten checks for $800, each dated one day after the other. By emptying the change from the machines daily, he was able to make the deposits to cover every check. He also bought and equipped an abandoned movie theater, all with no money down, and got a similar deal on equipment to open an ice cream store, continuing to grow all these business lines with little more than his industrious reputation as collateral.

By age twenty, Wilson had saved up $1,700 to build a house for himself and Doll on a lot that cost an additional $1,000. Three years later, he borrowed $6,500 against the house to purchase a Wurlitzer jukebox dealership. Although he became a top-performing jukebox seller, the awareness that a $2,700 outlay on real estate could return more than double its value in capital convinced him that home building had prospects of payoff superior to any of his other business ventures. Over the next several years, Wilson added this activity to his portfolio, financing everything with his typical high leverage.

When he entered the U.S. Air Force as a pilot during World War II, Wilson sold off all his business holdings, believing that managing them in his absence would place too great a burden on Doll and his young wife, Dorothy. He cleared a net of $250,000 cash on the deal—a haul worth about $3 million in today's terms. After flying the so-called Hump route from India through the Himalayas during the war, bringing supplies into China to enable the country's continued resistance of the Japanese, Wilson returned to reestablish his business activities in Memphis. He focused on real estate, building starter homes for young families. Ever looking for an edge, he was one of the first local builders to construct air-conditioned homes. He also started an insurance company to provide economical policies on his properties.

Wilson's story had already passed the rags-to-riches test with flying colors, but a bigger triumph was yet to come. His inspiration came in August 1951 on a vacation drive to Washington, D.C., with Doll, Dorothy, and the five Wilson children, aged eight to two. Covering the nearly 900 miles from Memphis to Washington in an un-air-conditioned car with such a multigenerational traveling party naturally required several overnight stops. The thrifty Wilson was irked to find that, despite the bedrolls he'd packed for his children, there would be a two-dollar charge per child for them to stay overnight in his room. Given the size of his family, this surcharge more than doubled the nightly cost of a typical motel room at the time.[59] To top it off, these roadside accommodations were at best irregular in quality; the smart traveler asked to inspect a room before renting it.

During the return drive to Memphis, Wilson was cooking up a business plan, perhaps informed by thoughts of all those young families who had been buying the homes he built. He told his wife that he planned to build a chain of quality motels catering to the needs of families. Dorothy, well schooled by now in the reception of her husband's nascent enterprise concepts, asked, patiently enough, how many he thought he'd build. He tossed out a figure of four hundred, a number he later claimed to have calculated in his head to cover the breadth of the United States, figuring 150 miles between motels on twenty major highways (ten north-south, ten east-west) crisscrossing the roughly 3,500-by-2,500-mile area of the forty-eight contiguous states.[60] Dorothy might have been forgiven for harboring doubts about the plan, but her husband's track record in fact offered little reason for them.

On the journey home, he used his ever-handy tape measure to take measurements of their hotel rooms and later spent hours perfecting the layout he presented to an architectural draftsman who would prepare formal plans for his first hotel. As it happened, the draftsman had spent the previous night watching the classic 1942 Bing Crosby film *Holiday Inn* and fancifully inscribed this name, which Wilson instantly deemed perfect for his enterprise, on the renderings of this ideal motel. Its site would be east of Memphis alongside U.S. Highway 70, a major east-west route stretching from North Carolina to Los Angeles. The location was nearly ten miles outside the town center, leaving some scratching their heads about why anyone would stay in such a remote area. Wilson's vision, though, was to attract highway travelers who would want easy access to lodging and had no need to brave the downtown congestion.[61] The financing needed was large even by Wilson's standards, however, and, unlike his loans for building homes, it wouldn't be readily paid out by a cash sale when the property was completed. He managed to negotiate a deal with an insurance company to buy out the bank loan at the end of two years, making the terms palatable for a local lender.

Ever attentive to efficiencies in construction, Wilson brought the building in under budget, but there was one area in which he didn't skimp. He knew from his days operating movie houses that an eye-catching sign was crucial for attracting passers-by to one's business. He laid out $13,000, about 5 percent of the total construction cost, for a gaudy, green, lighted sign some fifty feet tall, bordered in flashing yellow and topped by a twinkling star.[62] In August 1952, almost exactly one year after that pivotal family vacation, the five Wilson children cut the ceremonial ribbon to open the first Holiday Inn hotel, with the distinctive sign filling the sky behind them. Naturally, most prominent among the new property's policies was that youngsters could stay free in a room with their parents. By the following month, Wilson, confident of success, was already publicizing locations for his next three inns on major highways north and south of Memphis, staking claim to each major approach route. In early 1953, all the properties were open or well on their way toward operation.

To obtain the resources needed to turn four hotels into four hundred, even Wilson, the master of leverage, knew he needed help. He turned to Wallace Johnson, a successful Memphis builder with a rising national profile—Johnson had been featured in a 1952 *Saturday Evening Post* article dubbing the devout Johnson "that prayin' millionaire from Memphis."[63] Wilson offered Johnson half of the budding Holiday Inn enterprise in exchange for his help in presenting a rudimentary franchise offer: for a fee of $500 and monthly royalties of five cents per room, the partners would grant to a builder the right to construct and manage a Holiday Inn. Sixty homebuilders came to hear the business pitch, and most agreed to the terms. By June 1954, the first franchised Holiday Inn was up and running in Clarksdale, Mississippi. Few other builders followed through, which was a disappointment to Wilson at the time but a relief much later, when he realized what a bargain-basement deal he had given.[64] He and Johnson shifted their marketing efforts to target wealthy doctors and lawyers willing to invest in a franchise site where the partners made arrangements for construction. This approach bore fruit more rapidly, and by the end of 1955, there were twenty Holiday Inns in eleven states, earning the enterprise a blurb in *Fortune* magazine.[65] The U.S. interstate highway system, approved for funding in 1956, promised a fortuitous complement to the business concept. In August 1957, Holiday Inn went public, finally providing a cash infusion for which Wilson didn't have to sign a note. As the tenth anniversary of the first Holiday Inn neared, 275 hotels, about three-quarters of them franchise owned, dotted the United States and Canada. By now the terms for franchisees had changed significantly—the upfront fee was $10,000, and the monthly royalty $4.50 per room, or 2.5 percent of gross sales, whichever was higher.[66] The following year, Wilson's early prediction of four hundred hotels was a mere blip in the rearview mirror; the chain had grown nearly as large in room count as the Sheraton and Hilton hotels combined.[67]

Wilson, a polyglot entrepreneur if ever there was one, also pursued vertical integration with a vengeance and forged a prototypical conglomerate a decade

*C. Kemmons Wilson, founder of Holiday Inns, relaxing on one of his company's beds in the early 1980s.* (Source: Time Life Pictures/Getty Images)

or two before its time. He created or acquired subsidiaries to provide virtually everything needed for the inns, from kitchen wares and housekeeping necessities to room decorations, furnishings, and prefabricated building structures.[68] Further, he exploited synergy well before the word was commonly used in business. He struck cross-promotional deals such as that with Gulf Oil, which provided some $46 million in capital and loan guarantees, along with an agreement making Gulf credit cards accepted at Holiday Inns, no small benefit in the days before bank cards became common.[69] The clinching innovation for the chain came in 1965 with the Holidex reservation system, designed by IBM on the condition that Wilson and Johnson personally endorse an $8 million note for its cost. "I never wanted to *own* a million dollars— I wanted to *owe* a million dollars," said Wilson, who got his wish several times over.[70] The gamble on Holidex more than paid off, as the system was the first to offer the now-standard capability of booking rooms anywhere in a chain with a single toll-free telephone call. By 1972, the number of rooms had nearly doubled, approximating the total of not just the next two but the next *four* largest U.S. lodging competitors combined.[71] Green-and-yellow neon bulbs were flashing on signs in some twenty countries, including Morocco and Swaziland.

The following year's oil embargo and ensuing gasoline shortages and recession stalled the chain's growth, however, and the stock price plunged. Wilson, while retaining the title of chairman that he had held essentially from the company's start, began in 1974 to bring in new management to help reshape Holiday Inn's operations.[72] He finally resigned in 1979, when, from the hospital bed where he was recovering from a heart attack and bypass operation, he was unable to dissuade the board from an acquisition in the restaurant business—a transaction he considered unwise.[73] Lacking majority control, he decided it was time to move on, and he wasted no time finding other interests.

When he visited a friend's time-share home in Florida and learned that the modest two-bedroom house was being sold in two-week increments for ten thousand dollars each, Wilson crunched the numbers and figured out, as he had with his mother's house, that this type of real-estate venture had a lucrative future. He promptly acquired over 350 acres of land in the outer orbit of Walt Disney World, which was in its first decade and still developing as a tourist attraction. The Orange Lake Country Club, a time-share community that Wilson outfitted with all the amenities of an upscale resort, opened in 1982. Ultimately, he claimed, it made him more money than Holiday Inn, because he owned 100 percent of it.[74] Until his death in 2003 at age ninety, Wilson continued his enterprising ways, launching outlet malls, a brand of tortilla chips and salsa, a candy made of chocolate-coated roasted corn kernels, and more hotels under the Wilson World and Wilson Inn names. Having started with nothing but an appreciation for the power of leverage, Wilson built an empire that delivered the kind of legacy he never enjoyed. When he died, his children, such a critical part of the inspiration for his greatest success, were overseeing the management of more than a hundred enterprises.[75]

## Family Business Declining As Source of Prominent Leaders

Although Wilson handed down his businesses, another change evident over the century was the declining role of inheritance in the success stories of top leaders. In other words, going by Taussig and Joslyn's strict definition, the caste-like threshold was never attained. While a peak of nearly 30 percent of leaders ascending in the 1920s and 1930s ran family businesses, this mechanism of direct legacy was producing less than 5 percent of our leaders in the century's last two decades, as hired CEOs multiplied (figure 6-4).

The remnants of large, family-controlled businesses, in fact, were more likely to be found in the West and in Wilson's home territory, the South. These regions, whose business development was at a younger stage earlier in the century, saw significant enterprises in the hands of family leadership long after the reins of such businesses in the Northeast and Midwest had been passed to professional management. The Brown-Forman Corporation, a Kentucky-based liquor distiller and distributor, offers a typical glimpse at a large, late-century Southern family business.

**FIGURE 6-4**

**Fewer family business leaders, more hired CEOs**

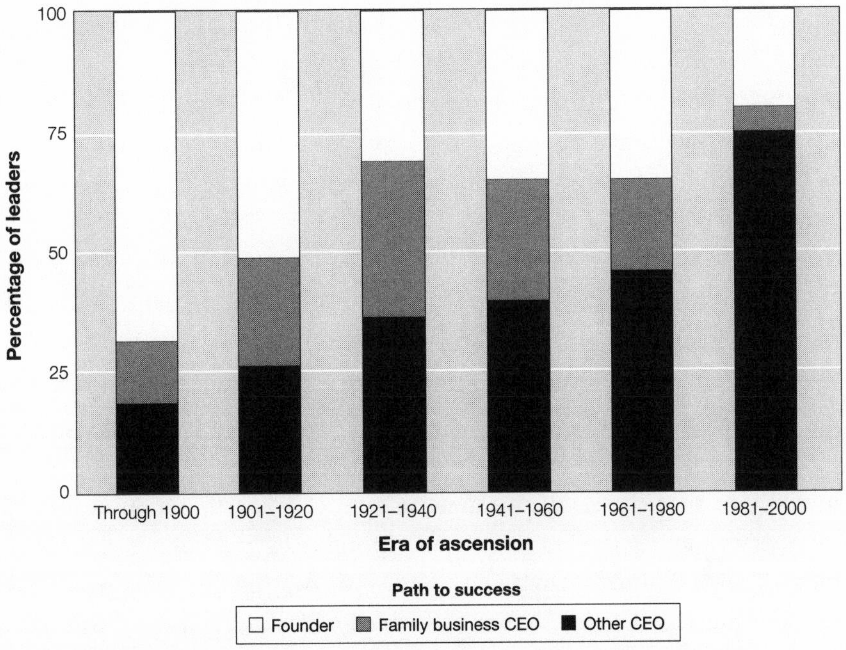

*Source*: HBS Leadership Initiative's "Great American Business Leaders of the 20th Century" database.

Back in 1870, George Garvin Brown and his half-brother formed a distillery in Louisville, bottling a brand of bourbon whiskey called Old Forester. George had been working for a medicine wholesaler and was aware of physicians' complaints about consistent quality in whiskey for their prescriptions. He designed a product to meet their concerns, making what the company claims was a unique innovation by packaging his whiskey in sealed, clear glass bottles to highlight that there had been no dilution or tampering.[76] A handwritten guarantee of quality also graced the label. The brand's reputation for medicinal use helped it earn a license to continue manufacturing for prescriptions during Prohibition. The company also survived the distilling hiatus mandated during World War II by fortuitously planning production so as to create back-stocks before the war, then producing industrial alcohol from 1941 to 1945. The crucial 1950s acquisition of a little Tennessee distillery that produced Jack Daniel's whiskey provided a flagship for the company's marketing for decades to come, and the Southern Comfort brand, acquired in the 1970s, would be almost as successful.

The *Forman* portion of the company name came from an early minority partner, whose shares George bought out after the partner's death in 1901. For more than a century, the company had a distinctly "Brown" cast to its leadership. George begat sons Robinson and Owsley; Robinson begat Robinson Jr., who begat Robinson III, and Owsley begat W. L. Lyons and George Garvin II. The key leadership posts of the company passed from father to son, brother to brother, or cousin to cousin until 1966, when a non-Brown, Daniel Street, was named president.[77]

Three years later, Street was succeeded by another non-Brown, William F. Lucas, but after that, the members of a fourth Brown generation were ready to move into leadership. Among them, Owsley Brown II, a son of W. L. Lyons, was the leader to make our list. Owsley Brown II gained his first national notice at age twenty-eight in a 1970 *Wall Street Journal* article that described the unabated "Brown-ing" of the company in some detail.[78] The bemused tone of the piece demonstrates how such "official" nepotism was by then viewed as a rather suspicious anachronism by the business establishment. Brown-Forman management, however, was quite unapologetic, acknowledging that "planned nepotism" was something it regarded as part of its strategy for success. Lucas had proudly trumpeted in a speech earlier that year, "We don't just accept the boss's son, we go out to get him."[79] In fact,

*Owsley Brown (right), head of Brown-Forman, toasting with Prince Felipe of Spain during the Prince's visit to the firm's Kentucky distillery in 1999.* (Source: CORBIS SYGMA)

Brown-Forman habitually recruited the sons of not only the Browns but all employees, from executives to janitors, estimating at the time that 200 of its 1,800 workers were relatives of at least one other employee. One screening mechanism was that the nepots, as they were known within the company, must have a college diploma and at least one postgraduate degree, although the latter could be earned after the employee had started employment and could be financed, if needed, by a corporate tuition-reimbursement program. Although this educational requirement might seem to restrict the qualified nepots to those born of families with somewhat greater means, management claimed that the requirement's purpose was to screen out freeloaders. Leaders of the company also asserted that those of the next generation who didn't produce were dismissed, most often through direct intervention by their fathers. The *Wall Street Journal* article nevertheless supplied quotes from unnamed employees past and present who grumbled about competing with the fast-rising nepots.

In 1993, Owsley Brown II, who had fulfilled the firm's educational requirements via college at Yale and a Stanford MBA, ascended to the office of president and CEO. He succeeded his older brother, W. L. Lyons Brown Jr., who had served eighteen years, during which time the company grew to exceed $1 billion in annual sales. Owsley II presided over consistent growth in sales and earnings, outpacing the Standard & Poor's 500 in shareholder return over the period through 2004.[80] His commitment to maintaining premium pricing, and thus profits, through strong branding and advertising—the same strategy that served his dad, granddad, and even his great-granddad, now practiced on a global scale—positioned Brown-Forman as a growth champion and darling of stock analysts.[81] In 2005, Owsley II concluded his tenure as CEO and was succeeded by a non-Brown, Paul C. Varga. Pro-nepotism rhetoric is no longer trumpeted in the company's presentations, and Owsley, still serving as chairman in 2006, is the only identifiable Brown listed among the executive officers. Browns still dot the board of directors, but they do not constitute the majority, a sign that times there may at last be changing.[82]

## But the More Things Change . . .

With family business no longer dominating the leadership pipeline, entrepreneurship recovering, and advancement from the bottom ranks fueling the rise of more and more CEOs, an increased openness in the ranks of business leaders seems likely by the end of the century. If we categorize leaders on the basis of father's occupation, however, the picture appears relatively static (figure 6-5).

From the first half of the twentieth century to the second half, we see mainly substitutions rather than changes in the parentage of leaders—poor farmers are replaced by poor blue-collar laborers, for example. Small-business owners become slightly less prominent, but increased proportions of white-collar workers and professionals (the latter mostly doctors, lawyers, and engineers) more than fill the gap, reinforcing a robust middle class. As this occupational chart suggests, the overall picture by class background for leaders thus remains almost identical throughout the century—approximately 20 percent wealthy, 30 percent poor, and 50 percent middle class. Neither the increasing closure predicted by Sorokin nor the increasing openness expected by Newcomer has occurred. Given the shifts toward less-prestigious undergraduate educational venues that we saw in chapter 5 for leaders rising later in the century, this result comes as something of a surprise.

**FIGURE 6-5**

## "New" club mostly the same?

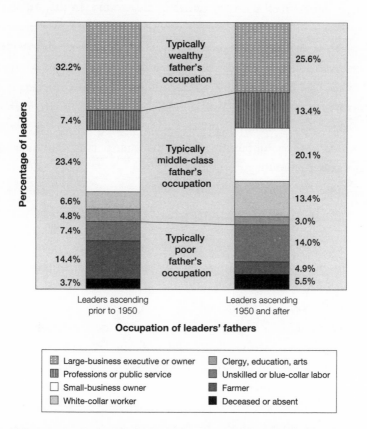

**Occupation of leaders' fathers**

*Source*: HBS Leadership Initiative's "Great American Business Leaders of the 20th Century" database.

The key, however, is that over 80 percent of leaders from poor families prior to 1950 had no college education at all, compared with around half of those from middle-class and wealthy families. In the second half of the century, though a gap remained, all the groups were considerably more educated. The net effect is that poor leaders made up over 27 percent of those with college educations after 1950 versus around 16 percent earlier in the century, an 11 percentage point difference that neatly corresponds with the increase in the percentage of degrees gained in "other public" institutions shown in figure 5-4.

The difference in prestige of undergraduate institutions is thus due to the education being received, perhaps in some measure because of the GI Bill, by those who wouldn't have gotten it earlier in the century. In that earlier era, however, those without college degrees were nevertheless accepted in leadership, because of higher education's limited role in business advancement. Leaders without college degrees rising in the first half of the century thus represent, for the most part, the same socioeconomic group as do leaders in the second half with degrees from "other public" institutions. Newcomer was right in her assessment that more poor individuals could earn college degrees than could start successful businesses, but that didn't translate into a larger percentage making it to the top.

## Toward an Equal-Opportunity Elite?

The observation that prominent business leaders of the early twentieth century were primarily from families of middle-class origins or better, with fathers employed in business, is certainly not unexpected. The lack of change in our leaders' economic backgrounds from the 1950s through the end of the century is more surprising, given the apparently increased egalitarianism of leader selection in dimensions like religion, birthplace, and college affiliation. The common denominator in those who became accepted, though, has been a rise in their economic standing: Catholic leaders were accepted largely after they (e.g., Dennis Sheedy) or their fathers (e.g., Thomas Murphy) had crossed into prosperity; immigrants were hired as CEOs when they had money and education, and so on.

With nearly 30 percent of the leaders consistently coming from relatively poor backgrounds and, because of their success, passing on wealthy or at least quite comfortably middle-class upbringings to their own children, genuine upward mobility is undoubtedly represented for almost one in three of these leaders. Still, countermeasures such as the GI Bill and trends toward professional management, rather than improving the chances of those from poorer backgrounds, appear to have only held the line against an inexorable advance of those with advantages. While social signals may be fading in importance in leadership selection, signals of merit and competence such as advanced degrees, primarily MBAs, are replacing social status. Although the gap in college degrees between rich and poor leaders narrowed for those born in 1930 or later (70 percent of poor leaders versus more than 80 percent of others), the gap in graduate degrees remained larger (33 percent versus nearly 50 percent). This suggests that, despite subsidies and scholarships, economic status continued to play a role in access to further educational opportunities, now the gateway to critical factors in business credibility. Although early predictions of caste-like exclusivity in the ranks of business leadership did not come to pass, of all the barriers we've discussed so far, the class boundary structure appears the most durable. We have yet to look, of course, at boundaries those earlier scholars were not even discussing—those of sex and race.

# SEVEN

# Gender and Race

## How Ultimate Outsiders Inch Inward

*I want you to know that whatever I have accomplished in life I have paid for it by much thought and hard work. If there is any easy way, I haven't found it. My advice to every one expecting to go into business is to hit often and hit hard; in other words, strike with all your might.*

—Madam C. J. Walker, addressing her sales delegates, August 1918

THE WORDS of Madam C. J. Walker could well have come from the pen of Horatio Alger, but it's hard to know how enthusiastic he, or, for that matter, most of his white male readers, would have been about the success of Madam C. J. Walker, a hair products entrepreneur who rose from plantation work to become widely credited as America's first African American woman millionaire. Even Booker T. Washington, a champion of the cause of African American entrepreneurs but opposed to African American women's use of such cosmetics and hair treatments, publicly snubbed her at his National Negro Business League conference before eventually coming to accept her accomplishments.[1] Walker, one of only six African American women among the twentieth-century U.S. business leaders on our list, was an ultimate outsider on two counts—gender and race. As we've seen in the preceding chapters, white males outside the mainstream of business circles, even early in the century, had at least some avenues of assimilation available to them. A German immigrant could network with more established fellow countrymen, a Catholic leader could accumulate wealth in the wide-open West and leverage that into credibility elsewhere, a son of poor parents could start at the lowest job in a company and work up over the years, and so on. For both women and African Americans, however, the factors that separated them from the majority of American business leaders were impossible to hide. The differences stared right back at them every time they looked at themselves in the mirror and rendered easy assimilation impossible. Not surprisingly, the two groups combined make up less than 7 percent of our leaders over the century.

## Strike with All Your Might

The tough road to business success faced by African Americans and women is best illustrated by the degree to which they founded companies rather than rose as CEOs. Two-thirds of the female leaders and about 83 percent of the African Americans (including all the women) founded their own companies (figure 7-1).

The entrepreneurial route, always a harder path, has been pursued more frequently (out of necessity, it is implied) by leaders who fell into an outsider category, a delineation that would interfere with their acceptance in existing enterprises. This ratio of entrepreneurship for African Americans and women is rivaled by no significant subgroup of white men except the pre-1950 foreign-born leaders, of whom more than 70 percent founded their own companies. White males from poor backgrounds also were nearly two-thirds founders before 1950. We've seen, however, that both these groups of white men attained significant acceptance in the CEO track to leadership after mid-century. In contrast, the proportions of founders among women and African Americans remained virtually identical before and after 1950.

## Outsiders Pay the Cost of Struggles

These ultimate outsiders, moreover, were not garden-variety entrepreneurs. Their struggle is apparent in statistics that suggest the unique difficulties they faced. Among African American leaders ascending prior to 1950, over 60 percent died while still holding their leadership positions, compared with less than 25 percent of white leaders in the same period. Not even the comparably disadvantaged white groups just discussed—poor men and foreign-born men arising in leadership before 1950—shared this extreme fate. Just over a third of

FIGURE 7-1

## Ultimate outsiders mostly entrepreneurs

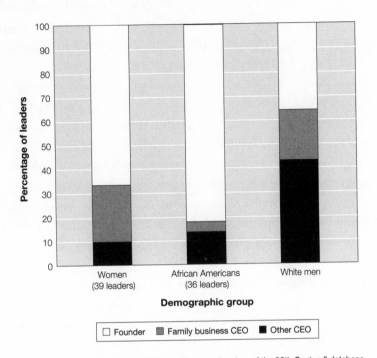

*Source*: HBS Leadership Initiative's "Great American Business Leaders of the 20th Century" database.
Six African American women were included in totals both for women and for African Americans.

foreigners died in office, and poor leaders did so at rates almost identical to other whites. African American leaders in this period lived on average less than four years after their retirement, compared with nearly eleven years for white leaders. Although life expectancies for African Americans overall have been shorter than for whites, the African American leaders averaged not only shorter life spans but longer tenures and later retirement ages than white leaders—a rather distressing combination that suggests the disparity between the groups' options for developing financial security. African Americans were inclined to stick with the businesses they had built, because there was no better deal around the corner.

For the women on our list, a similar indication of struggle is apparent in their general lack of happy marriages. Nearly half of the female leaders were divorced—of these, almost 40 percent experienced more than one divorce. About 12 percent of the women were single, and of those without divorces, close to half were widowed before assuming their leadership role and remained unmarried for the rest of their lives. In all, only about one-quarter of the female leaders were married continuously throughout their business leadership activities. By contrast, a mere 14 percent of male leaders on our list were divorced and less than 2 percent were bachelors. Even allowing for the possibility of undisclosed divorces among the men, these dramatic differences suggest corresponding, if not unexpected, differences in the experiences of male and female leaders. Granted, singleness was an initial condition of leadership for several women who inherited their roles from a deceased husband. Furthermore, for a few whose divorces preceded their leadership role, their divorce might have precipitated their pursuit of a career. It's nevertheless hard to ignore the data's implications that being unmarried made it easier for a woman to maintain a high-profile career and that the stresses of such a career were more likely to affect the marriages of women than of men.

In Dorothy Schiff's case, divorce preceded her business involvement, but a second marriage that drew her into leadership didn't last long, either. Schiff was a granddaughter of one of the leaders already discussed—German immigrant Jacob Schiff, who had succeeded on Wall Street with Kuhn, Loeb. The young Schiff's early life suggested the typical path of an heiress—graduation from New York's fashionable Brearley School, a year at Bryn Mawr, marriage at age twenty to a man about six years her senior, and two children within the first two years after the wedding. That the love and purpose soon departed from the marriage, and that she and her husband soon led essentially separate lives, is a sad but also not atypical part of the story. Her parents died within a few years of each other in the early 1930s, leaving Schiff independently wealthy, and she took advantage of that independence to divorce her husband. The second chapter of her life began when she wed George Backer within a year after ending her first marriage. She and Backer also had a child quickly, but her life after that would hardly remain domestic.

Backer broadened Schiff's already-wide circle of acquaintances to include prominent writers and political figures, and she forsook the Republican leanings of her family to become a New Deal Democrat. She met First Lady Eleanor Roosevelt and then, in 1936, President Roosevelt himself, with whom she developed a strong bond. Her biography contained ambiguous and rather suggestive statements she made about her relationship with FDR, but she later dismissed the innuendoes, denying that she and Roosevelt were more than friends.[2] Whatever the case, her new party loyalties led her to stand in 1937 as a Democratic candidate for delegate to New York's Constitutional Convention. Running in Nassau County, where she and her husband had a summer home, she lost in a Republican sweep of the district. Meanwhile, George Backer himself was nursing political hopes—in the same election, he made an unsuccessful bid for Congress from Manhattan as an American Labor Party candidate.[3] He would repeat the exercise and lose again in 1938, but was subsequently appointed to fulfill the term of a deceased New York City councilman from that party. By 1939, Backer had apparently decided that it would be prudent to find a way to gain a voice that didn't depend on winning an election. He made a commitment to buy the *New York Post*, which was then mired in financial difficulty and just one of a collection of afternoon papers in the city. It was his wife's money, of course, that made the deal possible—she acquired the paper in exchange for assuming its debts. George Backer took the title of president and publisher of the newspaper, while Schiff initially served as vice president, director, and treasurer.

Unfortunately, Backer's lack of managerial acumen threatened to exhaust even his wife's deep pockets, as she lost some $2 million in the first two years of owning the paper. Backer, enamored with winning an intellectual audience, wasn't building the circulation numbers needed to sell advertising. Ultimately, Schiff took control, shifting the *Post* to a tabloid format and adding comics, columns, and other more popular features. In public reports, the transition of "Mrs. Backer" to publisher in 1942 was attributed to George's "protracted ill health," although his leadership in philanthropic activities continued without apparent interruption, and he was robust enough to live some thirty-two more years.[4]

Schiff divorced Backer in 1943 and immediately thereafter married one of the *Post*'s executive editors, Ted Thackrey. They began to turn around the paper, widening circulation by purchasing the *Bronx Home News* in 1946, and also branching out into a handful of radio and television stations. At the same time, however, Ted Thackrey's politics were traveling further and further left, testing the patience of even the paper's relatively liberal readership, not to mention Schiff, who began penning counterpoint editorials that ran alongside his perspectives. The distance between their leanings was evident in their stances in the 1948 presidential race: while they both opposed Truman, Thackrey endorsed the Progressive Party's Henry Wallace, a candidacy noised to have Communist backing, and Schiff gave her support to the Republican candidate, Thomas Dewey.[5] The divided masthead led to another divided marriage, and the couple separated late that year. In January 1949, Schiff tried to wash her hands of the editorial issues by stepping away and naming Thackrey sole publisher, but the paper's finances were under too severe a strain for that arrangement to last. By April, he had left the paper, and their divorce was settled in August. For the rest of her life, including a final marriage (outside the publishing business) that also ended in divorce, she would be known, somewhat incongruously, as "Mrs. Schiff." Her brother felt that *Miss* wasn't suitable for a woman with children, and Schiff declared that *Ms.*, after it became an option, "sounds funny, looks awful and just shouldn't be."[6]

With Thackrey gone, Schiff again retained custody of the *Post* after a marital split, and the newspaper was now hers to run without a partner for the first time. She had earned this solo leadership "opportunity" by putting in more of her own money to bail the paper out of its financial crisis, however, and the

*Dorothy Schiff posing with the first edition of the* New York Post *to be published after an eighty-seven-day long newspaper printers' strike in 1963. Schiff's paper returned to publication one month before others in the city.* (Source: Bettmann/CORBIS)

odds remained against its success, given a competitive three-paper afternoon field in New York. Her newly appointed editor, James Wechsler, later said he would have made the *Post* a thousand-to-one shot in this race for survival.[7] Still, Schiff found her stride as a manager and writer, beginning in September 1951 a series of personal columns that became a hallmark of the paper. She worked with Wechsler to maintain at the *Post* a political voice that was distinctive and generally liberal but free to call anyone to account. No party could take her endorsement for granted, as she proved with an election-eve stunner in 1958, backing Republican Nelson Rockefeller over incumbent Democrat Averell Harriman in the New York gubernatorial race.[8] By 1963, her independent spirit prompted her to break ranks from other New York publishers (who, all men, had largely excluded her from negotiations, anyway) to settle with unions during a lengthy newspaper strike, returning to publication a month before the other papers. Two years later, however, she showed herself no pushover to labor, withstanding a one-day shutdown to get her printers to implement a trial of automated typesetting.[9] She couldn't make it stick, but no other major New York paper would get as far for almost a decade.[10] The Typographical Union president, Bert Powers, called her "the only publisher with balls."[11] While rivals merged and folded, her scrappy *Post* remained the last New York afternoon paper standing in 1967. By 1976, when Schiff sold the *Post* to Australian Rupert Murdoch for an estimated $31 million, the paper had rebounded from the brink of bankruptcy to enjoy some twenty-five consecutive years of positive cash flow.[12]

## Opportunity Is (Only) Where You Find It

Schiff's newspaper success notwithstanding, most women on our list gained their leadership roles in businesses that sold products to other women. In this relatively narrow niche of opportunities their experience paralleled that of African Americans. Prior to 1950, over half of the women focused in personal care products or foods. What is even more striking, over 80 percent of the period's African American leaders were concentrated in just two main industry groupings (financial services and publishing). This slim array of industries was further limited in potential because the businesses offered products and services almost exclusively to African American consumers. Across the full century, even white men born in non-English-speaking countries—a group whose numbers were roughly equivalent to African Americans and women—had a significantly wider spread of industry penetration than either group, and of course, other white men had a still wider distribution of opportunity (figure 7-2 and table 7-1).

The persistence of constraints on the markets available to African American leaders for most of the century differs notably from experiences such as that of Amadeo Giannini, who, though he initially capitalized on ethnic affinity and developed a business among fellow Italians, broke through those boundaries and attained success in a generalized market (see chapter 4). Of the firms African Americans founded in the early part of the century, those that survive to the present day still serve race-based niche markets, and those

**FIGURE 7-2**

**African Americans and women have narrow niches of opportunity**

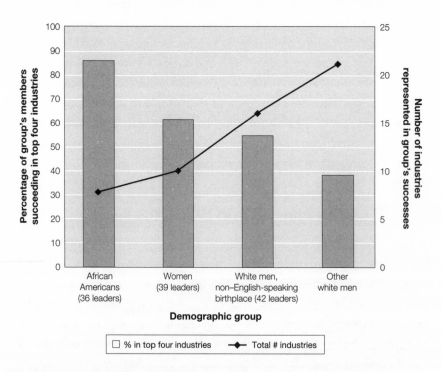

*Source*: HBS Leadership Initiative's "Great American Business Leaders of the 20th Century" database.

Six African American women were included in totals both for women and for African Americans.

**TABLE 7-1**

## Top four industry sectors by demographic group, before 1950 (and number of business leaders in each sector)

| African Americans | Women | White men, non-English-speaking birthplace | Other white men |
|---|---|---|---|
| Finance (14) | Personal care and home products (6) | Entertainment and broadcast media (10) | Fabricated goods (106) |
| Publishing and print media (7) | Services (6) | Fabricated goods (6) | Food and tobacco (92) |
| Entertainment and broadcast media (6) | Food and tobacco (6) | Food and tobacco (4) | Finance (70) |
| Personal care and home products (4) | Fabric and apparel (6) | Tie at 3 each:<br>• Finance<br>• Chemicals<br>• Utilities and energy | Retail (67) |

*Source*: HBS Leadership Initiative's "Great American Business Leaders of the 20th Century" database.

Defined industries were developed from a modified version of standard industry code groupings. See appendix for details. Six African American women were included in totals both for women and for African Americans.

survivors constitute a fortunate few. All but the largest African American–owned insurance and newspaper firms from that earlier era are now either out of business, merged into other corporations, or mere shadows of their former selves. The walls erected by racism made enduring success almost impossible to establish. Women, by contrast, were much less limited by an implicit constraint to consumers of their sex. True, a *Fortune* writer in 1935 could sniff, "Success in style designing or in the sale of cosmetics or in the publicizing of women's wear implies little or nothing as to those activities in which womanhood is not a natural advantage . . . It is a career in itself but it is not a career in industry."[13] Whether or not their businesses were considered "in industry," white women had essentially as much access to the wealth of the white community through its women as through its men. This access provided a much larger potential market and thus made white women's prospects for building a large enterprise much rosier than such prospects were for either male or female African Americans.

Consider, for instance, the empire created by one Florence Nightingale Graham, whose name heralded greater prospects than her simple beginnings as one of five children of a produce merchant and his wife living on a farm twenty miles northwest of Toronto. As it happened, Flo did, like her namesake, pursue training in nursing, but only briefly, leaving in dismay after just three weeks. From the start, however, Graham had care in mind—skin care, that is. Her attempts to cook up a batch of face cream on her family's stove produced such a stench that a compassionate clergyman appeared on their doorstep with a basket of fresh eggs, convinced that the Grahams were trying to make do with rotten ones. This embarrassment led her father to deliver an ultimatum: Flo must get married or go find an "honest job" in Toronto.[14]

She elected to pursue employment, but none of several clerical positions in Toronto suited her bigger dreams. At last, over her father's strenuous objections, she went to join her brother William in New York City in 1908, and there, the small-town girl found her track to success. She began as a bookkeeper for E. R. Squibb, a pharmaceutical manufacturer whose laboratory offered her a chance to explore the science of skin-care preparations. She soon jumped ship, however, for a position even closer to her goals—cashier at a beauty salon specializing in facial beauty treatments. Graham quickly finagled her way into a better vantage point on the front line, applying the creams and potions on customers. It wasn't long before her success with clients and her continued ambition prompted her to open a salon on Fifth Avenue in 1910. She became partners with Elizabeth Hubbard, who had concocted skin-care products for use in their enterprise. Shortly, however, the two strong-willed women quarreled over finances and found it impossible to continue in partnership. Graham's lawsuit against Hubbard was listed in the *New York Times* on August 16, 1910, just three days after the death of the original Florence Nightingale.[15] The business had been founded under Hubbard's name, but Graham got to the landlord first, securing the continued use of the salon space she and her partner had rented. With Hubbard opening her own shop down the street, Graham needed a new business identity, but Nightingale's recent death offered rather somber connotations to her own name. Whether influenced by, as she would later say, her fondness for the popular novel *Elizabeth and Her German Garden*, or just a reluctance to pay for redoing the whole lettering job on the window, she retained in the salon's name the "Elizabeth"

*Businesswoman and beautician Elizabeth Arden (born Florence Nightingale Graham) posing with a group of nurses in 1935.* (Source: Getty Images)

of her former partner. For the rest, she claimed literary inspiration from the title hero of a maudlin Tennyson epic, *Enoch Arden*.[16] Thus was "Elizabeth Arden" born as Florence Nightingale died.

In years to come, Arden built her new name with creativity and salesmanship, convincing her clients that the "face paint" they'd once regarded disdainfully could indeed be both flattering and acceptable in the best social circles. Women's suffrage fueled further liberation in dress and makeup in the Roaring Twenties, also to Arden's advantage. By the late 1930s, her cosmetics and other beauty products were marketed on at least five continents, and her salons dotted twenty-nine of the most fashionable cities in the United States and abroad.[17] Earlier, that sardonic *Fortune* writer, so certain that women's successes were not careers "in industry," had asserted: "Elizabeth Arden is not a potential Henry Ford. She is Elizabeth Arden."[18] Indeed, attitudes of the time would have prevented even a woman with the drive of Arden from founding an automotive business. Her success, however, was of a scope that many would-be Fords might envy.[19]

## Born on the Wrong Side of the (Industrial) Track

Though similarities exist between the outsider situations of women and African American leaders, access to broader (i.e., white) markets by white women entrepreneurs is one of many significant differences between the groups. The women, about 85 percent of whom are white, largely mirror the white male leaders in their overall socioeconomic backgrounds, nearly half being middle class and close to 20 percent being wealthy. The not-insignificant percentage of women who gained opportunities through family connections (typically via a father or husband who led the business before she did) is an indicator of their relative prosperity. About 70 percent of the African Americans, on the other hand, grew up poor. The poverty of the group amplified its outsider status, if indeed the barriers created by racial prejudice could possibly have been made more rigid than they already were. Almost all these African American leaders arising before 1950 shared the further outsider element of being born in the South. These origins are themselves a legacy of the slave trade that initially brought most African Americans to this continent. Even after emancipation, former slaves and their descendants largely lived in the least industrialized area of the country and, as we have seen, an area from which relatively few business leaders emerged (only 16 percent of pre-1950 leaders).

This disadvantage of birthplace placed African American leaders squarely on the horns of a dilemma when it came to finding prospects for success. While having local roots might offer someone a head start in business, an African American born in the South found that home sweet home was not only a business backwater but an area of rigid, historically ingrained racial prejudice and segregation. These factors produced an unusual pattern that accentuated the difficulties of African Americans early in the century. Like U.S.-born white leaders of the period, around 40 percent of African Americans succeeded in their home state, but *unlike* the white leaders (even the poor ones), almost all the rest of African American leaders left their home region entirely to find success (figure 7-3).

Staying at home is the most logical option for a person who lacks the resources to travel, and most African Americans who succeeded in the South fit that description. In the case of Alonzo Herndon, founder of Atlanta Life Insurance, it's hard to imagine that a twenty-year-old African American man with less than a year of formal education and only about a decade removed from

**FIGURE 7-3**

## Early African Americans succeed either near home or very far from it

*Location of success versus birthplace for U.S.-born leaders ascending prior to 1950*

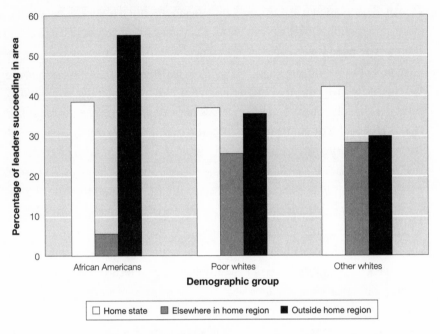

*Source*: HBS Leadership Initiative's "Great American Business Leaders of the 20th Century" database.

emancipation could have gotten very far with eleven dollars and a hand truck. That's all he took with him when he struck out from his birthplace in Walton County, Georgia, to find something better to do than work as a farmhand for his former master. Some seventy miles later, Herndon found himself in the Georgia town of Senoia, where he started as a farmhand but began supplementing his income as a self-trained barber. After only a few months, he opened his own barbershop in Jonesboro, near Atlanta. By 1883, about five years after setting out with his hand truck, he was a partner in an Atlanta barbershop, but he wasn't finished yet. He had his own barbershop in the city three years later. Over the succeeding years, he stepped up in size and scale until, by 1902, he opened a veritable palace for male grooming, the most lavish barbershop

Atlanta had seen, on distinguished Peachtree Street. The shop served an elite, all-white clientele of local businessmen and politicians. One of them offered Herndon a chance to invest in real estate, which he also did very successfully.

Soon, though, an even bigger opportunity emerged for Herndon. Small, African American–owned benevolent associations, often linked with churches, were growing to provide basic insurance coverage like death or disability payments. The need was created by the difficulty African Americans had in obtaining insurance of any kind from white firms. By 1905, however, a new Georgia state law—inspired by the lobbying of white insurance competitors, excessive defaults of the small African American associations, or quite likely both—required that all insurers maintain a minimum deposit of $5,000 with the state treasury as a guarantee of solvency. Two ministers who ran the Mutual Aid Association in Atlanta turned to the community's prosperous barber, Herndon, to provide the money to sustain their firm. In addition to the deposit, he decided to pay $140 to purchase the association outright, establishing what would become Atlanta Life Insurance Company. Within a year, fierce race riots rocked the city—whites vandalized Herndon's Peachtree barbershop and attacked several of his employees, killing one. Herndon was shocked at being a target of violence after years of community leadership, but he remained committed to the city and to Atlanta Life, which he continued to build, largely through successful mergers, into a multistate enterprise. By his death in 1927, the firm was generating over $1.8 million in income and some $190,000 in profit, and it has survived to 2006, operating in seventeen states with over $200 million in assets.[20]

## Most of the Successful African Americans Headed North

As the unrest encountered by Herndon suggested, for African Americans with any options at all, finding opportunity early in the twentieth century meant heading to the North. Northern cities offered jobs in industry and a chance for African Americans to sustain at least a lower-middle-class lifestyle in a community that, while essentially as segregated as in the South, felt like turf they could call their own. Chicago was a particular magnet, where a growing African American population supported the rise of enterprises like the *Chicago Defender*, a newspaper published by one of our leaders, Robert Abbott. The paper's wide circulation in the South only enhanced the city's attraction, as Abbott vigorously exhorted African Americans to come North.[21] Chicago, in the words of another leader who made his fortune in the city, "was a special place of special and sassy blacks who did things they didn't do on Broadway or anywhere else."[22]

That leader, born in Arkansas in 1918 into a family tree only two generations removed from slavery, was named Johnny Johnson. He grew up on the wrong side of the color line in Arkansas City with his mother, a domestic worker; his father was killed in a sawmill accident when Johnny was eight. The following year, a catastrophic flood washed through the Mississippi River valley, blurring racial lines in Arkansas City in the name of survival as African Americans and whites alike crowded on the levees and struggled to fortify them. Any illusions of equality, though, were just that. *New York Times* accounts of the flood carefully note the names of any white victims when available, but mention only the numbers and genders of anonymous "Negroes" who perished.[23]

Johnson and his mother survived the devastation but faced the continued racial constraints of their environment. The nearest school that would educate African Americans beyond the eighth grade was about seventy miles away in Pine Bluff, and money for boarding expenses was not in the family's budget. Instead, Johnson's mother, who had by now remarried, determined to get herself and her boy to Chicago—a friend of hers had moved there and was now sending back encouraging news about opportunities for African Americans. In Chicago, Johnny could attend public high school. To make sure he didn't get into trouble or become too comfortable with an Arkansas life, his mother insisted he repeat eighth grade while she worked extra jobs to assemble the funds for their journey.[24] In July 1933, over her husband's opposition (although he would join them within a year or so), she and Johnny followed the path of so many Southern-born African Americans of their day and took the train north.

Johnson's accent and shabby clothes made him the butt of jokes in his new school, but he practiced speaking in front of the mirror to improve his confidence, and his resourceful mother bettered his wardrobe significantly with hand-me-down suits from the family she served as a domestic. She lost the job not long thereafter, however, and her husband, when he arrived in Chicago, couldn't find employment. They rented out their apartment's bedroom for income and scraped by, going on welfare for about two years (and then only after his mother wrote an appeal directly to President Roosevelt when the local board turned them down).[25] Depression-era job opportunities with the Works Progress Administration (WPA) and National Youth Administration helped his stepfather and Johnny, respectively, contribute to getting the family on its feet again. Johnny's devotion to Dale Carnegie and other self-help writers paid off as he began to excel in school, immersing himself in extracurricular activities and being elected class president for both his junior and senior years. As he neared graduation in 1936, a favorite teacher suggested that "John" was a name that would suit him better for adult life. This mentor advised the young man to adopt a middle name also—henceforth, he would be known as John Harold Johnson. Under this distinguished name, he received a $200 scholarship to the University of Chicago, but that amount was only a fraction of the money needed for a year's tuition, and despite Johnson's precociously accomplished nature, jobs remained hard to come by. Drawing on his hard-won self-confidence, he approached Harry H. Pace, the CEO of Supreme Liberty Life Insurance, after a speaking engagement. Supreme Liberty was an African American–owned Chicago insurance company that, like Atlanta Life, had developed to serve the African American community. Fortunately for Johnson, Pace knew of his strong high school performance and offered him a job.

Johnson's initial responsibilities at Supreme Liberty amounted to sitting at a desk and waiting to be summoned, but his patience was gradually rewarded with work that was more interesting. He did take some courses at the University of Chicago and Northwestern University, but soon found his on-the-job education much more valuable and abandoned the classroom for good. A key early responsibility came when he was made editor of the company newsletter in 1939. Johnson was responsible not just to Pace but to Earl Dickerson and Truman Gibson, leaders whose success with Supreme Liberty also earned them places on our list. In 1942, at Pace's request, Johnson began creating for him a summary of news from the prominent African American newspapers and magazines of the day. Stories about African Americans, except when focusing on crimes committed, were rarely covered in mainstream media, and few African Americans had access to all these journals. Johnson soon noticed how the unique trove of knowledge he gleaned from these activities often made him the center of attention at parties.[26] He figured out that such popularity suggested potential profitability, and he began to consider how to produce a monthly publication collecting and reprinting African American–focused news.

The field was littered with failed publications started by African Americans, however, and not even in Chicago could Johnson find backers for his idea. Credit was also nearly impossible for an African American man to obtain, meaning the leverage formula that worked for Kemmons Wilson wouldn't help Johnson. Still, his relationship with Supreme Liberty provided some enviable resources. Among Johnson's office responsibilities was running the addressing system that produced mailings to Supreme Liberty policyholders; Pace gave him permission to use the list for a direct-mail solicitation. Johnson also negotiated with Dickerson for a rent-free "office" in the corner of Dickerson's law library at Supreme Liberty headquarters. Most notably, Johnson persuaded the printer who handled Supreme Liberty's business to print on credit a magazine "we" (a deliberately vague and essentially royal *we* in this case) were publishing. The only cash still needed up front was five hundred dollars for postage, and he managed to secure a loan for this by using his mother's furniture as collateral. Three thousand of the twenty thousand policyholders solicited sent back $2 for a year's subscription, a whopping 15 percent response that confirmed Johnson had tapped a felt need. What was more important, the response provided enough up-front cash to publish the first issue of *Negro Digest* in November 1942. He needed to sell the other two thousand copies of the print run, however, to pay off the balance of the costs.

To capture a white distributor's interest, Johnson dispatched friends and family to shop many different newsstands and request *Negro Digest*. After the distributor bit, Johnson bankrolled his shoppers to return to those newsstands and buy the magazine, building positive word of mouth and prompting newsdealers to hawk the publication themselves to African American patrons. (Several decades later, even after he'd made his fortune, Johnson would similarly seed the department store market with customers for his Fashion Fair cosmetics line.)[27] Johnson recruited a network of agents to sell the publication in other cities and regions; *Negro Digest* was being sold in New York

City within three months and, three months after that, in California. After eight months of circulation, fifty thousand copies were being sold per month, and Johnson was feeling confident enough to request a leave of absence from Supreme Liberty to focus his attention on the publication. The magazine needed a push to take interest to the next level, and Johnson came up with the idea of a series of original articles called "If I Were a Negro," penned by prominent white Americans such as Orson Welles, Pearl Buck, and, most notably, First Lady Eleanor Roosevelt, who each offered personal responses to dilemmas faced by African Americans. After Mrs. Roosevelt's column ran, circulation doubled again to one hundred thousand and kept rising.

The next month, Johnson bought a building to house his business, and with *Negro Digest* producing cash almost faster than he could reinvest it, he launched an even more ambitious project—a pictorial magazine for African Americans, in the style of *Life*. Two freelancers working for him had suggested an entertainment magazine for African Americans, but since Johnson put up all the money, he dictated a different focus. Where *Negro Digest* was information intensive and dealt with the rough realities of racism, the new publication would be more upbeat, presenting images of African American success and community life that couldn't be found even in African American newspapers. In November 1945, the first issue of *Ebony* was published. It was an almost immediate success in circulation, reaching nearly a half million in its first year, but given its more expensive paper stock and color printing needs, Johnson had creditors nipping at his heels and urgently needed to sell advertising to pay the bills. He created mail-order businesses of his own in cosmetics, books, vitamins, and wigs to fill ad space and create revenue. Nevertheless, he had to attract mainstream advertisers to the potential of the African American consumer. Zenith was among the first manufacturers to yield to his pitch, and the company advertised its radios in *Ebony*. Other major advertisers soon followed.

Johnson resisted resting on his laurels and repeatedly developed new magazines as he perceived a market for them in the African American community—two *True Confessions*–style romance magazines called *Tan Confessions* and *Copper Romance* were first published in the 1950s, along with the pocket-sized news magazine *Jet*. *Negro Digest* ceased publication in 1951, when *Jet* was launched, but the earlier periodical would be revived as *Black World* in the 1960s, when the news flow of the civil rights movement renewed the demand

*A 1985 photo of John Harold Johnson, publisher of* Negro Digest, Jet, *and* Ebony *and founder of Fashion Fair cosmetics, with his daughter Linda Johnson Rice, who took charge of the company in 2002.* (Source: Time Life Pictures/Getty Images)

for such content. *Black World* vanished for good in the 1970s, and the romance magazines also ran out of steam, but *Jet* and *Ebony* continued to thrive into the twenty-first century. By then, Johnson's business comprised not only the largest African American–owned publishing concern but also the dominant department store cosmetics line for African Americans (Fashion Fair). Back in 1972, the enterprises had attained their current home, a new building at a posh address on Chicago's Michigan Avenue. The same decade, Johnson had become chairman and CEO of his first employer, Supreme Liberty Life, finally terminating that original leave of absence. He had gained a controlling stake by investing in the company to keep it going during financial difficulties, returning the favor to the business that had helped get him started.[28] In 1991, he orchestrated the sale of Supreme Liberty, which at the time had assets valued over $50 million.[29]

Along the way, Johnson began to move in powerful circles, visiting the White House during the Eisenhower administration and making the acquaintance of every chief executive thereafter. During the Kennedy admin-istration, he traveled as a special ambassador in official delegations to Kenya and the Ivory Coast (now Côte d'Ivoire). His first national board membership came in 1971 with 20th Century Fox Films, on whose board he served with Princess Grace of Monaco, and board appointments with major manufactur-ers such as Zenith and Chrysler followed. In the early 1980s, he made the *Forbes* list of the four hundred wealthiest Americans and was one of the first African Americans to do so. Finally, in April 2002, at age eighty-four, he stepped down as CEO of Johnson Publishing and was succeeded by his daughter, Linda Johnson Rice.[30] He always insisted that there be no forced retirements in his company and, sure enough, remained as chairman until his death in 2005.[31]

## African Americans Work Their Way Up by the Books

Johnson's mother moved him northward for high school, but many African American leaders traveling that path pressed even higher in their educational goals. African American leaders arising prior to 1950, in fact, were as a group just as educated as, or more educated than, white ones (figure 7-4). Despite the relatively small numbers of African Americans, it's a bit startling that, in a time when they would have faced far fewer options for college education than whites did, almost half of this minority group of leaders had college degrees, a proportion almost identical to white leaders. A third overall pursued graduate studies also, compared with only about 8 percent of whites. The comparison suggests that education was a bigger factor for African Americans in gaining access to business opportunities, even though none of these leaders were in-volved in managing white-owned enterprises. Racial prejudice in the white-dominated business community also reduced the likelihood that attractive opportunities would pull African Americans away from schooling—with no better options, they did well to get as advanced an education as they could to draw upon any possible advantage.

In the life of Robert Vann, for example, his persistent pursuit of education suggests how essential he considered it for his success in the world. He was born in North Carolina to a teenage single mother in 1879, a grandson of for-mer slaves. His mother followed a tradition held over from slavery and gave

**FIGURE 7-4**

**Early African American leaders advance through education**

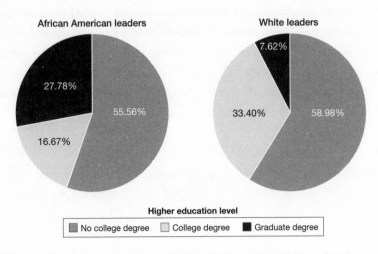

Source: HBS Leadership Initiative's "Great American Business Leaders of the 20th Century" database. For African American and white leaders ascending before 1950.

him the surname of a family in whose home she worked as a domestic servant. The lifestyle of one of those affluent families, observed at close range by Vann as a child, fueled his own aspirations. He applied himself diligently in a local school for African Americans, but when Vann graduated at thirteen, his recently acquired stepfather immediately put him to work in farming and other manual labor. At sixteen, his big break came in the form of a job as janitor and part-time clerk at the local post office. Modest though it sounds, the job allowed Vann to save enough to enter a private secondary school and to pay his ongoing tuition through working as he completed his education. Graduating at twenty-two, he attended Virginia Union's preparatory school and then the university itself. After a successful year of studies there, he continued his trek northward. He entered Western University of Pennsylvania (now the University of Pittsburgh), finishing his bachelor's degree at age twenty-seven and his law degree three years later. One of only a handful of African American students, he nevertheless became editor in chief of the school newspaper, a hint of things to come.

By now, Vann's ambition far outstripped the limited opportunities for African Americans offered in the South, and his mother's death left him with no family connections to inspire his return there. He settled in Pittsburgh and began practicing law, though with limited monetary reward, as even African Americans in the North preferred white lawyers for important cases. He married in 1910 and the same year began his relationship with the *Pittsburgh Courier*, providing legal help to incorporate the tiny African American–run newspaper. Just as Earl Babst did at Nabisco, Vann jumped from the legal world into his client's operations, taking over editorial responsibilities when the paper's first editor left.

A happy side benefit was the chance to use the paper to publicize his legal successes and to enlarge his law practice, but building the newspaper as a voice for African Americans became his real passion. With minimal advertising revenues and no sales through newsstands (which were generally white-owned), the *Courier* had only subscription revenues to depend on, but Vann toughed it out and circulation grew. He made key hires on both the business and editorial side, eventually retaining a white-owned agency to attract national advertising contracts. By the late 1920s, the *Courier* was deemed the nation's best African American weekly and had also provided a political platform for Vann. He was appointed assistant city solicitor of Pittsburgh, the first African American to hold such a high office in that city. He gained a federal appointment in the attorney general's office after his support for Franklin Delano Roosevelt in 1932 significantly helped sway African American voters, who had largely been loyal Lincoln Republicans, toward the Democrats. Disappointed with the scope of responsibilities assigned to him in D.C., however, Vann left after only a few years and returned northward to enjoy continued success with the paper in Pittsburgh. In the late 1930s, buoyed by the popularity of its extensive coverage of two major stories—the rise of African American boxing hero Joe Louis and Ethiopia's resistance to the Italian invasion—the *Courier*'s circulation hit 250,000, only about 30,000 of which was local to Pittsburgh.[32] Its distribution reached nationwide and to Canada, Europe, the Caribbean, and even the Philippines. Vann's own life ended in 1940, but the paper he nurtured continued as arguably the most influential of its kind, cresting at a circulation of over 357,000 in 1947, the largest of any African American newspaper.[33]

## Women Start and Stay in the Urban Northeast

While African Americans faced a disadvantage in origins that tended to pull all who had any chance to depart away from their Southern birthplaces, the female leaders of the early twentieth century, mostly white, were mainly born in the same already-advantaged areas that produced our white male leaders— the Northeast and Midwest. Given that several women gained their access to business opportunity through a father or husband and that most came from relatively prosperous, business-oriented families, it's no surprise that the women were born in places linked with business activity. Moreover, the kinds of industries in which most of these women succeeded, as discussed, largely served female consumers with discretionary purchasing power. Such consumers were more likely to be found in areas where many businesses were established, and with the businesses, large numbers of successful men. The origins of female leaders thus matched the places where ready markets for their products existed, making it even more likely the women would find their best prospects for business near their roots in industrialized areas.

In the first half of the century, in fact, only around a quarter of women succeeded anywhere outside the Northeast. The wide-open West, so friendly a territory to early male outsiders of other stripes, saw no female leaders on our list arising prior to the 1970s. Instead, almost half of our female leaders made their success in the bustling business hub of New York City, a proportion much higher than for male leaders (figure 7-5). Ironically, the prime location for these particular ultimate outsiders was in the shadow of the entrenched business establishment that drove so many male outsiders elsewhere. New York was, of course, the center of the nation's fashion and advertising industries. Advertising represented one of the first professional service sectors to see significant numbers of women in its ranks, again because women were often the buyers being targeted by those pitches.

The only female CEO in our group to rise through corporate ranks before the 1980s, for instance, did so in the Big Apple. This barrier breaker, one Dorothy Shaver, was born in 1893 in Center Point, Arkansas. Her birthplace seems decidedly ill named, as it is in fact near the Arkansas-Oklahoma border, in the center of nothing in particular. Roughly equidistant from the larger cities of Dallas, Little Rock, and Oklahoma City, it is equally disconnected

**FIGURE 7-5**

## Women find way to success in the Big Apple

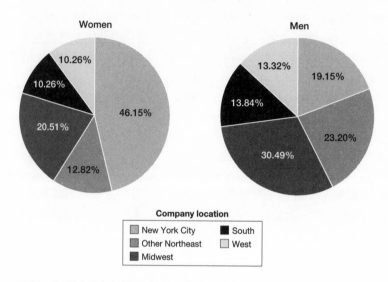

Women

Men

Company location

New York City · South
Other Northeast · West
Midwest

*Source*: HBS Leadership Initiative's "Great American Business Leaders of the 20th Century" database.

from all of them. Even in such a backwater, however, Shaver had connections on her side. Her father was an attorney and later a judge. He soon moved the family to Mena, the county seat, where he built one of the most distinguished homes in town. Shaver's maternal grandfather was also an attorney by training but gained notoriety in Arkansas working in publishing and academia: in the 1840s, he had owned one of the state's major newspapers, the *Arkansas Gazette* and, after selling it, had headed a military academy in Tulip, Arkansas. Her paternal grandfather commanded an Arkansas regiment in the Confederate army.[34] In short, the Shavers had a noteworthy local profile making them relatively big fish in an admittedly small pond. It was obviously a beginning far more advantaged than that of her fellow Arkansan, Johnny Johnson, who came along a couple of decades later.

About the only thing that didn't go Shaver's way was an intended elopement at age eighteen, but she later regarded the intervention as "fortuitous."[35] She was instead sent for two years of college at the University of Arkansas and then went to the University of Chicago, accompanying her younger sister, Elsie, who was attending that city's Art Institute. Before long, the ambitious women had set their sights on the enticing territory of New York City, and with their parents' blessing (and financial stipend), they took the train there in 1920.

At this stage, perhaps the most advantageous of family connections entered the picture, as Shaver's mother posted a note asking Samuel W. Reyburn, her cousin's son, to check in on her daughters in New York.[36] Reyburn was then president of Lord & Taylor, the marquee property of Associated Dry Goods, a holding company controlling a collection of stores from Minneapolis to Newark. After establishing a bank in Arkansas, Reyburn had gotten his ticket to the big city in 1914, when he was invited to New York by a J. P. Morgan–backed banking group to reorganize a group of retail properties.[37] His success earned him a leadership role in Associated, the reincarnation of the troubled stores. By the time he paid a Sunday call on the Shaver sisters, he was a rising member of Manhattan's business elite: he would soon be named to the board of the Guaranty Trust Company, and, a few years after that, would become a director of New York's Federal Reserve Bank. Not only was his own star on the ascent, but Reyburn was already making a habit of helping friends from Arkansas find their way into New York business circles.[38] All these things, plus perhaps thoughts of his own three daughters, about ten years younger than Dorothy and Elsie, made him an ideal prospect for encouraging their ambitions. The Shavers shared with him a hand-painted rag-doll collection that artist Elsie had created, and Reyburn quickly found a window placement at Lord & Taylor for the "Little Shavers." Orders for the dolls came in rapidly, and the sisters stepped up production, with Elsie the artisan and Shaver the business manager.

This business arrangement lasted several years, by which time Elsie had wearied of the exercise and wanted to return to painting without the production-line pressures. Reyburn wasn't through mentoring, however, and he offered Shaver a job evaluating Lord & Taylor's comparison shopping program, which gathered competitive price and product data. She analyzed the effort and didn't hesitate to share her conclusions that the whole approach was wrongheaded. She felt that the subterfuge required was distasteful and that the endeavor sent the wrong message. Lord & Taylor, she argued, should spend more time establishing excellence in its own lines and less time worrying about the standards of other stores.

From such bold statements are stars often born, and Reyburn recognized the quality of Shaver's insights. He made her the first-ever head of design for a retail store, and by 1927, she was a member of Lord & Taylor's board of directors. Nor was Reyburn her only fan—he resigned from Lord & Taylor's presidency to focus on managing the holding company in 1931, with Shaver then a vice president. In 1937, after yet another change in management, she ascended to the title of first vice president, a second-in-command post supervising advertising and public relations as well as promotion and display. This exhibition of survival skill in the typically cutthroat retail environment culminated when Lord & Taylor's president, Walter Hoving, resigned in December 1945 and Shaver was chosen by the all-male Associated Dry Goods board to take his place. The headline in the normally stolid *Wall Street Journal* read: "Woman to Succeed Hoving as Head of Lord & Taylor," betraying a certain astonishment in its emphasis on not the name but the sex of the new president.[39] Her only female counterparts running large retail stores (including Beatrice Fox Auerbach of G. Fox & Co., a leader also on our list) had inherited their roles. Shaver was, articles noted, the first woman to head a store of such size, which amounted to about $30 million in annual sales at the time, and within six months, she would also be sitting on Associated's board.

Even before claiming the presidency, Shaver had been bringing a distinctive tone to Lord & Taylor's merchandise and marketing. In one window display during an unseasonably warm November, she produced a simulated blizzard with a half-ton of specially treated cornflakes and had the frosted glass etched with the warning, "It's coming! Sooner or later!" Winter clothing sales reportedly spiked upward by 50 percent the first day of the display.[40] Such brashly inventive marketing exemplified what came to be known as the Shaver Touch—a touch that migrated from New York City to newly established branch stores in suburban locations, sites that Lord & Taylor was first among Manhattan department stores to pursue. Fanciful mural decorations, even in fitting rooms and stairwells, clouds of perfume wafting through the air in stores, and the store's long-standing American Beauty rose motif, were just a few of the innovations in Shaver's Lord & Taylor.[41]

Shaver's most noted crusade was on behalf of American designers, reminding stylish women that Europe wasn't the only origination point for fashionable attire. Beginning in the 1930s and gaining momentum during World War II, her efforts to promote the American look elevated many previously

*Dorothy Shaver (rear, center), president of Lord & Taylor department stores, having lunch with her executives in 1946.* (Source: Time Life Pictures/Getty Images)

anonymous U.S. designers into demanded names. Her focus on the importance of design led to the establishment of the Lord & Taylor American Design Awards in 1938. At first, the awards recognized achievements in the design of items such as gloves, refrigerators, costumes, and cameras, but over time, the focus was broadened sufficiently to honor such diverse recipients as U.S. Army and Navy engineers (for attaining American air superiority), the United Nations, and Albert Einstein. ("What is a Lord & Taylor?" the famous scientist reportedly queried when notified of the recognition.)[42] The relative incongruity of a department store presenting awards in such arenas reflected Shaver's drive to distinguish Lord & Taylor as a glamorous and unpredictable store brand. The awards essentially ended with her death in 1959, showing what a part she had personally played in keeping them going.

The dynamic and endlessly creative personality that Shaver brought to Lord & Taylor fueled what would be the store's most glorious years of success. Far from contributing style alone, she understood the dynamics of building traffic and turning inventory, and sales more than doubled during her tenure as president. If it was lonely being a woman at the top (she remained single and shared a home with her sister throughout her life), she refused to dwell on it, pooh-poohing the uniqueness of her success: "All this fuss about a woman making good is a left-over from the time when women were not considered men's equals," she scoffed in the enlightened day of 1947.[43] Still, she took pride in the fact that she'd retained, hired, and developed strong male executives when it had been speculated that none would tolerate working for a woman.[44] It was an era when companies still looked for "the best possible man for the job," but the directors of Associated Dry Goods saw no contradiction in claiming this accomplishment for themselves when they promoted Dorothy Shaver.[45]

## Education for Women Is the Only Real Change by Midcentury

Shaver's bold words in 1947 were not borne out by an immediate increase in success stories for women, however. After her death in 1959, it would be more than twenty-five years before another woman on our list rose to the top of an existing enterprise other than through family inheritance. Mabel Newcomer's exhaustive 1955 study included only the following two incisive sentences on the topic: "Insofar as there is discrimination in employment or business dealings on account of sex, race, nationality, religion, and politics, it will probably be most apparent at the top levels. And it may be said without further comment that no woman and no Negro has been found among the top executives of this study."[46] W. Lloyd Warner and James Abegglen, rather than refrain from comment, made the following, apparently unstudied, observation: "The life careers of ambitious women usually are not in professional roles but are realized by marriage to 'a successful catch.'"[47] Given such assumptions, it's not surprising that their book included an exploration of how much businessmen who marry women of higher social status thereby boost their career prospects, plus a chapter entitled "The Kinds of Women Who Make Successful Wives." This was a time, after all, when esteemed Harvard Business School professor Georges Doriot (also a business leader on our list) regularly invited students' wives to one session of his class specifically to impress on them their appropriate role in supporting their husbands.[48] Midway through the century, neither the achievements of Shaver, Arden, and Schiff nor the massive and successful entry of females into diverse workforce sectors to replace males during World War II had made a dent in traditional conceptions about women in the workplace.

Change was occurring, however, in the level of women's enrollment in higher education, and we have already seen how critical educational credentials were becoming in the selection of second-half leaders. Throughout the century, female leaders, unlike male ethnic outsiders, had tended to be much less educated than their male peers. Only three of the twenty-six women on our list born before 1930 had college degrees, compared with over half the men born in that period. After that date, however, women began catching up, and more than half of those born 1940 or later were college educated (figure 7-6).

Although the women in our group still trailed the men (about 80 percent of men born from 1940 onward had college degrees), this shift reflects

**FIGURE 7-6**

## Women's education levels rising later in century

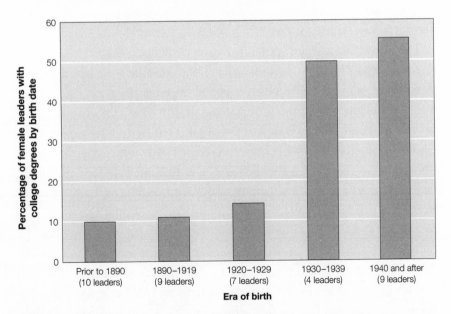

*Source*: HBS Leadership Initiative's "Great American Business Leaders of the 20th Century" database.

women's participation in the overall trends boosting U.S. education levels after midcentury. A U.S. woman born in the 1940s was roughly twice as likely as one born in the 1920s to have attended at least four years of college, an even sharper rise than that of similar statistics for men.[49] Not surprisingly, both of our women with MBAs and all of those hired as CEOs after Dorothy Shaver belong to this post-1940 generation.

Born in 1947, Rochelle Lazarus is a leader fitting squarely into this new era for women. More familiarly known as Shelly, she had a rise to leadership virtually indistinguishable from the typical path followed by men in her era, fitting in every respect but her sex the characterization of a long-tenured company man. She made her first acquaintance with advertising while a senior at Smith College, attending an industry career conference in New York City with a friend more or less on a lark. A psychology major, Lazarus loved learning about the techniques employed to influence and persuade consumers through advertising. Moreover, she knew that the sooner she got a job, the sooner she and her Yalie fiancé, then in medical school, could get married.[50] She pursued an MBA at Columbia University and was one of only four women in the 275-person class of 1970.[51] After graduation, she was hired by Clairol—just over a year later, now a "hair expert," as she would later joke, she came over to the advertising agency side with Ogilvy & Mather (O&M), expecting to stay a couple of years.[52]

This instead marked the beginning of over *thirty* years with O&M, a period interrupted only by a two-year sojourn in Ohio when her husband, by then a pediatrician, was obliged to satisfy a period of military service. The timing wasn't great—their departure in 1974 came shortly after Lazarus, then seven months pregnant, had been named O&M's first female account supervisor.[53] Upon her return to New York, however, she picked up where she had left off, working on key client accounts such as American Express. In 1987, in a move that puzzled some but would pave the way for advancement, Lazarus transferred into the agency's direct-marketing subsidiary. Within two years, she became its president, and two years after that, she was named overall head of O&M's New York office, a prime leadership role that promised more good things. She was appointed president of O&M North America in 1994, a year that also saw her play a leading role in consolidating IBM's extensive advertising relationships from forty-odd agencies into the O&M fold.[54] Her further journey to the top was a relatively quick one—to president and chief operating officer in 1995, CEO the following year, and then chairman in 1997. "I'm proof the glass ceiling is history," she declared at the time.[55] Lazarus wasn't even a trailblazer at O&M: she succeeded a woman, Charlotte Beers, in the top post. The woman-to-woman leadership transition sparked talk of O&M's being a haven for female success, but Lazarus insisted that this wasn't the root of the matter. The critical factor leading to Beers's rise and hers, she argued, was that the firm was "a true meritocracy."[56] In 2005, she continued to assert that a fair chance to demonstrate their skills was all that women needed for advancement: "We don't need remedial programs or special help . . . We don't need mentors or whatever."[57] She remains at the top of the worldwide agency in 2006 with a continued record of success. Given the prevalence of divorces and singleness among women leaders from earlier in the century, it's perhaps just as significant an indicator of change in societal attitudes that Lazarus, a mother of three, has a marriage lasting even longer than her career at O&M.[58]

## Continued Industry Segregation for African Americans, but Markets Broaden

African Americans, like women, remained off the radar screen of scholars analyzing executive mobility midcentury. Warner and Abegglen, noting only in the book's final pages the absence of any "Negroes" among the business elite in their study, acknowledged that this group's full integration into business leadership "may be the ultimate test of free competition for jobs" in the years to come.[59] In fact, there is only marginal improvement in representation from minorities among our leaders after 1950. The percentage ticks slightly upward, from 3.3 percent to 3.8 percent, but no African American leaders emerged in white-majority firms—all these minority leaders either built their own businesses or worked in African American–owned firms. Moreover, there were almost 50 percent more white women on our list in the second half of the century than African American men, a decided reversal from earlier in the century, when African American men were more numerous. Only one African American leader (a man) had an MBA, also a slightly lower proportion than for white women.

The one sign of progress in a situation with little apparent good news was that African Americans after 1950 were able to build businesses that marketed to anyone, regardless of color. Barry Gordy and Russell Simmons were among the African American leaders who were on our list and who used the entertainment industry as a business foothold. Their enterprises succeeded largely by producing music rooted in African American culture and by building the wider appeal of that music into a mass-market success. Even more notable than such industrial crossovers, however, was the achievement of Reginald Lewis. In 1987, he engineered a successful $1 billion leveraged buyout of the international holdings of Beatrice Companies, a global conglomerate of consumer food and household products. As a result, TLC Beatrice (TLC being an acronym for his investment firm, The Lewis Company) became the largest African American–owned firm in America. Nothing about its products or markets, however, carried a racial focus. Before acquiring Beatrice, Lewis had bought, turned around, and sold McCall Patterns, Inc., netting himself a cool $50 million on a $1 million initial personal investment. The degree of leverage in these activities shows how much things had changed since John Johnson needed furniture as collateral for even a $500 loan; spinning debt into gold was no longer just a white man's game. By the late 1980s, Lewis's personal wealth was estimated at $400 million, and he enjoyed all the perks of a top Wall Street financier—corporate jet, fine cigars, and homes in New York and Paris. A graduate of Harvard Law School, he was a regular at the Harvard Club in Manhattan. Among his many philanthropic activities was a $3 million donation to the law school, at the time the largest gift it had ever received from an individual.[60]

Lewis, sadly, spent all too short a time at this pinnacle of success, dying of brain cancer in 1993. TLC Beatrice, over ten times larger in sales than the next-largest African American–owned business when Lewis acquired it, was still the largest African American firm at his death by a whopping margin.[61] The company's $1.5 billion in sales stood over a third higher than sales of the remaining nine of the top ten African American–owned industrial/service firms combined, according to the list published in mid-1992 by *Black Enterprise*.[62] TLC Beatrice alone, moreover, accounted for about a third of the overall sales of the top *one hundred* such firms. In other words, Lewis had made it into the business elite, but he didn't have a lot of company from other African Americans. After his death, his widow extended his enterprise to further success, topping $2.2 billion in sales before electing to sell off the assets in 1998.[63] Other African American leaders on our list became as wealthy, but Lewis stood alone for both the scale of his success and its accomplishment on the hitherto lily-white turf of Wall Street.

## The Devil or the Deep Blue Sea

Considering the evidence of significant difficulties for both groups, whether in deaths or divorces, it's hard to say which of these two types of ultimate outsiders, African Americans or women, had a tougher time finding a pathway into American business leadership in the twentieth century. On the one hand, African Americans faced a disadvantage of origins in the nonindustrialized South. Even outside that region, they faced a severely segregated society that initially constrained business development to markets only within their own race—markets that, moreover, remained under threat of competition from any white-owned firms that might choose to pursue the same opportunity. On the other hand, even with these disadvantages, African American leaders outnumbered females prior to 1950. In the corporate arena, women faced a gender-based segregation in work roles that raised barriers fully as rigid as those encountered by African Americans. Certainly, "women's industries" like beauty, fashion, and prepared foods, which were generally open to women, offered much larger potential markets than those enjoyed by early African American entrepreneurs. However, while virtually all the African American leaders achieved success from impoverished beginnings, the large percentage of women leaders coming from affluent or at least middle-class families suggests that socioeconomic advantages were almost essential for women in gaining business leadership posts.

By the second half of the century, however, the economic advantages of white female leaders paid dividends that advanced their situation beyond that of African Americans, as the women pursued further education and gained opportunities for assimilation into "male-style" professional management careers, increasing their representation among second-half leaders to over 4 percent. African American women, as well, more than doubled their admittedly tiny proportion of leaders. The picture for African American men stands out as most noticeably *un*changed over the century, with flexibility apparent in the chance for African American–owned businesses to serve broader markets but no evidence of improved access for African Americans to managerial tracks in white-majority business settings. Then again, only one of the African American leaders appearing on our list was born after the *Brown v. Board of Education* decision, and only three were sixteen or younger at the passage of the Civil Rights Act. Similarly, just two of the women on our list came of college age after the passage of Title IX. If we are to see significant change in the diversity of America's business leadership in terms of race and gender, in other words, it would most likely come at least a generation beyond those individuals who occupied the top rungs of business by the close of the twentieth century. With a century's worth of evidence about the dimensions that created outsiders and insiders, we now turn from history to the task of examining the present for any sign of change that may yet be forthcoming.

# EIGHT

# Into the Twenty-First Century

## Open Doors or Glass Ceilings?

*I hope that we are at a point that everyone has figured out that there is not a glass ceiling. My gender is interesting but really not the subject of the story here.*

—Carly Fiorina, president and CEO of Hewlett-Packard

IN 1999, according to Carly Fiorina, it was no longer big news that a woman was taking over the second-largest computer manufacturer in the world, a company in the top third of the *Fortune* 100.[1] Obviously, many disagreed with her opinion—less than six years later, when Fiorina was discharged from her position at Hewlett-Packard in an equally high-profile manner, much of the press coverage centered on what the firing meant for other women aspiring to top corporate roles. In a way, though, Fiorina's story was the ultimate sign of equality. If she were hired without regard for her sex, then, when her strategic choices (most notably a merger with Compaq) were perceived to be weakening the company's performance, she could be fired in like manner. Another woman, Patricia Dunn, was one of the board members who pressed Fiorina the hardest (and the one who succeeded her as chairman), bolstering the argument that the saga signaled progress for women, not a setback.

The dearth of women in top corporate roles nevertheless remains a point of focus. Catalyst, a research organization founded in 1962, studies a variety of issues related to women's career paths and opportunities. In 2002, the group conducted a survey of *Fortune* 500 companies and found that women occupied just 5.2 percent of top-earning corporate positions, among them the slots held by Fiorina and her five compatriot female CEOs.[2] This is equal to the percentage of women in our list of leaders from 1950 on. There are, nevertheless, signs of movement in the Catalyst statistics. In 1995, when Catalyst first undertook such a study, only 8.7 percent of corporate officers were women. By 2002, the percentage had nearly doubled, standing at 15.7 percent. The women's percentage of top earners, meanwhile, had more than doubled. There were only six CEOs in 2002, but in 1995, there had been just one. By March 2005, despite Fiorina's firing the previous month, nine female CEOs headed companies listed in the *Fortune* 500, a 50 percent bump upward from the numbers for 2002.[3] Nearly 86 percent of *Fortune* 500 companies had at least one female corporate officer in 2002, and for sixty of those companies, women constituted 25 percent or more of all officers. But more companies than that (seventy-one) had no female officers at all, and thus the question of gender bias still looms.

The even more challenging question of bias in leadership swirls around race, a topic not so easily surveyed and becoming more complex by the minute as Americans of Hispanic origin emerge alongside African Americans as a significant minority group, exceeding 10 percent of the population overall and growing.[4] Asian Americans, while constituting a much smaller group

*Carly Fiorina, former CEO and president of Hewlett-Packard, speaking at a press conference in 1999 to unveil the firm's new logo and market positioning.* (Source: AFP/Getty Images)

than either African Americans or Hispanic Americans, exert an influence well beyond their numbers. Making up less than 5 percent of the population aged eighteen to twenty-four in the 2000 U.S. Census, they received 6.5 percent of the bachelor's degrees granted by U.S. schools that year.[5] And those degrees were likely to be prestigious—a study of attendance at top American schools in the 1990s found that Asian Americans who enrolled in college were more than twice as likely as Hispanic Americans, African Americans, or non-Hispanic whites to attend one of the top fifty national universities.[6] Population projections, moreover, show the white, non-Hispanic population shrinking as a percentage, so that by 2050, "minority" ethnic groups are expected, in total, to exceed 40 percent of the population and to outnumber the so-called majority group at all ages up to thirty-five.[7] How long will it take for this increasing diversity to find its way into the business sector? Would a list of similar top U.S. business leaders over the next century be as white-male-dominated as ours for the twentieth century? Foresight is much harder than hindsight, but we can look for clues.

## A Changing Pipeline

As we saw in the characteristics of our business leaders toward the close of the century, social and demographic signals were beginning to be superseded by educational credentials—particularly the MBA degree—in qualification for leadership. The idea that education (a college degree, at least) can override factors of origin and create a level playing field for occupational and economic mobility has been reinforced in other studies of American mobility.[8] While advancement to the top rungs of corporate leadership certainly draws on personal qualities not taught in academia, and some people with lesser levels of schooling still find ways to succeed, holders of MBA degrees constitute an increasingly significant pool of candidates for the bigger prizes in American business. Accordingly, greater diversity among those obtaining the degree suggests greater potential leadership diversity to come.

Without a doubt, a critical event in broadening access to graduate education for women was the passage of the Education Amendments of 1972. Ironically, press coverage at the time focused on the bill's failure to establish limits on school busing. "Not in the course of this Administration has there been a more manifest Congressional retreat from an urgent call for responsibility," said President Nixon, who signed the bill despite his express reservations over its noncommittal busing provisions.[9] What were apparently utterly uncontroversial to both the president and Congress were the provisions of Title IX, which prohibited institutions of higher education that receive federal funding from discriminating on the basis of sex. Even today, the most frequent discussions of the implications of Title IX relate to its impact on collegiate athletics. In fact, however, this legislation had a dramatic effect on the entry of women into graduate programs, including business schools. The timing of the act in 1972 corresponded with a sea change, in which the percentage of women among graduating MBAs ramped up from the 3–5 percent range (where it had held steady for more than a decade) to quickly double twice from 1973 to 1980, when it passed 20 percent and kept on climbing (figure 8-1). Since the

**FIGURE 8-1**

## Number of women getting MBA degrees multiplies after Title IX

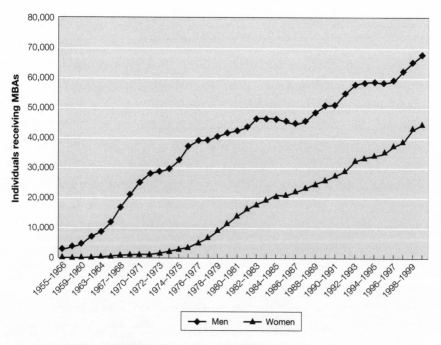

*Source*: U.S. Department of Education, National Center for Education Statistics, *Digest of Education Statistics, 2001*, table 284, available at http://nces.ed.gov/programs/digest/d01/dt284.asp. Data collected biennially from 1956 to 1970, then annually through 2000.

1970s also marked the beginning of a massive expansion in the overall number of MBA degrees awarded in the United States, year-by-year proportional gains made by women translated into a significant impact on the group's cumulative number of MBAs. Women received over 30 percent of all MBA degrees awarded in the United States between 1973 and 2000 and, for the 2000 academic year, made up nearly 40 percent of MBA recipients.[10]

These new numbers deliver at least the potential for significant changes in the population of business leaders within the coming decades, changes already hinted at by the shifting numbers in the Catalyst survey. Some may argue that the growth in female corporate officers as reported by Catalyst is a result of title inflation or of companies' response to the publicity generated by this measurement. Still, Catalyst's first survey occurred in 1995, a year when the MBA generation of 1975 and onward, which included a dramatically higher proportion of women, was just starting to come into its own. Perhaps the doubling of corporate officer proportions within the seven years of the Catalyst survey period from 1995 to 2002 bears some correspondence to the quadrupling of the women's share of MBAs awarded in the seven years from 1973 to 1980, a time frame almost exactly twenty years prior.

In our pool of leaders, the proportion of women leaders by birth years tracks well with the proportion of women earning MBAs in the United States during a corresponding period approximately twenty-five years later (figure 8-2). Not all our leaders (male or female) had MBAs, of course, but the level of women's access to MBA programs could offer a proxy for their overall access to business opportunities.

Since careers that bring individuals to the top of significant enterprises typically take twenty to thirty years, and tenures in a leadership post average five to ten years, such posts are generally occupied by people born forty-five to sixty-five years earlier. Accordingly, the top level of large firms in 2005 substantially reflected a cohort of individuals who were born from 1940 to 1960 and thus attended college and postgraduate training from 1960 through the mid-1980s. For the year 2020, leaders of top firms would largely be those educated from about 1975 through 2000, a generation for which the percentage of women MBAs is nearly 33 percent. To suggest that one in three corporate leaders might be a woman by 2020 is aggressive but not beyond the realm of possibility, given the 16 percent of *Fortune* 500 officers observed in 2002 by Catalyst. If the proportion of women officers could double in seven years

**FIGURE 8-2**

## Women's leadership progress tracks with MBA expansion

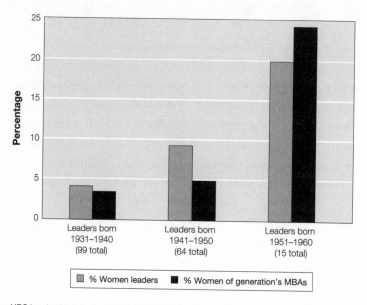

*Sources*: HBS Leadership Initiative's "Great American Business Leaders of the 20th Century" database; U.S. Department of Education, National Center for Education Statistics, *Digest of Education Statistics, 2001*, table 284, available at http://nces.ed.gov/programs/digest/d01/dt284.asp.

The generation matched to a birth cohort was the group receiving MBAs in a period twenty-five years after the birth-year range. To compensate for biennial data collection from 1956 to 1970, counts of male and female MBAs for odd-numbered years were estimated at the midpoint between figures for preceding and subsequent years.

(from 1995 to 2002), might it not also double over the subsequent eighteen years, particularly given the nearly proportionate rise in women MBAs over the comparable prior period?

In fact, *Fortune*'s 2004 list of the fifty most powerful women in business suffered no shortage of worthy candidates; most of the women listed held titles of president, CEO, or chairman, with 80 percent having been born after 1950 and educated mainly in the post–Title IX era. Just two had family connections in their firms, and only two were entrepreneurs, showing significant changes from twentieth-century patterns. Similarly, only two leaders worked in cosmetics, and just twenty worked in food, retail, advertising, or media—the "softer" industry entry points that had previously represented the primary turf accessible to women. Instead, most of these executives were leaders in high-tech, financial services, pharmaceuticals, or telecommunications firms.[11] The number of women in top corporate positions may be rising slowly, but the difference in industries penetrated by women leaders is, in light of our findings from the past century, an important sign of the group's ongoing shift from outsiders to insiders on the paths to power.

Despite these signs of progress, it appears aggressive to predict that 9 *Fortune* 500 female CEOs in 2005 will by 2020 increase in number to 150, an amount required to approach the one-third proportion discussed above. To project the likely composition of a list of top business leaders of the early twenty-first century comparable to our list for the twentieth century, though, we must consider not just women who head large companies, but entrepreneurs and high-achievers in smaller companies as well. Meg Whitman of eBay, to name an obvious example, would already be on a short list of candidates for comparable twenty-first-century leaders, although her company hadn't crept into the *Fortune* 500 as of 2005. Entrepreneurial activity by women in the United States has expanded significantly over recent years, with the numbers of women-owned firms and of people employed by such firms growing about twice as fast as comparable figures for all U.S. firms between 1997 and 2004.[12] In some ways, this looks like a second wave of the entrepreneurial path that was pursued by poorer, non-WASP male outsiders in the early twentieth century: unaccepted in the mainstream, those who can't "join 'em" try to "beat 'em." Women came later into these possibilities, at least in terms of opportunities beyond the traditional "women's industries," but there is evidence that the late start is being offset by rapid gains.

Funding for business expansion, however, whether via credit or venture capital, continues to be highlighted as a particular obstacle for women. The Committee of 200, an organization benchmarking women's parity with men in business since 2002, rates venture capital funding as the area in which women's disadvantage in access relative to men remains the greatest by far. Its 2005 report estimated that women-led businesses were at less than 10 percent of parity versus others in receipt of venture capital funds.[13] With women making strides as executives in the high-tech and biotech arenas, however, this venture capital obstacle, too, seems likely to fall. Although deposed from HP, Carly Fiorina, for example, would be capable of inspiring a venture capitalist to ante up significant cash for any new venture she headed. In any case, opportunities for entrepreneurship in a broader range of industries than before should improve the potential for women to gain prominence in business leadership. While a fifty-fifty split remains a long way off, the coming decades can be expected to show continued shifts in the gender mix for top U.S. business leaders, and a list chosen on a basis similar to ours for the first half of the twenty-first century could be expected to contain around 20 percent women.

## And a Bit More Colorful . . .

If we look at the MBA pipeline in an attempt to forecast racial diversity in business leadership, the picture is murkier than it is for women. The challenges in interpreting the data increase because the expanding Asian American and Hispanic ethnic groups are often summarized together with African Americans in minority-student statistics. For African Americans specifically, as for women, much has demonstrably changed in access to business education over the past several decades. A survey in the mid-1960s counted fewer than 50 African American students among the 12,000 students enrolled in MBA programs in the United States. African Americans thus constituted less than 0.5 percent of all students.[14] By 2000, however, statistics from the Department of Education indicated that African Americans received 8,630 MBAs, nearly 8 percent of all such degrees awarded.[15] Though this still falls short of proportional representation (African Americans made up close to 14 percent of the population aged 25–29 in 2000), it is a significant jump.[16] The National Black MBA Association, founded in 1970, claimed in 2005 a membership of over 6,000, of whom nearly 90 percent were age 40 or younger, meaning virtually all of the association's members grew up in the era following *Brown v. Board of Education* and the Civil Rights Act.[17] In the summer of 2005, three *Fortune* 100 companies, including powerful brand names like Merrill Lynch, American Express, and AOL Time Warner, had African American CEOs (Stan O'Neal, Kenneth Chenault, and Richard Parsons, respectively).[18] While heading just 3 percent of such companies does not represent a proportional gain for African Americans over their representation in our list of twentieth-century leaders, none of the African American leaders on our earlier list had risen to the top of a company that wasn't minority owned. As with the broader array of industries in which women currently

*Kenneth Chenault (left), chairman and CEO of American Express; Richard Parsons (center), chairman and CEO of Time Warner, Inc.; and Stan O'Neal (right), chairman, president, and CEO of Merrill Lynch.* (Source: Getty Images)

hold prominent roles, this shift in the ownership composition of businesses headed by African Americans is a signal of important changes in access.

Also as in the case of women, however, the penetration made by African Americans into business circles appears meager, leading many observers to focus on continued disadvantages. A survey of twenty-five leading business schools in 2002 showed the percentage of African American students to be about 5 percent, only a slight improvement over the proportion of African Americans in comparable schools in 1999. The authors of the study decried the "snail-like progress" being made by African Americans in business school enrollment; they cited legal challenges to race-based affirmative action programs as the cause for drops of 25 percent or more in African American enrollment at the MBA programs of certain state universities. The study highlighted the University of Texas, where African Americans constituted less than 1 percent of MBA students, and the University of California, Los Angeles, and University of California, Berkeley, business schools, where just 3.2 percent and 2.1 percent, respectively, of those enrolled were African American.[19] As an illustration of the new variety of perspectives on minority opportunities, however, all three of those business schools appeared in a 2002 list of the top ten MBA programs for Hispanic students, as rated by *Hispanic Business* magazine.

The University of Texas topped the list for its "extensive support" of Hispanics, who made up 14 percent of the total MBA enrollment. UCLA ranked number seven in the *Hispanic Business* survey, showing 10 percent Hispanic enrollment, and UC Berkeley ranked number ten (9 percent Hispanic).[20]

The advance of "newer" minorities such as Hispanic Americans and Asian Americans in business leadership continues to boost diversity statistics, even if it obscures the less rosy situation of African Americans. The National Society of Hispanic MBAs, founded in 1988, claimed six thousand members in 2005, as many as the National Black MBA Association, though the Hispanic organization has existed less than half as long.[21] In the MBA pipeline, the presence of foreign students is yet another complicating factor for those wishing to decipher trends in U.S. minority access. White, non-Hispanic U.S. students received about 65 percent of MBAs awarded by U.S. schools in 1999–2000, a lower share than the proportion of such students obtaining degrees as doctors, lawyers, or other professions.[22] Taken on its own, this statistic suggests minorities found an open door in MBA programs. Students earning MBAs in the United States, however, include a sizable percentage of nonresident aliens, a population cohort largely not found in other professional programs. That group (whose racial makeup is not reported in institutional statistics) exceeded 16 percent of those receiving MBA degrees in 1999–2000, nearly equaling the percentage of all U.S. minorities combined.[23] In the most prestigious MBA programs, the percentages of foreign students averaged even higher, hovering at or above 30 percent of the graduating class, almost always higher than the percentage of U.S. minorities (figure 8-3).

Globalization is obviously playing its own part in shifting the composition of business leadership. The only Hispanic or Asian leaders on our twentieth-century list were foreign born, and many more recent successful leaders with those backgrounds came from abroad as well. Nor are these groups uniform in their advances. Different countries of origin present different levels of economic prosperity, and Asian or Hispanic immigrants with higher-status backgrounds are likely to find their way upward faster. Asians and Hispanics who were born outside the United States and who have already succeeded in the hallowed halls of established corporations include Hector Ruiz (born in Mexico), president and CEO of Advanced Micro Devices; Andrea Jung (born in Canada to Chinese immigrant parents), CEO of Avon Products, Inc.; John Chen (born in Hong Kong), president and CEO of Sybase; Indra Nooyi (born

**FIGURE 8-3**

## Foreign students exceed U.S. minorities at most top business schools

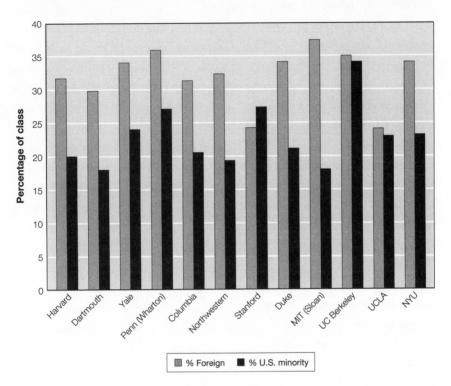

*Source*: Individual institution Web sites. Statistics for class of 2004 at Dartmouth University, Yale University, University of Pennsylvania, Duke University, University of California—Berkeley, University of California—Los Angeles, and New York University; class of 2003 at Stanford University; class of 2002 at Harvard and Northwestern universities; fall 2002 enrollment at Columbia University; and class of 2000 at Massachusetts Institute of Technology. It is not always clear whether the percentages of U.S. minority students reported by schools refer to the percentage of the class as a whole or the percentage of U.S. students only. This comparison assumes the former, which gives the institutions the benefit of the doubt by suggesting the highest possible overall proportion.

in India), president and CEO of PepsiCo; Maria Elena Lagomasino (born in Cuba), CEO of J.P. Morgan Private Bank; and, finally, Rajat Gupta (born in India), former managing director of McKinsey and not to be confused with Raj Gupta (also born in India), CEO of Rohm and Haas.

Even with such gains in corporate offices, minorities often still rely on entrepreneurship as a significant path to business success. There are already signs, particularly in the technology sector, of just how big a force foreign-born entrepreneurs can be. In Silicon Valley, Chinese and Indian entrepreneurs headed 29 percent of all firms started up between 1995 and 1998, for example.[24] Again, "frontier" industrial arenas such as the Internet and its related opportunities presented open territory for those on the outside of the majority business networks. As with women-owned businesses, minority-owned businesses are multiplying at rates faster than those of other firms, echoing the trend of outsider entrepreneurship in the previous century. In 2002, Hispanic-owned firms outnumbered those of African Americans or Asian Americans, although Asian Americans owned the most firms with paid employees and had the highest average revenues.[25]

Many Hispanic Americans have started businesses with an ethnic-affinity focus similar to that of earlier African American–owned media or financial companies, but others have achieved notable mass market successes. Real estate developer Jorge Perez, of Cuban family roots but born in Argentina. spearheaded pricy condominium developments in Florida and elsewhere, creating a company with over $2.1 billion in 2004 revenue.[26] While Hispanic-owned businesses tend to be concentrated in Sun Belt states such as Florida, Texas, and California, along with concentrations of the Hispanic American population, the current economic growth in those areas of the United States means that Hispanic Americans, unlike African Americans in the early twentieth century, find themselves in an entrepreneurial hotbed rather than a

*Andrea Jung (left), chairman and CEO of Avon Products, Inc.; Hector Ruiz (center), chairman and CEO of Advanced Micro Devices, Inc.; and Indra Nooyi (right), president and CEO of PepsiCo.* (Sources: left and center, Getty Images; right, Zack Seckler/CORBIS)

business backwater. With the projected growth of Asian American and Hispanic American populations, it's hard to envision that a comparable list of top American business leaders for the first half of the twenty-first century wouldn't be at least 15 percent minority. The overall figure approaches the proportion at which U.S. minorities as a whole currently earn MBAs, and, while the figure may sound conservative, it is more than double the level of minority representation in the previous half-century. For African Americans, however, the picture is not as encouraging. Although the nature of the companies led by African Americans has undeniably broadened, the low growth in the number of MBAs for this group offers little hope that, by 2050, the proportion of top leadership for African Americans will have increased much beyond the 4 percent seen in the prior century.

## What About Ragged Dick?

Ironically, after legislation has done what it can to eliminate barriers based on race and gender, the most persistent hurdle to be overcome on the way to business leadership remains the one that faced Ragged Dick—that is, being poor. As statistics showed, very little changed in the economic backgrounds of our business leaders over the century; from the beginning to the end of the period the leadership group was dominated by individuals from the middle and upper middle class. Regardless of whether someone's parent, grandparent, or distant ancestor lived the Horatio Alger story of rising from poverty, the present generation is better positioned for success because of that heritage. Today's rising class of leaders may not be as likely as in former generations to inherit an enterprise from a tycoon father, but today's group is just as likely, or more so, to be dominated by the offspring of prosperous doctors, lawyers, or engineers. Indeed, most of the white women and Asian Americans forming an increased presence in corporate leadership found open doors because of educational credentials supported by their relatively affluent socioeconomic origins rather than because of any genuine broadening of minds in the majority "white male" American business culture. Economic advantages explain in part why members of those outsider groups, though still underrepresented at the top, moved from the back room to the boardroom at a pace exceeding that of African Americans or Hispanic Americans. On our list of twentieth-century leaders, family assets opened up opportunities for relative outsiders ranging from Jacob Schiff to his granddaughter Dorothy, and the twenty-first century promises to be no different.

Parental assets may not directly pave the way into the business leadership club, but they enhance the chances of obtaining the increasingly critical educational qualifications for such opportunities. Someone lacking conventional education can still stake a claim on the frontiers of technology with a brilliant discovery or insight; on our list of twentieth-century successes, Edwin Land of Polaroid, Bill Gates of Microsoft, and Michael Dell of Dell Computers are examples of leaders who took that path. Though none of the three finished college, however, they could be termed discretionary dropouts. That is, their parents had the means to pay tuition if these budding entrepreneurs had elected to stay in school. Socioeconomic disadvantages, however, reduce the likelihood that even a gifted child will finish college. In a study tracking a group of eighth-grade students in 1988 who had all scored in the top quartile of mathematics aptitude on a standardized test, less than 30 percent from the lowest socioeconomic quartile had obtained a bachelor's degree twelve years later, while nearly three-quarters of those from the highest socioeconomic quartile had done so.[27]

Parental education in particular, often linked with wealth, remains a strong factor in predicting an individual's likelihood of attending and completing college, a critical step now that educational qualifications act as such a prominent filter on access to leadership. A study of 1992 high school graduates, for instance, revealed that over 92 percent of graduates who had at least one parent with a college diploma were enrolled in college within two years of graduation, while less than 60 percent of those whose parents had high school diplomas or less were enrolled.[28] Similarly, a study of individuals entering postsecondary education in 1989 showed that only 13 percent of those whose parents were not college educated had obtained a bachelor's degree five years later, a proportion less than half that of other students. Almost half of the first-generation college students had left without obtaining any type of postsecondary degree—vocational, associate's, or otherwise.[29] In some hopeful instances, however, the disadvantages dissipate. Of the 1992 high school graduates studied who gained acceptance to a four-year college, almost 90 percent successfully enrolled, with no significant differences in the level of enrollment between groups with differing levels of parental education.[30] Financial aid can definitely open the door to college for students without socioeconomic advantages. Given that open door, first-generation students who persisted to a bachelor's degree were shown in one study to obtain initial employment and salaries comparable to fellow graduates with college-educated parents, and to be as likely as those peers to enter MBA programs.[31] The idea that higher education creates a level playing field regardless of origins is legitimate—the catch is that lower socioeconomic origins continue to stack the odds against completing higher education in the first place.

Awareness of these challenges has prompted elite schools to consider ways to increase the proportion of enrolled students from lower socioeconomic classes. In 2004, Harvard University, after revealing statistics that showed less than 7 percent of its U.S. students came from the lowest quartile of socioeconomic status, announced a new financial aid plan that eliminated any requirement of parental contribution toward tuition from families earning less than forty thousand dollars per year.[32] Others advocate an even more aggressive approach that would give preference, when choosing between applicants with relatively equal levels of achievement, to the applicant of lower socioeconomic status.[33] So long as education remains the primary gateway to business leadership, institutional actions that help boost college enrollment for those with socioeconomic disadvantages remain critical to broaden leadership composition. An elite education is one of the few weapons an outsider can obtain to neutralize the advantages in business access that inevitably accrue to the offspring of well-established families.

The problems for socioeconomic outsiders pursuing business success are exacerbated by changes in the openings for entrepreneurship. In a geographic sense, few U.S. regions present the frontier profile of "clean slate" economic development and rapid population growth that the West did in the early twentieth century, for example. The biggest businesses increasingly maintain national and even global operations that make finding local footholds more difficult, and a successful newcomer is likely to be gobbled up by a larger firm before growing to scale. In an industrial sense, the obvious frontiers center on technology—the Internet or health sciences, for example—making education at least as much of a prerequisite for entrepreneurship as for corporate life. The dominance of MBA-carrying venture capitalists in these arenas also means that access to funds or leadership roles is likely to be restricted to those possessing a similar educational credential. Entertainment and professional athletics are, effectively, the only remaining avenues whereby someone without a diploma can build the kind of wealth that provides easy access to business opportunities, but these endeavors are limited to a select and talented, not to mention lucky, few. The bootstrapping options available to earlier generations, such as the generation of immigrants who originally built the film industry, appear elusive today, particularly when the needs for capital to enter prominent areas of opportunity seem to be rising. To the extent that entrepreneurial entry points have declined in number, poorer candidates face reduced prospects for business achievement.

In Horatio Alger's writings, a benefactor told Ragged Dick, "Poverty in early life is no bar to a man's advancement."[34] This may be true in the strictest sense: unlike race or sex, growing up in a poor family has never absolutely excluded candidates from business opportunities. Such a background does, however, present a daunting obstacle that shows no sign of diminishing as the wealth gap between richest and poorest, both in America and the world, continues to grow. There exist no benchmarking organizations to measure the advancement of poorer candidates into business leadership, as such organizations do for women and racial minority groups, meaning that the dimension of socioeconomic diversity is easier to ignore. For all these reasons, a mid-twenty-first-century list of leaders seems highly unlikely to improve on the 30 percent proportion of leaders coming from poor backgrounds on our twentieth-century list. Indeed, even maintaining that level may be less likely than attaining the projected increases among women and minorities.

## Clogs in the Pipeline?

Our considerations of the future thus far have largely assumed a continuation of the picture we saw shaping access to U.S. business leadership in the late twentieth century—that the MBA would be as much if not more significant as a leadership qualification than it now is, and that professional management career paths would largely continue to dominate U.S. corporate leadership selection. Under this scenario, access to an MBA can be justified as a strong predictor of access to leadership. However, we've seen that the turns in the road over the twentieth century often surprised those who explored the trends of access to leadership. F. W. Taussig and C. S. Joslyn didn't expect that professional management tracks would provide a countervailing influence against the "caste-like" formation of an inherited ownership class. And Mabel

Newcomer, prescient as she was about the rise of MBAs and educational credentials in leadership qualifications, somewhat misjudged how much education's new prominence would enhance social mobility. Surprises in the future could likewise interfere with the accuracy of our predictions.

One obvious and often-noted element slowing the rise of women MBAs, for example, has been their tendency to drop off the fast track to business leadership at rates higher than those of comparably qualified men, with the women either opting for part-time work or taking time off from careers entirely, often to devote time to child rearing.[35] Although the ratio of difference appears to be dropping, women continue to spend more time on household and parenting responsibilities than men.[36] It remains to be seen how these factors will impact the generation of 1990s MBAs, in which the number of women in elite business schools significantly increased. If women continue to opt out of careers in business at higher rates than men do, that trend would threaten the projected increases of women in leadership. Still, a larger number of women who possess credentials marking them as leadership candidates should translate to some increase in representation for women at the top.

In another scenario, there is potential for change in the value of the MBA itself as an equalizer of access to the leadership track. As the number of such degrees granted in the United States grows, the credential is threatened by a commodity status, which is likely to result in a focus on the "brand" value of MBAs earned at elite institutions. Favoritism toward elite MBAs flows back downstream to imply advantages for those affiliated with certain elite colleges and early-career employers (large investment banks and consulting firms, for example). Such affiliations may offer applicants an edge in getting into the "right" MBA programs, as business colleagues or fellow college alumni who have already earned MBAs constitute a rich network of potential advisers on the admissions process. Again, initiatives to ensure that the educational chain leading to elite undergraduate schools is accessible to those from all backgrounds, and that hiring in key feeder firms and business segments operates with an increasing consciousness of diversity, would be necessary to avoid tighter closure on the path to leadership.

Still another possibility that could increase rather than diminish the dominance of an elite majority in top American corporations is the extent to which corporate leadership posts are filled by external versus internal candidates. Rakesh Khurana, analyzing the characteristics of searches for external CEO candidates, has suggested that searches are often conducted in a relatively closed fashion that narrows the pool of candidates considered and prompts a focus on charisma or other signaling factors at the expense of a substantive exploration of capabilities and qualifications.[37] Under the hot lights of today's high-powered financial press and heightened investor scrutiny, even a CEO with mixed performance at another company can have perceived public-image advantages over "slow and steady" internal climbers. In search of a name that will bump up the stock price, particularly when the market implicitly demands change in the face of bad numbers, board members are likely to jump at the "star" outsider candidate. Connections formed via elite educational networks can also enhance the star's reputation or bring him or her to a board member's attention. Though the numbers are small, there is some hint of this phenomenon in the late twentieth century: on our list, CEOs hired from the outside into top roles in the 1980s and 1990s were over four times more likely than internally promoted leaders to have both undergraduate *and* graduate degrees from Ivy League schools. In other words, the profile of outside hires more closely matches that of prototypical insiders to business circles.

Finally, there remains the very real question of whether a century from now, the composition of American business leadership will still be defined as we think of it today. Global conglomerates, spread more and more broadly across national boundaries, have made the location of an organization's headquarters less and less determinative of its identity, changing our sense of who American business leaders are. DaimlerChrysler executives, for example, are by no means American business leaders in anything like the sense that Lee Iacocca of Chrysler clearly was. In fact, DaimlerChrysler, with 45 percent of its revenues and over a quarter of its employees in the United States, had in 2005 only one American among its ten board members, of whom eight were German and one Canadian, all of them white males.[38] This all-male composition is quite different from what's increasingly expected of boards in comparably-sized U.S. companies.

For U.S.-based firms operating globally, exporting American ideals of diversity based upon race and gender is not easy. A recent study of European subsidiaries of U.S.-based multinational firms illustrated the forms that local resistance can take. European managers voiced frustration at a one-size-fits-all diversity program that included American-specific language such as references to the Ku Klux Klan.[39] Some managers in the situation responded by redefining the dimensions of diversity to focus on the relative lack of non-American personnel in top management. This tactic points to yet another way global businesses may impact the composition of leadership: if employees from other nations take top positions at the expense of U.S.-born minority candidates, is it a victory or a setback for diversity? American ideals of diversity, in short, may or may not carry the day in global companies, and this will affect top leadership composition in the future.

## Facing the Old Legacies in a New Century

In considering how the trends we observed in the twentieth century will continue in the twenty-first century, we arrived at different conclusions for different outsider groups. For women, increased enrollment in MBA programs should continue to increase their numbers in leadership, perhaps to a level as high as 20 percent of top business leaders in the first half of the new century. For African Americans and others who are outsiders because of ethnicity, the group's penetration into leadership over a wide range of industries and large publicly held companies is encouraging. However, the growth trend in business leadership looks stronger for Asian Americans and Hispanic Americans than it does for African Americans. While we project overall growth to a level of 15 percent nonwhite representation in top business leadership over the next fifty years, there is little reason from present trends to expect that representation for African Americans in particular will increase much over the 4 percent level in our list for the twentieth century. Finally, for those who are outsiders by virtue of low socioeconomic status, there is no question that disadvantages will endure and may even increase if countermeasures are not taken to improve college enrollment and persistence among first-generation collegians. A 30 percent representation, as seen on the prior century's list, of those from lower socioeconomic backgrounds will be hard to match in the future.

We acknowledge, however, that our perspective is no less subject to unexpected future developments than the perspectives of past researchers who studied U.S. business leadership composition. Our predictions are subject to contingencies, and we identified several such possible threats to accuracy. The prevalence of women's departures from the career track could diminish their projected increase in leadership. The proliferation of MBAs could accelerate formation of a new status structure that distinguishes elite MBAs from the crowd of degree holders, a system that would renew the advantages of elite families. More recruitment of CEOs from outside the organization to head top firms could revive the importance of elite networks in identifying leadership candidates. What is perhaps most significant, the expansion of multinational businesses could change conceptions of diversity altogether, meaning that race and gender differences take a back seat to those of nationality.

Both our conjectures about the next century and our consideration of potential roadblocks, though, pale in importance to larger questions: Why does it matter? Why should Americans care about how the paths to business leadership operate? We feel that when a nation screens its leaders, whether in business or otherwise, by qualities not related to their competence, it suffers a competitive disadvantage by failing to place the best people in power. As the emerging global economy presents increasing challenges to our country's position of economic leadership, the question of what kinds of biases persist in corporate America becomes more critical.

At the close of the twentieth century, we saw business leadership largely bidding good-bye to screening by social factors such as religious denomination and national origin, factors which governed leadership selection earlier in the century. As the twenty-first century began, even the more stubbornly held exclusionary barriers toward women and ethnic minorities seemed to be falling, albeit by dint of legislation rather than enlightenment. Previous screening factors have been superseded by a new common denominator of educational attainment—at minimum a college degree, and increasingly an MBA—which constitutes the ticket for possible admission to the upper ranks of business. Practitioners of the all-too-human instinct to open doors for, and follow, leaders "like us" are largely swearing a new allegiance to the "tribe of MBA." For members of this tribe, more and more of the old barriers to entry are no longer relevant.

What remains undeniable, however, is that disadvantages in income and education are still sustained through generations. Just as was the case throughout the twentieth century, today only an exceptional individual can break through socioeconomic barriers and rise to business leadership. Because educational attainments, including the MBA, continue to be linked to socioeconomic origins, use of education as the filtering mechanism for leaders still skews the selection toward middle-class and higher socioeconomic groups. This skewing, in turn, remains harmful to the country's competitiveness, if we assume that competence in leadership is not confined to the advantaged and educated set. Ultimately, the generational cycle of advantages cannot be eliminated without a challenge to the principles of capitalism itself, but the imbalance can be ameliorated by intentional business practices, public policies, and philanthropic activities that acknowledge the wealth gap and reach across it to offer opportunities, especially in education. In other words, in this brave new era, hard work and benefactors remain the keys to business success for the disadvantaged—whatever progress we'd like to think we see, Alger's formula has not changed a bit.

# "Great American Business Leaders of the 20th Century Database"; Background and Data

### *Leader Selection*

The individuals included in this book were drawn from the "Great American Business Leaders of the 20th Century" database, which was compiled by the Harvard Business School Leadership Initiative from 2001 through 2004. The dataset was initially used as the basis of Anthony J. Mayo and Nitin Nohria's *In Their Time: The Greatest Business Leaders of the Twentieth Century* (Boston: Harvard Business School Press, 2005). The methodology used to select the one thousand business leaders in the database was outlined in the appendix of *In Their Time*, and we have reproduced significant portions of that section here.[1]

The candidates that were included in our pool of one thousand business executives had to have been a founder or chief executive officer (CEO) of a U.S.-based company for at least five years between 1900 and 2000. Consequently, any CEO whose tenure began after 1996 was automatically excluded. At the other end of the century, we included individuals whose tenures began before 1900 if they held the CEO or top company official position for at least five years in the first decade. For the earlier decades of the twentieth century, we drew on the work of Richard S. Tedlow, Courtney Purrington, and Kim Eric Bettcher. In their working paper, "The American CEO in the Twentieth Century: Demography and Career Path," they chronicle the evolution of the CEO title, citing its first official use in business in 1917 by the U.S. Steel Corporation. In accordance with their research findings, we have chosen to designate an individual a CEO, regardless of specific title, if he or she was regarded as the primary and, sometimes, sole individual setting the company's direction, allocating resources, and monitoring its progress.[2] Prior to the common usage of the CEO title, the top company business official may have been labeled president, partner, managing director, or chairman. Several candidates on our list, especially those whose tenures occurred before 1920, held one of these titles. Whenever a company used the CEO title (typically after 1917), this individual was always chosen for our study.

We used a minimum five-year tenure screen to ensure that we captured a relevant time frame in which a CEO or founder could make an impact on an organization. The five-year tenure was adapted from a research study conducted by John J. Gabarro, who evaluated the timing of an executive's impact on an organization. Through his research on the process of taking charge, Gabarro determined that a new executive's full impact on a company was not felt immediately, but over the course of several months in office. Further, a full assimilation of all the executive-level decisions of the previous administration typically took two years. The first few years also provided an opportunity for a business official to set his or her strategic course of direction and to determine its initial impact on the organization. According to Gabarro's study, new executives orchestrated their most significant structural changes during their third year within the organization. Although his study examined the actions of senior executives, not necessarily CEOs, we believe that his findings are applicable to CEOs.[3] In fact, the taking-charge process for CEOs is often considerably shorter and scrutinized even more closely. By using a minimum five-year tenure threshold, we believe that we provided a conservative time frame in which CEOs could have a meaningful and lasting impact on the performance of their company. As a point of reference, the average CEO tenures for our pool of business executives ranged from a high of thirty years in the beginning part of the century to just under eight years today. Beyond this five-year-tenure requirement, business executives had to have achieved either, or both, of two specific accomplishments: demonstrate at least four consecutive years of top financial performance or lead a business or service that changed the way Americans lived, worked, or interacted in the twentieth century.

The financial performance criteria were demonstrated through three primary metrics: (1) Tobin's Q performance (market to book value), (2) return-on-assets ratios, and (3) market-value appreciation. Given the sparse availability of easily accessible and complete financial information across the twentieth century (especially before 1925), we used a multitiered financial-analysis approach. Through a combination of manual research in Moody's and Standard & Poor's references, we captured asset performance for the two hundred largest U.S. corporations (defined by gross sales or revenues) between 1900 and 1925. This initial set of companies was drawn from research on the largest industrial corporations in the United States in 1917.[4] Using the CRSP (Center for Research in Security Prices) database of the Wharton School of the University of Pennsylvania, we evaluated market-value appreciation data between 1925 and 1950 for the 1,250 largest companies in the United States.

Finally, we used the Compustat Database to obtain performance metrics for all three variables (Tobin's Q, return on assets, and market-value appreciation) between 1950 and 2000 for the largest 1,250 companies in the United States (ranked by gross sales or revenue). CEOs who produced at least four consecutive years of top-level performance on at least one of these metrics were included. Top-level performance was defined as having achieved a financial metric (Tobin's Q, return on assets, or market-value appreciation) within the top 10 percent of all businesses for a given year. Being a part of the top 10 percent of any of these metrics for four consecutive years earned the CEO a spot on our list. The financial-screening process yielded approximately 260 candidates.

Measuring a leader's impact on society, on business, or on both is admittedly a subjective task. Approximately three-quarters of the individuals included in our candidate pool of one thousand did not qualify when we applied our financial thresholds. The bulk of these individuals were culled from an extensive review of historical biographical references and business rankings. The rankings included historical lists by *Fortune*, *Forbes*, *Time*, the *Wall Street Journal*, the *New York Times*, business encyclopedias, and other sources. A list of references is included in the bibliography. In many cases, these individuals were cited for the advances that they made in American business—opening new markets, creating industries, instituting modern management practices, or advancing technology. Though dominated by *Fortune* 100–type CEOs, the list is much broader. It endeavors to capture impact beyond that simply created by size of enterprise, and it seeks to capture individuals outside the normal or traditional business realm. As a result, the list includes heads of many smaller businesses. Leaders of small businesses who made our list were typically recognized because they built business legacies that endured the test of time, because they opened up new opportunities for others, or because they did both. Many women and minority group members on our list are individuals who broke through barriers to establish themselves in business, thereby forging a path for future generations.

Given the thousands and thousands of individuals who served as the heads of both large, public enterprises and small, private ones during the last hundred years, we have sought to capture only the small fraction who sit at the pinnacle of success—individuals whose accomplishments were truly lasting and noteworthy. Though we tried to be vigilant in the selection, our personal judgments and interpretations of historical information played a significant role. As a result, there is certainly room to argue with some of our choices. Throughout this book, we have only been able to profile a few dozen individuals in depth. Information on all one thousand business leaders is included on the HBS Leadership Initiative Web site, http://www.hbs.edu/leadership/.

### *Attribute Coding*

All attributes were coded on the basis of research through biographical dictionaries, biographies, newspaper and magazine articles, company histories, and other relevant sources, including *Who Was Who in America, Moody's Industrial Manuals,* and *Standard & Poor's Register of Corporations, Directors, and Executives.* No questions were directed to living leaders to fill in gaps, although once the list was made public on the HBS Leadership Initiative Web site, members of leaders' families have contacted the Leadership Initiative with some corrections. The following section outlines the specific coding process for several demographic characteristics that were used extensively in this publication.

> *Path to success:* Leaders were categorized as *founders* if they either began their enterprise from scratch or acquired a budding or troubled enterprise and shepherded it to success. *Family business leaders* were those who joined and led an enterprise owned or substantially controlled by family members or in-laws. Those who married into a family *after* joining an enterprise

(as in the case of Jacob Schiff at Kuhn, Loeb) were not considered family leaders. Those whose fathers or other family members preceded them in the management of an enterprise that was not family controlled also were not considered family leaders. All leaders not fitting the founder or family business leader definition were classed as *other CEOs*.

*Company location:* The location of the company headed by a leader was coded on the basis of the site of the company's headquarters during the leader's tenure as CEO. If a company's headquarters moved during the tenure, the site that was used for the longest or most significant period of leadership was chosen.

*CEO tenure:* The years of CEO tenure were dated from when a leader began and then subsequently terminated serving in the role that placed him or her in effective control of the firm's operations. For most leaders, it began when they acquired the title of CEO and ended when they relinquished it, even though the title of chairman was commonly taken or retained by many at that stage. As outlined above, the use of such titles was inconsistent throughout the century, so some judgment was exercised in determining what constituted a leader's taking control or retiring.

*Colleges:* Undergraduate colleges were only recorded for leaders who could be reliably identified through consulted sources as having earned a bachelor's degree. Colleges were not coded for those who dropped out short of graduation, however much progress they made toward a degree, or for those who earned junior college degrees or other nonbaccalaureate degrees. Graduate degrees and schools were only recorded for those confirmed to have earned a master's level degree or higher, with the exception of law school graduates. (Those receiving LLB degrees after first receiving a different bachelor's degree were recorded as completing graduate studies.)

*Religion:* Religious affiliation was coded on the basis of evidence suggesting a leader's adult identification with the religion, not just evidence of the religious affiliation of his or her parents. Charitable involvements and sites of funeral services were used as evidence of affiliation in some cases.

*Socioeconomic status:* Leaders were coded as *wealthy, middle class*, or *poor* where there was available evidence of the economic status of the family during the years of the leader's childhood and adolescence. Generally, a *wealthy* code was reserved for those of notable wealth for their era, an assessment based on contemporary descriptions of the family's wealth or status and other evidence such as college attended and manner of life. For instance, a leader embarking on a European tour prior to beginning college would be likely to be classified as wealthy. As with *wealthy*, the *poor* coding was reserved for those for whom evidence of hardship such as early childhood employment, limited education, or parental absence was known. *Middle class* thus includes a broad grouping of leaders whose backgrounds range from simple but comfortable working-class homes through relatively prosperous upper-middle-class lifestyles. In the absence of some specific description of the leader's early family life, no code for socioeconomic status was assigned.

*Industry codes:* A code was assigned to the leader on the basis of the industry considered to dominate the firm's activities during his or her tenure. The codes in general conform to the top-level industry classifications provided by OneSource, a business information service owned by infoUSA. However, additional classifications were introduced to identify more explicitly a range of activities commonly grouped under the broad heading of *services*. Subcategories for publishing, broadcast media, and hospitality industries were created. Also, a single category, personal and home products, was created distinct from the industrial *chemicals* coding. In total, the coding used included twenty-one industry classifications:

1. Agriculture and mining
2. Automotive and aerospace
3. Chemicals, industrial
4. Communications
5. Computers and electronics
6. Construction and real estate
7. Fabric and apparel
8. Fabricated goods
9. Finance
10. Food and tobacco
11. Health care
12. Metals
13. Retail
14. Services
15. Transportation
16. Utilities and energy
17. Wood, paper, and forestry
18. Restaurants and lodging
19. Personal care and home products
20. Publishing and print media
21. Entertainment and broadcast media

Because industry focus, like company location, is subject to change over time, the industry code was selected based on the category best describing the company's activities during the leader's tenure.

### *"Unknown" Codes*

The fields with the largest proportion of unknown values were religious affiliation, father's occupation, and family socioeconomic status. Leaders with unknown values in these categories were more likely to fall into the category of *other CEOs*, because of the larger proportion of leaders following this path to success later in the century, a time period for which biographical compilations were less likely to be available. Arguably, the disproportionate absence of detailed information for *other CEOs* may also be due to the tendency of popular biographical accounts to provide more early-life details in the start-up stories of entrepreneurs. Religious affiliation was the hardest code to ascertain, with approximately 46 percent of leaders (mostly in the second half of the century) having unknown affiliations. Unknown family socioeconomic status or father's occupation also was more prevalent for leaders after 1950, but was confined to only about 20 percent for each of those attributes over the century. Approximately 11 percent of leaders overall had unknown values for all three characteristics. By comparing the other characteristics (e.g., birthplace, education, path to success) of this uncoded group with the group of leaders whose attributes for these categories are known, we can make the case that the majority of these leaders with unknown attributes are probably, like the majority of the leaders in the group with known attributes, nominally Protestant individuals of middle-class upbringing. No data fields other than these three (religious affiliation, father's occupation, and family socioeconomic status) had a percentage of unknown values in excess of 1 percent.

## Chapter 1

1. Horatio Alger Jr., *Ragged Dick, or, Street Life in New York with the Boot Blacks* (New York: Signet Classic/New American Library edition, 1990), 77 and 185.

2. Charles R. Geisst, *The Last Partnerships: Inside the Great Wall Street Money Dynasties* (New York: McGraw-Hill, 2001), 49.

3. Among studies of the elite from a variety of periods, see C. Wright Mills, *The Power Elite* (New York: Oxford University Press, 1956); William Miller, "American Historians and the Business Elite," *Journal of Economic History* 9, no. 2 (November 1949): 184–208; Michael Useem, "The Inner Group of the American Capitalist Class," *Social Problems* 25 (February 1978): 225–240; Richard L. Zweigenhaft and G. William Domhoff, *Diversity in the Power Elite: Have Women and Minorities Reached the Top?* (New Haven, CT: Yale University Press, 1998); E. Digby Baltzell, *The Protestant Establishment: Aristocracy and Caste in America* (New York: Random House, 1964); Ferdinand Lundberg, *America's 60 Families* (New York: Vanguard Press, 1937); Pitirim Sorokin, "American Millionaires and Multi-Millionaires: A Comparative Statistical Study," *Journal of Social Forces* 3, no. 4 (May 1925): 627–640.

4. Among the more notable of such historical studies, see F. W. Taussig and C. S. Joslyn, *American Business Leaders: A Study in Social Origins and Stratification* (New York: Macmillan, 1932); C. Wright Mills, "The American Business Elite: A Collective Portrait," in "The Tasks of Economic History," supplement, *Journal of Economic History* 5 (December 1945): 20–44; W. Lloyd Warner and James C. Abegglen, *Big Business Leaders in America* (New York: Harper and Brothers, 1955); Mabel Newcomer, *The Big Business Executive: The Factors That Made Him, 1900–1950* (New York: Columbia University Press, 1955); Peter Temin, "The Stability of the American Business Elite," *Industrial and Corporate Change* 8 (June 1999): 189–210; Richard S. Tedlow, Kim Eric Bettcher, and Courtney A. Purrington, "The Chief Executive Officer of the Large American Industrial Corporation in 1917," *Business History Review* 77 (winter 2003): 687–701.

## Chapter 2

1. Proportions compiled from U.S. Census data, Historical Statistics Compilation HS-4, "Resident Population by State: 1900 to 2002," http://www.census.gov/statab/hist/ 02HS0004.xls; and for periods prior to 1900, U.S Census Bureau, *Statistical Abstract of the United States: 2004–2005*, 124th ed. (Washington, DC: 2004), 7, available at http://www .census.gov/prod/2004pubs/04statab/pop.pdf; and Historical Census Browser, University of Virginia, Geospatial and Statistical Data Center, http://fisher.lib.virginia.edu/ collections/stats/histcensus/index.html.

2. U.S. Department of the Interior, *Report on the Manufactures of the United States at the Tenth Census* (June 1, 1880) (Washington, DC: Government Printing Office, 1883), 7–8.

3. Our comparison used numbers of U.S.-born white males, aged eighteen to forty-four, as determined in the 1900 Census and as obtained from U.S. Department of Commerce and Labor, *Statistical Abstract of the United States, 1903* (Washington, DC: Government Printing Office, 1904), 492–493, available at http://www2.census.gov/prod2/statcomp/documents/1903-02.pdf.

4. Herkimer County Historical Society, *Story of the Typewriter, 1873–1923* (Herkimer, NY: Press of A. H. Kellogg Company, 1923), 31.

5. Richard N. Current, *The Typewriter and the Men Who Made It* (Urbana: University of Illinois Press, 1954), 61.

6. "Henry H. Benedict, Art Patron, Dead," *New York Times*, June 13, 1935, 23.

7. Herkimer County Historical Society, *Story of the Typewriter*, 64.

8. Ibid., 84.

9. Current, *The Typewriter*, 105.

10. Herkimer County Historical Society, *Story of the Typewriter*, 89.

11. Additional sources: Donald R. Hoke, *Ingenious Yankees: The Rise of the American System of Manufactures in the Private Sector* (New York: Columbia University Press, 1990), 132–150; Bruce Bliven Jr., *The Wonderful Writing Machine* (New York: Random House, 1954); Alden Hatch, *Remington Arms in American History* (New York: Rinehart & Company, 1956), 167–176.

12. William P. Tolley, *Smith Corona Typewriters and H. W. Smith* (New York: Newcomen Society, 1951), 13.

13. Quoted in ibid., 18.

14. Quoted in John A. Zellers, *The Typewriter: A Short History, on Its 75th Anniversary, 1873–1948* (New York: Newcomen Society, 1948), 17.

15. Economic backgrounds of leaders were defined as poor, middle class, wealthy, or unknown, on the basis of available biographical data. See the appendix for more details. Percentages calculated are of those whose background could be identified.

16. Elmer M. Shankland, "Gordon Rentschler," in *America's 50 Foremost Business Leaders*, ed. B. C. Forbes (New York: B. C. Forbes & Sons Publishing, 1948), 477.

17. "George Adam Rentschler," in *A History and Biographical Cyclopaedia of Butler County, Ohio* (Cincinnati: Western Biographical Publishing, 1882), available at www.rootsweb.com/~ohbutler/cyc/356.htm.

18. "Historical Sketch," Archives of the Flood of 1913, Dayton Metro Library Web page, home.dayton.lib.oh.us/Archives/Flood1913/FloodHistorSketch.html.

19. "City Bank's New Chief Rose Rapidly to Power," *New York Times*, April 7, 1929, XX5.

20. "George Adam Rentschler Weds Rita Rend Mitchell," *New York Times*, November 12, 1936, 32.

21. "G. S. Rentschler, Financier, Is Dead," *New York Times*, March 5, 1948, 21.

22. "History of Niles," www.niles-simmons.de/englisch_neu/chronik/chronik_content1.htm.

23. Additional sources: *The Pratt & Whitney Aircraft Story* (Hartford, CT: Pratt & Whitney Aircraft Division of United Aircraft Corporation, 1950); "Engineering Success:

Pratt & Whitney Aircraft, 1925–1940," *Business & Economic History* 27, no. 1 (October 11, 1998): 162ff.; "F. B. Rentschler, Air Leader, Dead," *New York Times*, April 26, 1956, 33; United Technologies Web page, www.utc.com; John N. Ingham, "Rentschler, Frederick Bent," in *Biographical Dictionary of American Business Leaders* (Westport, CT: Greenwood Press, 1983), 1,153–1,154.

24. William H. Whyte Jr., "The Corporation and the Wife," *Fortune*, November 1951, 109.

25. "In Praise of the Ornery Wife," *Fortune*, November 1951, 75.

26. William H. Whyte Jr., *The Organization Man* (New York: Doubleday & Company, 1956), 192–193.

27. Osborn Elliott, *Men at the Top* (New York: Harper and Brothers, 1959), 106.

28. "Minnesota Mining—A New Ball Game?" *Forbes*, July 1, 1976, 34.

29. "3M Chooses 'Delegation of Authority,'" *BusinessWeek*, September 24, 1949, 26, 32, and 34.

30. "3M's Way: Patents Plus Labs," *BusinessWeek*, October 4, 1958, 126.

31. Jack B. Weiner, "3M: Management, Marketing and Momentum," *Dun's Review* 89, no. 3 (March 1967): 76.

32. Lee Smith, "Lures and Limits of Innovation," *Fortune*, October 20, 1980, 86.

33. Thomas Gunning, "3M Taps Former Omahan as New Chairman, CEO," *Omaha World-Herald*, February 11, 1986 (via Factiva).

34. Additional sources: "Herbert Buetow, Manufacturer, 73," *New York Times*, January 11, 1972, 40; Lee Egerstrom, "Former 3M CEO, Minnesota Civic Leader [Bert Cross] Dies," *St. Paul Pioneer Press*, May 11, 2001, 9B (via Dow Jones Interactive); "Raymond Herzog, 81, Executive," *New York Times*, July 22, 1997, A17; Richard Gibson, "Minnesota Mining's Allen Jacobson Rose to Top Post by Focusing on Bottom Line," *Wall Street Journal*, February 10, 1986, 17.

35. James Marshall, *Elbridge A. Stuart, Founder of Carnation Company* (Los Angeles: Carnation Company, 1949), 25.

36. Ibid., 39.

37. Ibid., 65–66.

38. Paul Dorpat, "Kent's Carnation: When the Hops Failed, Cows and Cans Took Over," *Seattle Times*, February 2, 1986, 15 (via Factiva).

39. Christine Savage Palmer, "Historic Overview: Carnation, Washington," report prepared for the King County, Washington, Cultural Resources Division, Parks, Planning and Resources Department, September 1995, http://www.ci.carnation.wa.us/library/carnation-historical-context.pdf.

40. Additional sources: "Elbridge Stuart, Founded Milk Farm," *New York Times*, January 15, 1944, 13; Priscilla Long, "Carnation Condensed Milk First Manufactured in Kent on September 6, 1899," August 6, 1999, at http://www.historylink.org/essays/output.cfm?file_id=1608; James R. Warren, "Stuart, Elbridge A.," October 11, 1999, at http://www.historylink.org/essays/output.cfm?file_id=1733; John N. Ingham, "Stuart, Elbridge Amos," in *Biographical Dictionary of American Business Leaders* (Westport, CT: Greenwood Press, 1983), 1,396–1,397.

41. John Accola, "Denver Behemoth Had Humble Beginnings," *Rocky Mountain News*, December 11, 1994, 116a (via Factiva).

42. Ken Auletta, "John Malone: Flying Solo," *New Yorker*, February 7, 1994, 54.

43. Ibid.

44. Mark Ivey, Frances Seghers, and Matt Rothman, "The King of Cable TV: Meet the Man Who Makes the Networks Tremble," *BusinessWeek*, October 26, 1987, 88ff. (via Factiva).

45. Auletta, "John Malone," 54.

46. John Accola, "Fast Track to the Top: No. 3 Cable Company Zoomed to Become World's Largest in Only Nine Years," *Rocky Mountain News*, December 11, 1994, 120a (via Factiva).

47. L. J. Davis, "Cable Television: Television's Real-Life Cable Baron," *New York Times*, December 2, 1990, SMA50.

48. Laura Landro, "Tele-Communications Sets Cable-TV Agenda," *Wall Street Journal*, February 11, 1986, 6.

49. Auletta, "John Malone," 53.

50. Geraldine Fabrikant, "The Markets: Marketplace—Tracking the Rich Deals of TCI's Chairman Is No Easy Job," *New York Times*, July 27, 1998, D1.

51. Philip Hamburger, "Ah, Packages!" *New Yorker*, May 10, 1947, 40.

52. Ibid., 41.

53. James R. Warren, "United Parcel Service," September 20, 1999 at http://www.historylink.org/essays/output.cfm?file_id=1679.

54. Hamburger, "Ah, Packages!" 45.

55. "Delivery Specialists," *BusinessWeek*, April 14, 1934, 24–25.

56. Ibid., 24.

57. Additional sources: Wolfgang Saxon, "James E. Casey Is Dead at 95; Started United Parcel Service," *New York Times*, June 7, 1983, B8; William A. Ulman, "Casey the King of the Errand Boys," *Saturday Evening Post* 226, no. 1 (July 4, 1953): 24ff.; "The UPS Story," at www.ups.com/about/story.html.

58. Texas State Library and Archives Commission, "Votes for Women! The Women's Suffrage Movement in Texas," www.tsl.state.tx.us/exhibits/suffrage; Jack Alexander, "Just Call Me C. R.," *Saturday Evening Post* 213, no. 31 (February 1, 1941): 69.

59. George James, "C. R. Smith, Pioneer of Aviation as Head of American, Dies at 90," *New York Times*, April 15, 1990, B13.

60. Alexander, "Just Call Me C. R.," 70.

61. "Amon Carter Dies in Fort Worth; *Star-Telegram* Publisher Was 75," *New York Times*, June 24, 1955, 21.

62. F. Robert van der Linden, *Airlines and Air Mail: The Post Office and the Birth of the Commercial Aviation Industry* (Lexington: University Press of Kentucky, 2002), 237–238.

63. Robert J. Serling, *Eagle: The Story of American Airlines* (New York: St. Martin's Press, 1985), 72.

64. "Confirmed by Mother and Son," *New York Times*, June 9, 1933, 2.

65. Bill Fairley, "FDR's Maverick Son Was Fort Worth Fixture in '30s," *Fort Worth Star-Telegram*, September 4, 2002, 3B; "Elliott Roosevelts Parents of Daughter," *New York Times*, May 10, 1934, 26.

66. On the wedding, see "Elizabeth L. Manget Bride of C. R. Smith," *New York Times*, December 30, 1934, N5; on the job with Barrett, see Fairley, "FDR's Maverick Son."

67. Charles J. Kelly Jr., *The Sky's the Limit* (New York: Coward-McCann, 1963), 220.

68. "American Airlines Had $213,262 Profit," *New York Times*, March 16, 1939, 44; "United Airlines Reports $997,221 Loss for 1938," *Wall Street Journal*, March 17, 1939, 8; "TWA Shows Loss of $773,263 for Year Ended December 31, 1938," *Wall Street Journal*, February 23, 1939, 5.

69. "Airline in the Black," *Fortune*, February 1939, 115.

70. Alexander, "Just Call Me C. R.," 72.

71. "Jets Across the U.S.," *Time*, November 17, 1958, 87.

## Chapter 3

1. Henry Clews, *Fifty Years in Wall Street* (New York: Irving Publishing, 1908), 1,061.

2. Ibid.

3. Ibid., 8.

4. "President Sees New Play," *New York Times*, October 6, 1908, 9; Peter Jennings and Todd Brewster, *In Search of America* (New York: Hyperion, 2002), 249–250.

5. Clews, *Fifty Years in Wall Street*, 1,061.

6. U.S. Department of Commerce, *Statistical Abstract of the United States: 1920* (Washington, DC: Government Printing Office, 1921), 45, available at http://www2.census.gov/prod2/statcomp/documents/1920-01.pdf.

7. Ibid.

8. Ibid.

9. Joseph G. McCoy, *Historic Sketches of the Cattle Trade of the West and Southwest* (Washington, DC: Rare Book Shop, 1932; orig. published 1874), 396.

10. Richard H. Peterson, *The Bonanza Kings: The Social Origins and Business Behavior of Western Mining Entrepreneurs, 1870–1900* (Lincoln: University of Nebraska Press, 1977), 32.

11. "American Smelting Company in Court," *New York Times*, February 17, 1901, 1.

12. "R. L. Livingston Has Heiress Bride," *New York Times*, February 16, 1911, 11.

13. "Pope's Blessing on Burden Wedding," *New York Times*, June 18, 1911, 11.

14. Additional sources: Lewis Atherton, *The Cattle Kings* (Bloomington: Indiana University Press, 1961); John N. Ingham, "Sheedy, Dennis," in *Biographical Dictionary of American Business Leaders* (Westport, CT: Greenwood Press, 1983), 1,289–1,291.

15. Stephen J. Whitefield, "Strange Fruit: The Career of Samuel Zemurray," *American Jewish History* 73, no. 3 (March 1984): 310.

16. "United Fruit II: The Conquest of Honduras," *Fortune*, March 1933, 32.

17. Lester D. Langley and Thomas Schoonover, *The Banana Men: American Mercenaries and Entrepreneurs in Central America, 1880–1930* (Lexington: University Press of Kentucky, 1995), 145–148.

18. Charles Morrow Wilson, *Empire in Green and Gold: The Story of the American Banana Trade* (New York: Henry Holt, 1947), 224–225.

19. Thomas P. McCann, *An American Company: The Tragedy of United Fruit*, ed. Henry Scammell (New York: Crown Publishers, 1976), 21.

20. Additional sources: "Samuel Zemurray, 84, Is Dead; Headed United Fruit Company," *New York Times*, December 2, 1961, 23; United Fruit Historical Society Web site, www.unitedfruit.org.

21. "Does a Star Lose Prestige by Acting for the Movies?" *New York Times*, July 18, 1915, X2.

22. Janet Staiger, "Combination and Litigation: Structures of U.S. Film Distribution, 1896–1917," *Cinema Journal* 23, no. 2 (winter 1984): 45–47.

23. Neil Gabler, *An Empire of Their Own: How the Jews Invented Hollywood* (New York: Doubleday [Anchor], 1988; orig. published by Crown Publishers), 127.

24. John Drinkwater, *The Life and Adventures of Carl Laemmle* (New York: G. P. Putnam's Sons, 1931), 68–71.

25. Bernard F. Dick, *City of Dreams: The Making and Remaking of Universal Pictures* (Lexington: University Press of Kentucky, 1997), 27–29.

26. Gabler, *Empire of Their Own*, 68.

27. Ibid., 30–31; Benjamin B. Hampton, *A History of the Movies* (New York: Covici, Friede Publishers, 1931), 108–110.

28. Hampton, *History of the Movies*, 74.

29. Ibid., 79.

30. Gabler, *Empire of Their Own*, 117.

31. Ibid., 408.

32. A. Scott Berg, *Goldwyn: A Biography* (New York: Alfred A. Knopf, 1989), 63.

33. See, for example, "Goldwyn Scores Film 'Monopolies,'" *New York Times*, January 14, 1948, 31; and "Producers Allege Movie House Trust," *New York Times*, August 25, 1948, 29.

34. Cited in Stephen Birmingham, *"Our Crowd": The Great Jewish Families of New York* (New York: Harper & Row, 1967), 156.

35. Cyrus Adler, *Jacob H. Schiff: His Life and Letters* (New York: Doubleday, Doran & Co., 1929), 1:9.

36. Birmingham, *"Our Crowd,"* 164 and 176.

37. Additional sources: "Made Kuhn, Loeb Co. Big Banking House," *New York Times*, September 26, 1920, 3; Howard Calkins, "Kuhn, Loeb & Co. 75 Years Old Today," *New York Times*, February 1, 1942, F1; "Mrs. Jacob Schiff Dies at Age of 78," *New York Times*, February 27, 1933, 15; John N. Ingham, "Schiff, Jacob Henry," in *Biographical Dictionary of American Business Leaders* (Westport, CT: Greenwood Press, 1983), 1,249–1,253.

38. U.S. Department of Commerce, Bureau of the Census, *Sixteenth Census of the United States: 1940; Population: Nativity and Parentage of the White Population, General Characteristics* (Washington, DC: Government Printing Office, 1943), 194.

39. See, for example, the following items, all from the *New York Times*: "Explosive Teeth," September 16, 1875, 4; "Set Fire to His Eye-Glasses," May 1, 1882, 5; "Flames Visible for Miles," April 15, 1884, 2; "Panic Narrowly Averted," February 27, 1900, 1; and "Celluloid Comb Caught Fire," January 22, 1901, 1.

40. "Swiss Family Dreyfus," *Fortune*, October 1933, 139.

41. Ibid., 140.

42. "Cellulose Co. Changes Name," *New York Times*, April 29, 1927, 34.

43. See these items from the *New York Times*: "Earnings Record Set by Celanese," November 12, 1940, 38; "Sales of Celanese Reach a New High," March 8, 1943, 21; "Celanese Business Reaches a Record," March 7, 1944, 21; "Sales by Celanese Set Record in 1944," March 9, 1945, 26; and "Celanese Report Lists 5 New Highs," March 15, 1949, 46.

44. Additional sources: "Celanese's Origin in Test Tubes; Use Now Wide," *Wall Street Journal*, April 23, 1935, 17; "Camille Dreyfus," *Current Biography Yearbook, 1955*, ed. Marjorie Dent Candee (New York: H. W. Wilson, 1955), 174–175; Celanese Corporation, "Celanese: A Company with a Tradition," Web page, www.celanese.com/index/about_index/history-1999-1980/history-1918-1863.htm; Celanese Acetate LLC, "Our History," Web page, http://www.celaneseacetate.com/index/about_us-acetate/our_history-acetate.htm; Plastics Historical Society, "Celluloid," Web page, www.plastiquarian.com/celluloi.htm.

45. U.S. Department of Homeland Security, *Yearbook of Immigration Statistics, 2003* (Washington, DC: Government Printing Office, 2004), 12–15, available at http://uscis.gov/graphics/shared/statistics/yearbook/2003/2003Yearbook.pdf.

46. Joseph Gilpin Pyle, *The Life of James J. Hill* (New York: Doubleday, Page & Co., 1917), 1:18.

47. Ibid., 1:22.

48. "J. J. Hill Dead in St. Paul Home," *New York Times*, May 30, 1916, 6.

49. Additional sources: Michael P. Malone, *James J. Hill: Empire Builder of the Northwest* (Norman: University of Oklahoma Press, 1996); John N. Ingham, "Hill, James Jerome," in *Biographical Dictionary of American Business Leaders* (Westport, CT: Greenwood Press, 1983), 577–582.

50. U.S. Bureau of the Census, *Statistical Abstract of the United States: 1953* (Washington, DC: Government Printing Office, 1953), 42, available at http://www2.census.gov/prod2/statcomp/documents/1953-01.pdf.

51. Immigration totals from U.S. Department of Homeland Security, *Immigration Statistics, 2003*, 11, available at http://uscis.gov/graphics/shared/statistics/yearbook/2003/2003Yearbook.pdf; and U.S. population data from U.S. Bureau of the Census, *Statistical Abstract of the United States: 2001* (Washington, DC: Government Printing Office, 2001), 8, available at http://www.census.gov/prod/2002pubs/01statab/pop.pdf.

52. "Renaissance Miner," *Forbes*, August 21, 1978, 118.

53. Robert H. Ramsey, *Men and Mines of Newmont: A Fifty-Year History* (New York: Octagon Books [Farrar, Straus & Giroux], 1973), 181.

54. Ibid., 195–196.

55. "Newmont Mining Elects Malozemoff President, Searls Board Chairman," *Wall Street Journal*, December 16, 1953, 13.

56. "From Shotguns to Rifles," Forbes, June 15, 1971, 48; "The Engineer Who's Domesticating Newmont," *BusinessWeek*, October 5, 1974, 104.

57. "Newmont Mining's Fourth Generation of Gamblers," *Fortune*, October 1965, 132–133.

58. Maria Shao, "Malozemoff, Newmont's Guiding Force for 26 Years, Preaches Diversification," *Wall Street Journal*, September 23, 1980, 22.

59. Additional sources: Stefan Wagstyl, "Tough Act to Follow for Newmont Chairman," *Financial Times* (London), April 15, 1986, 31; "Vice Chairman Named at Newmont Mining," *New York Times*, September 12, 1988, D3; "Plato Malozemoff, 88, Retired Executive," *New York Times*, August 18, 1997, B8; Newmont Mining Company Web page, www.newmont.com.

# Notes

## Chapter 4

1. Catholic and Orthodox Christians, both being generally associated with immigrant populations, were grouped together in much of this chapter's analysis, but Catholics constitute the vast majority of this group. There are only three Orthodox-affiliated leaders versus sixty-three Catholics in total on our list.

2. Religious statistics from William M. Newman and Peter L. Halvorson, *Atlas of American Religion: The Denominational Era, 1776–1990* (Walnut Creek, CA: AltaMira Press, 2000), 49; 1890 population totals and age divisions from U.S. Department of the Interior, Census Office, *Report on the Population of the United States at the Eleventh Census: 1890, Part I* (Washington, DC: Government Printing Office, 1895), 829–831. Raw census statistics alone would suggest approximately a 50 percent level of church affiliation among those fifteen and older, but Newman and Halvorson have reestimated statistics from the census, incorporating other sources, to address undercounting in the original figures.

3. Newman and Halvorson, *Atlas of American Religion*, 18.

4. Ibid., 19–20.

5. John T. Flynn, *God's Gold: The Story of Rockefeller and His Times* (New York: Harcourt, Brace and Company, 1932), 394.

6. John D. Rockefeller, *Random Reminiscences of Men and Events* (New York: Doubleday and Page, 1909), 142.

7. Herbert Adams Gibbons, *John Wanamaker* (New York: Harper and Brothers, 1926), 1:183.

8. Additional sources: Friends of the Wanamaker Organ, "A Short History of the Life of John Wanamaker," Web page, www.wanamakerorgan.com/johnw.html; Bethany Collegiate Presbyterian Church, "Church Profile," Web page, www.bethanycollegiate.com/church_profile.html.

9. Flynn, *God's Gold*, 396.

10. "J.P. Morgan Criticised," *New York Times*, November 6, 1901, 6.

11. "Full Text of the Will of J. Pierpont Morgan," *New York Times*, April 20, 1913, 2.

12. For examples, see "Clergy Discuss Morgan's Will," *New York Times*, April 23, 1913, 3; "Morgan's Will Recalls Quaint Phraseology of Olden Days," *New York Times*, May 4, 1913, SM4.

13. Additional sources: Herbert L. Satterlee, *J. Pierpont Morgan: An Intimate Portrait* (New York: Macmillan, 1939); Frederick Lewis Allen, *The Great Pierpont Morgan* (New York: Harper and Brothers, 1949); Jean Strouse, *Morgan: American Financier* (New York: Random House, 1999); W. S. Rainsford, *The Story of a Varied Life: An Autobiography* (London: George Allen and Unwin, 1922); "Morgan As a Man Praised by Pastors," *New York Times*, April 7, 1913, 9.

14. "At Church of J. P. Morgan," *New York Times*, March 7, 1932, 11. See also "Morgan Attends Church," *New York Times*, May 29, 1933, 2.

15. Mabel Newcomer, *The Big Business Executive: The Factors That Made Him, 1900–1950* (New York: Columbia University Press, 1955), 48.

16. Flynn, *God's Gold*, 396. See also Lucy Kavaler, *The Astors: A Family Chronicle of Pomp and Power* (New York: Dodd, Mead & Co., 1966), 15 and 43.

17. "Fashionable Wedding," *Andover Townsman*, November 28, 1902.

18. Divorce records of Genevieve Joyce Fahey and Frank Joseph Fahey filed in Essex County, Massachusetts, including divorce petition of Genevieve Joyce Fahey, May 9, 1916, and deposition of Thomas James Orbison, May 29, 1916.

19. "John Joyce Passes Away on Coast," *Lawrence Sun-American*, January 27, 1917, 1 (also obituary articles in *Boston Globe* and *Lawrence Telegram* on the same date).

20. "Fahey, Frank J.," in *National Cyclopaedia of American Biography* (New York: James T. White, 1948), 34:391.

21. Additional sources: Gordon McKibben, *Cutting Edge: Gillette's Journey to Global Leadership* (Boston: Harvard Business School Press, 1998); Russell B. Adams Jr., *King C. Gillette, the Man and His Wonderful Shaving Device* (Boston: Little, Brown, 1978); John N. Ingham, "Fahey, Frank Joseph," in *Biographical Dictionary of American Business Leaders* (Westport, CT: Greenwood Press, 1983), 357–359.

22. U.S. Department of the Interior, Census Office, *Report on Statistics of Churches in the United States at the Eleventh Census: 1890* (Washington, DC: Government Printing Office, 1894), 39. Because of a lack of state or regional level detail in Newman and Halvorson, raw census figures were used for this and the subsequent calculation.

23. Ibid., combined with 1890 state population totals in U.S. Department of the Interior, Census Office, *Report on the Population of the United States at the Eleventh Census: 1890, Part I* (Washington, DC: Government Printing Office, 1895), 829.

24. Deanna Paoli Gumina, *The Italians of San Francisco, 1850–1930* (Staten Island, NY: Center for Migration Studies of New York, Inc., 1978), 11, 13.

25. "San Francisco Keen for Giannini to Win," *New York Times*, December 20, 1931, E5.

26. Regarding Giannini's influence on Capra and Columbia, respectively, see Joseph McBride, *Frank Capra: The Catastrophe of Success* (New York: Simon & Schuster, 1992); and Clive Hirschhorn, *The Columbia Story* (New York: Crown Publishers, 1989).

27. Additional sources: Felice Bonadio, *A. P. Giannini: Banker of America* (Berkeley: University of California Press, 1994); Gerald Nash, *A. P. Giannini and the Bank of America* (Norman: University of Oklahoma Press, 1992).

28. Moses Rischin, *The Promised City: New York's Jews 1870–1914* (Cambridge, MA: Harvard Press, 1962), 261.

29. Ibid., 261–262; John Steele Gordon, *The Great Game: The Emergence of Wall Street As a World Power, 1653–2000* (New York: Scribner, 1999), 174–175.

30. "Checks for Wedding Presents," *New York Times*, January 4, 1884, 2.

31. "John M. Hancock, Financier, Dead," *New York Times*, September 26, 1956, 33.

32. "Herbert Henry Lehman," in *Dictionary of American Biography, Supplement 7: 1961–1965*, ed. John A. Garaty (New York: American Council of Learned Societies/Charles Scribner's Sons, 1981), 466–468.

33. Additional sources: *A Centennial: Lehman Brothers, 1850–1950* (Lehman Brothers: New York, 1950); Barry E. Supple, "A Business Elite: German Jewish Financiers in 19th Century New York," *Business History Review* 31, no. 2 (summer 1957): 143–177; John N. Ingham, "Lehman Family," in *Biographical Dictionary of American Business Leaders* (Westport, CT: Greenwood Press, 1983), 782–787.

34. Charles E. Silberman, *A Certain People: American Jews and Their Lives Today* (New York: Summit Books, 1985), 85.

35. Ibid., 86.

36. Russell Porter, "Government Argues That 'Intent' Convicts the Communist Leaders," *New York Times*, June 24, 1950, 2.

37. Peter Vanderwicken, "Irving Shapiro Takes Charge at Du Pont," *Fortune*, January 1974, 81.

38. Richard L. Zweigenhaft and G. William Domhoff, *Jews in the Protestant Establishment* (New York: Praeger Publishers, 1982), 45.

39. Gerd Wilcke, "Chemical Producer Reassigning Some Key Executives," *New York Times*, July 17, 1973, 53.

40. Silberman, *A Certain People*, 85.

41. Gerd Wilcke, "Shapiro: du Pont Chief of a New Mold," *New York Times*, December 19, 1973, 65.

42. Patricia Bonfield, *U.S. Business Leaders: A Study of Opinions and Characteristics* (New York: Conference Board, 1980), 15.

43. On Shapiro's retirement and son's employment, see Tamar Lewin, "Irving Shapiro, Attorney at Law," *New York Times*, August 8, 1982, F1, F15. For additional sources on Shapiro's life and career, see: Gerd Wilcke, "Du Pont Expected to Pick Shapiro As New Chairman," *New York Times*, December 14, 1973, 71; Jeffrey M. Sheppard, "Way to Executive Suite: Through Law School," *New York Times*, January 6, 1974, 163; Claudia H. Deutsch, "Irving S. Shapiro, 85, Lawyer and Ex-Chairman of DuPont," *New York Times*, September 15, 2001, B7.

44. Advertising Club, "About Us," Web page, www.theadvertisingclub.org/aboutus_past.html.

45. Marylin Bender, "Quaker Hill, Where Lowell Thomas Is Patriarch of the Quiet Celebrities," *New York Times*, November 10, 1968, 90.

46. "Three Named for Bench in Brooklyn Deal," *New York Times*, August 4, 1947, 19.

47. Leo Egan, "C. E. Murphy Gets Appellate Post," *New York Times*, January 1, 1954, 24; "Charles Murphy, Justice, Is Dead," *New York Times*, November 23, 1959, 31.

48. "Lowell Thomas Jr. Weds Mary Pryor," *New York Times*, May 21, 1950, 100.

49. Joseph M. Guilfoyle, "Trend-Bucker: WVEC-TV Breaks into Black As Many UHF Stations Fold," *Wall Street Journal*, January 19, 1955, 1.

50. "Asks Voiding of TV Deal," *New York Times*, December 7, 1954, 49.

51. "TV Outlet Discontinues," *New York Times*, February 1, 1955, 35.

52. William M. Blair, "Hagerty Disavows Influencing F.C.C. in Albany TV Case," *New York Times*, February 8, 1959, 1ff.

53. "Licensing Payola Charged to F.C.C.," *New York Times*, June 21, 1960, 23.

54. "Capital Cities Cleared by FCC, 4–2, to Acquire TV Station, Sell Another," *Wall Street Journal*, June 19, 1967, 6.

55. Additional sources: Walt Hawver, *Capital Cities/ABC, the Early Years, 1954–1986: How the Minnow Came to Swallow the Whale* (Radnor, PA: Chilton Book Company, 1994); David Callahan, *Kindred Spirits: Harvard Business School's Extraordinary Class of 1949 and How They Transformed American Business* (Hoboken, NJ: John Wiley and Sons, 2002), 49–53, 147–153, 243–245; Guy Lometti, "Murphy, Thomas S.," in *Encyclopedia of Television*, ed. Horace Newcomb (Chicago: Fitzroy Dearborn Publishers, 1997); Museum of Broadcast Communications, "Murphy, Thomas S.," Web page, www.museum.tv/archives/etv/

index.html; Christine Foster, "Couples," *Forbes*, December 2, 1996, 18ff.; Allan Sloan and Thomas Baker, "Murphy's Law," *Forbes*, March 16, 1981, 66ff.; "The National Business Hall of Fame," *Fortune*, April 5, 1993, 108ff.; "Focus on Growth at Capital Cities," *New York Times*, July 2, 1966, 3.

## Chapter 5

1. Henry Clews, *Fifty Years in Wall Street* (New York: Irving Publishing, 1908), 27.
2. Roger Ward Babson, "Is It Wise to Spend Four Years at College If Planning to Enter Business?" (Babson Park, MA: undated pamphlet). Emphasis added.
3. "James Buchanan Duke, Tobacco King, 68, Dies of Pneumonia," *New York Times*, October 11, 1925, 25.
4. Robert F. Durden, *Bold Entrepreneur: A Life of James B. Duke* (Durham, NC: Carolina Academic Press, 2003), 176, 190.
5. The Duke Endowment, "2004 Grants," Web page, www.dukeendowment.org/resources/grantsbyyear/2004.
6. U.S. Department of Commerce, Bureau of the Census, *Sixteenth Census of the United States: 1940, Population: Nativity and Parentage of the White Population, General Characteristics* (Washington, DC: Government Printing Office, 1943), 194.
7. Though the official organization of "Ivy League" schools did not occur until mid-century, we used as a definition for our analysis throughout the century the list of schools that form today's Ivy League—Brown, Columbia, Cornell, Dartmouth, Harvard, Penn, Princeton, and Yale. All were well-established and prestigious schools in the early part of the century as well.
8. "Bunyan in Broadcloth: The House of Weyerhaeuser," *Fortune*, April 1934, 170.
9. Additional sources: Charles E. Twining, *F. K. Weyerhaeuser: A Biography* (St. Paul: Minnesota Historical Society Press, 1997); Ralph W. Hidy, *Frank Ernest Hill, and Allan Nevins, Timber and Men: The Weyerhaeuser Story* (New York: Macmillan, 1963); "Weyerhaeuser Picks Successor to President," *New York Times*, February 11, 1988, D5; Weyerhaeuser Web page, www.weyerhaeuser.com; John N. Ingham, "Weyerhaeuser Family," in *Biographical Dictionary of American Business Leaders* (Westport, CT: Greenwood Press, 1983), 1,594–1,600.
10. George Wilson Pierson, *Yale College: An Educational History, 1871–1921* (New Haven, CT: Yale University Press, 1952), 103.
11. Lewis Sheldon Welch and Walter Camp, *Yale, Her Campus, Class-rooms and Athletics* (Boston: L. C. Page & Co., 1899), 56.
12. Ibid., 65; J. Wilbur Chapman, "The Funeral," chapter 27 in *The Life and Work of Dwight Lyman Moody* (originally published 1900), available at www.biblebelievers.com/moody/27.html.
13. Cited in Pierson, *Yale College*, 12.
14. Statistics for 1904–1905 as shown in George Wilson Pierson, *A Yale Book of Numbers: Historical Statistics of the College and University, 1701–1976* (online version published 1983), at www.yale.edu/oir/pierson_original.htm, 80.
15. Welch and Camp, *Yale, Her Campus*, 536–538. See also Pierson, *Yale College*, 19.

16. Edwin E. Slosson, *Great American Universities* (New York: Macmillan, 1910), 59–60.

17. Marcia G. Synott, "The Admission and Assimilation of Minority Students at Harvard, Yale, and Princeton, 1900–1970," *History of Education Quarterly* 19, no. 3 (autumn 1979): 288 and 290.

18. Ibid., 290–291.

19. "Earl Babst, Industrialist, Dead," *New York Times*, April 25, 1967, 43.

20. William Cahn, *Out of the Cracker Barrel: The Nabisco Story from Animal Crackers to Zulus* (New York: Simon & Schuster, 1969), 118, 120, 142, 174.

21. "American Sugar Refining Co.," *Wall Street Journal*, December 10, 1907, 7; "The Reform of a 'Bad' Trust," *New York Times*, June 19, 1911, 13. See also "Mr. Havemeyer on Trusts," *New York Times*, June 15, 1899, 1; and "Mr. Mellen and Mr. Havemeyer," *Wall Street Journal*, January 26, 1904, 1.

22. "American Sugar Closes Its Big Chalmette Refinery," *Wall Street Journal*, December 23, 1914, 3. See also "Closing New Orleans Refinery Scares the Politicians," *Wall Street Journal*, December 31, 1914, 6.

23. "American Sugar Wins Ouster Suit in Louisiana," *Wall Street Journal*, May 31, 1915, 6; "American Sugar Refining Under the Louisiana Law," *Wall Street Journal*, June 26, 1915, 5.

24. Earl D. Babst, *Occasions in Sugar* (New York: private printing, 1940), 12. See also "American Sugar Refining's Policy in Louisiana," *Wall Street Journal*, November 25, 1915, 3.

25. "American Sugar," *Wall Street Journal*, January 12, 1916, 6.

26. "Louisiana Sugar Law Found Unconstitutional," *Wall Street Journal*, January 19, 1916, 6; "American Sugar's Victory in Louisiana," *Wall Street Journal*, April 26, 1916, 8.

27. "Am. Sugar Refining Suits May Be Settled," *Wall Street Journal*, September 27, 1916, 5.

28. "189 Sugar Suits Settled," *New York Times*, April 7, 1917, 14.

29. "Sugar Suit Settlement Pleases the Stockholders," *Wall Street Journal*, April 21, 1917, 5.

30. "American Sugar Wins," *Wall Street Journal*, July 20, 1918, 5; "No Sugar Monopoly Now, Says Decree," *New York Times*, December 21, 1921, 30.

31. Additional sources: "Babst, Earl D.," in *National Cyclopaedia of American Biography* (Clifton, NJ: James T. White, 1973), 54:471–412; "American Sugar Now More Liquid," *Wall Street Journal*, October 26, 1923, 9; "The Way of the Winner," *Wall Street Journal*, March 21, 1925, 6; Domino Sugar Web page, www.dominosugar.com.

32. Mabel Newcomer, *The Big Business Executive: The Factors That Made Him, 1900–1950* (New York: Columbia University Press, 1955), 151.

33. Statistics on college education in Newcomer's group extrapolated from chart in ibid., 68.

34. Marvin Bower, *The Will to Lead* (Boston: Harvard Business School Press, 1997), 10.

35. Elizabeth Haas Edersheim, *McKinsey's Marvin Bower: Vision, Leadership, and the Creation of Management Consulting* (Hoboken, NJ: John Wiley & Sons, 2004), 16.

36. Ibid., 17–18.

37. Ibid., 33; Bower, *Will to Lead*, 15.

38. Roger Lowenstein, "The Lives They Lived: The Purist," *New York Times*, December 23, 2003, section 6, 44 (via LexisNexis Academic).

39. John Huey, "How McKinsey Does It," *Fortune*, November 1, 1993, 77.

40. Bower, *Will to Lead*, 17.

41. John A. Byrne, "A Final Bow to McKinsey's High Priest," *BusinessWeek Online*, January 28, 2003 (via Factiva). See also Edersheim, *McKinsey's Marvin Bower*, 41, 71, 74.

42. Edersheim, *McKinsey's Marvin Bower*, 80.

43. John A. Byrne, "The McKinsey Mystique: Its Style and Influence Make It a Breed Apart," *BusinessWeek*, September 20, 1993, 67.

44. Newcomer, *Big Business Executive*, 75.

45. Richard Buck, "Rosenberg: Man in Motion—BankAmerica CEO Builds Reputation As Marketing Whiz," *Los Angeles Times*, August 15, 1991, E1 (via LexisNexis Academic).

46. Sanford Rose, "BankAmerica Makes a Politically Astute Choice for Chief Executive," *American Banker*, January 26, 1990, 11 (via LexisNexis Academic).

47. Ibid.

48. Sam Zuckerman, "Giannini's Heir: If Dick Rosenberg Can Get the Security Pacific Merger to Work, BankAmerica Could Be in Position to Become the First Truly Nationwide Bank," *American Banker*, January 23, 1992, 3A (via LexisNexis Academic).

49. Sam Zuckerman, "The Redemption of Richard Rosenberg," *USBanker*, September 1995, 30 (via LexisNexis Academic).

50. Additional sources: John W. Milligan, "Can Bank of America Become America's Bank?" *Institutional Investor* 25, no. 3 (March 1991): 46ff.; Saul Hansell, "Market Place: More Talk Than Fact, a Possible Bank Merger Titillates Investors," *New York Times*, October 24, 1995, D16; Victor F. Zonana, "Wells Fargo Names Hazen President, Operating Chief," *Wall Street Journal*, July 18, 1984, 44; Victor F. Zonana, "Crocker Appoints Morby to Oversee Several Divisions," *Wall Street Journal*, September 28, 1984, 16; Suffolk University, "A Brief History of Suffolk University," Web page, www.suffolk.edu/history.html; Golden Gate University, "History," Web page, www.ggu.edu/about/History.

51. For the 20 percent estimate, see Keith W. Olson, "The G.I. Bill and Higher Education: Success and Surprise," *American Quarterly* 25, no. 5 (December 1973): 605, citing Norman Fredriksen and William B. Schrader, *Adjustment to College* (Princeton: Educational Testing Service, 1951). For an estimate that college completion rates increased by 43 percent, hence 100 out of 143, or 70 percent of those completing, would have completed otherwise, see John Bound and Sarah Turner, "Going to War and Going to College: Did World War II and the G.I. Bill Increase Educational Attainment for Returning Veterans?" *Journal of Labor Economics* 20, no. 4 (October 2002): 806.

52. John K. Waters, *John Chambers and the Cisco Way: Navigating Through Volatility* (New York: John Wiley and Sons, 2002), 17–18.

53. Andy Reinhardt, "Meet Mr. Internet," *BusinessWeek*, September 13, 1999, 136.

54. Ibid., 136.

55. "Stockwatch: Cisco Up As Analysts Raise Targets After Q2 EPS Beats Estimates," *AFX European Focus*, February 9, 2000; transcript from February 8, 2000 broadcast of *Street Sweep*, CNNfn (both via LexisNexis Academic).

56. Peter Burrows, "Cisco's Comeback," *BusinessWeek*, November 24, 2003, 120.

57. "Cisco Systems—on the Record: John Chambers," *San Francisco Chronicle*, February 29, 2004, I1; Kevin Maney, "Chambers, Cisco Born Again," *USA Today*, January 21, 2004, 1B (both via LexisNexis Academic).

58. Additional sources: Andy Serwer, "There's Something About Cisco," *Fortune*, May 15, 2000, 114ff.; Andrew Kupfer, "The Real King of the Internet," *Fortune*, September

7, 1998, 84ff. (via Factiva); Mary Anne Ostrom, "Power in Silicon Valley: John Chambers," *San Jose Mercury News*, July 30, 2000, 1A; Mark Leibovich, "A Rain God Confronts a Harsh Climate; CEO's Optimism Tested by Downturn," *Washington Post*, April 6, 2001, A01 (via LexisNexis Academic); Fred Vogelstein, "Can Cisco Dig Out of Its Hole?" *Fortune*, December 9, 2002, 179ff. (via Factiva); Cisco Web page, www.cisco.com; Cisco Systems Annual Reports, 1997, 2000.

59. Newcomer, *Big Business Executive*, 146. Emphasis added.


## Chapter 6

1. Pitirim Sorokin, "American Millionaires and Multi-Millionaires: A Comparative Statistical Study," *Journal of Social Forces* 3, no. 4 (May 1925): 636.

2. Barry V. Johnston, "Pitirim A. Sorokin (1889–1968): Pioneer and Pariah," *International Sociology* 11, no. 2 (June 1996): 230.

3. Sorokin, "American Millionaires," 635.

4. F. W. Taussig and C. S. Joslyn, *American Business Leaders: A Study in Social Origins and Stratification* (New York: Macmillan, 1932), 114, similarly 119, also 235–239.

5. Ibid., 114.

6. Ibid., 241.

7. Ibid., 239.

8. Van Allen Bradley, *Music for the Millions: The Kimball Piano and Organ Story* (Chicago: Henry Regnery Co., 1957), 246.

9. Earl Chapin May, *The Canning Clan* (New York: Macmillan, 1937), 351.

10. James W. McKie, *Tin Cans and Tin Plate: A Study of Competition in Two Related Markets* (Cambridge, MA: Harvard University Press, 1959), 86.

11. "Profits in Cans," *Fortune*, April 1934, 80–81.

12. "Continental Can Co. Formed with Capital of $17,500,000," *Wall Street Journal*, December 11, 1912, 6.

13. Additional sources: "Conway, Carle Cotter," in *National Cyclopaedia of American Biography, Current* (New York: James T. White, 1930), C:249–250; "Norton, Edwin," in *National Cyclopaedia of American Biography* (New York: James T. White, 1937), 26:167–168; "Frank A. Assman, Financier, Is Dead," *New York Times*, February 20, 1936, 19.

14. See discussion in John B. Rae, "Why Michigan?" in *The Automobile and American Culture*, ed. David L. Lewis and Laurence Goldstein (Ann Arbor: University of Michigan Press, 1983), 2–5.

15. "Joy, James Frederick," in *National Cyclopaedia of American Biography* (New York: James T. White, 1901), 11:154.

16. "Newberry, John Stoughton," in *National Cyclopaedia of American Biography* (New York: James T. White, 1904), 12:554–555.

17. Beverly Rae Kimes, ed., *Packard: A History of the Motor Car and the Company* (Princeton, NJ: Princeton Pub., 1978), 53–54.

18. George S. May, *A Most Unique Machine: The Michigan Origins of the American Automobile Industry* (Grand Rapids, MI: Eerdmans Pub., 1975), 124.

19. Kimes, *Packard*, 63, 69.

20. Cited by May, *Most Unique Machine*, 339.

21. "Michigan Historical Markers: The Michigan Stove," Web page, http://www
.michmarkers.com/pages/S0661.htm.

22. Kimes, *Packard*, 664.

23. Additional sources: Charles K. Hyde, "Henry Bourne Joy," in *Encyclopedia of
American Business History and Biography*, vol. 6, *The Automobile Industry, 1896–1920*, ed.
George S. May (New York: Facts on File, 1990), 274–280; "Henry B. Joy Dead: Motor
Car Leader," *New York Times*, November 7, 1936, 17; Packard Club, "History: Company
Genesis," Web page, www.packardclub.org; Jason Stein, "Joy's Dream Spanned East to
West," *Las Vegas Review-Journal*, February 21, 2004, available on www.reviewjournal.com;
"Joy, Henry B.," in *National Cyclopaedia of American Biography* (New York: James T. White,
1939), 27:396–397.

24. W. Lloyd Warner and James C. Abegglen, *Big Business Leaders in America* (New
York: Harper and Brothers, 1955), 25.

25. Ibid., 27.

26. Ibid., 31.

27. Ibid., 33.

28. Emmet Hughes, "Joe Martino's National Lead," *Fortune*, July 1957, 104.

29. Ibid.

30. "National Lead Co. Veteran Elected a Vice President," *New York Times*, April 19,
1946, 39; "National Lead Company Elevates Two Officials," *New York Times*, November
27, 1946, 33; "Officers Advanced at National Lead," *New York Times*, April 18, 1947, 33.

31. Hughes, "Joe Martino's National Lead," 104.

32. Ibid., 101.

33. "Elected to Directorate of Chase National Bank," *New York Times*, October 23,
1952, 49.

34. For Smith's appointment, see "Rail, Airline Heads Join Bank Board," *New York
Times*, December 10, 1953, 77; on the continuing service of Smith and Martino, see "Directors Designated," *New York Times*, February 18, 1955, 29.

35. Philip Hawkins, "Edward R. Rowley Elected to Top Position at National Lead,
Succeeding J. A. Martino," *Wall Street Journal*, March 26, 1968, 10.

36. Additional source: Ronald Sullivan, "Joseph Martino Dies at 83; Ex–National
Lead Chairman," *New York Times*, November 6, 1983, 44.

37. Newcomer, *Big Business Executive*, 64; preceding statistics noted on pp. 57, 63, and 64.

38. Alexis de Tocqueville, *Democracy in America*, translated by George Lawrence and
ed. J. P. Mayer and Max Lerner (New York: Harper & Row, 1966), 605.

39. Faye Rice and Edward Prewitt, "Lessons from Late Bloomers," *Fortune*, August 31,
1987, 88.

40. Jennifer Bayot, "John Culligan, 88: Transformed Maker of Household Items,"
*New York Times*, December 21, 2004, A27; "Laporte's Successor," *BusinessWeek*, January 19,
1981, 36 (both via LexisNexis Academic).

41. See, for example, "Live Stock Dies in Nebraska," *New York Times*, January 30, 1932,
5; and "Nebraska Corn Damaged," *Wall Street Journal*, July 26, 1932, 11.

42. James C. Worthy, *William C. Norris: Portrait of a Maverick* (Cambridge, MA:
Ballinger Publishing, 1987), 18.

43. Robert Slater, *Portraits in Silicon* (Cambridge, MA: MIT Press, 1987), 114.

44. Worthy, *William C. Norris*, 24.

45. Carol Pine and Susan Mundale, *Self-Made: The Stories of 12 Minnesota Entrepreneurs* (Minneapolis: Dorn Books, 1982), 113.

46. Worthy, *William C. Norris*, 40.

47. For IBM figures, see "IBM 4th Period Gross Income, Net Hit Record Levels," *Wall Street Journal*, January 14, 1964, 26.

48. Worthy, *William C. Norris*, 44. See also Scott R. Schmedel, "Control Data Sues IBM for Damages in Antitrust Case," *Wall Street Journal*, December 12, 1968, 2.

49. "Data Processing Financial Sues IBM, Asks $1 Billion Damages; Suit Is Second by a Rival," *Wall Street Journal*, January 6, 1969, 34; "IBM Hit with Fourth Civil Antitrust Suit As a Software Concern Alleges Monopoly," *Wall Street Journal*, April 23, 1969, 5; Lewis M. Kohlmeier, "Justice Department Charges IBM with Monopolizing Computer Field," *Wall Street Journal*, January 20, 1969, 3.

50. Worthy, *William C. Norris*, 113.

51. See, for example, Michael W. Fedo, "How Control Data Turns a Profit on Its Good Works," *New York Times*, January 7, 1979, F3.

52. Eben Shapiro, "Founder of Control Data Plans to Leave Its Board," *New York Times*, March 30, 1991, 27.

53. On the restructuring, see Steve Gross, "Control Data to Split Itself in Two and Change Name; CDC to Spin Off Computer Business in Restructuring," *Star Tribune* (Minneapolis), May 28, 1992, 1D (via LexisNexis Academic); on the 1999 buyout, see "Control Data Systems, Inc., Renamed Syntegra," press release of BT, December 1, 1999, http://www.btconsulting.com/mediacentre/pressreleases/us/us_press_archive_1999_12 _01.htm.

54. Dick Youngblood, "Old CDC Worker Program Evolves, Thrives and Is Now Poised for Expansion," *Star Tribune* (Minneapolis), September 3, 1997, 2D (via LexisNexis Academic); Ceridian Corporation, 2004 Annual Report, available at www.ceridian.com.

55. Dick Youngblood, "Horton's High-Tech Plant Is an Inner-City Success Story," *Star Tribune* (Minneapolis), March 15, 1992, 2D; Neal St. Anthony, "On Business" column, *Star Tribune* (Minneapolis), April 28, 2000, 1D (both via LexisNexis Academic).

56. Plato Learning, Inc., 2004 Annual Report, available at www.plato.com.

57. Additional sources: Ralph Nader and William Taylor, *The Big Boys: Power and Position in American Business* (New York: Pantheon Books, 1986); Joseph J. Fucini and Suzy Fucini, *Experience, Inc.: Men and Women Who Founded Famous Companies After the Age of 40* (New York: Free Press, 1987); Patricia O'Toole, *Money and Morals in America: A History* (New York: Clarkson Potter, 1998).

58. Details of Wilson's life in the following paragraphs are from Kemmons Wilson with Robert Kerr, *Half Luck and Half Brains: The Kemmons Wilson, Holiday Inn Story* (Nashville, TN: Hambleton-Hill Publishing, 1996), 8, 11, 12, 15, 26, 27, and 33.

59. See figures of average nightly charges from five to seven dollars in 1952, cited in Robert B. Andrews, "Super-Motels: Roadside Hostelries Adopt TV and Swimming Pools," *Wall Street Journal*, August 18, 1954, 7.

60. Wilson and Kerr, *Half Luck and Half Brains*, 47.

61. Ibid., 51.

62. Ibid., 52–53.

63. Harold H. Martin, "That Prayin' Millionaire from Memphis," *Saturday Evening Post* 224, no. 30 (January 26, 1952): 36.

64. Wilson and Kerr, *Half Luck and Half Brains*, 63–64.

65. "Busiest Man in Town," *Fortune*, December 1955, 201.

66. "Motel Chain Finds Profits in Owning," *BusinessWeek*, July 14, 1962, 47.

67. "A Single Standard for Travelers," *BusinessWeek*, November 16, 1963, 114.

68. Wilson and Kerr, *Half Luck and Half Brains*, 133.

69. Ibid., 84; "A Single Standard for Travelers," 118.

70. T. G. Harris, "Southern Business: The Boom Man," *Look*, November 16, 1965, 44.

71. "Rapid Rise of the Host with the Most," *Time*, June 12, 1972, 81.

72. Barbara Lovenheim, "Holiday Inns Is Booming," *New York Times*, August 5, 1979, F1.

73. Wilson and Kerr, *Half Luck and Half Brains*, 152.

74. Ibid., 155.

75. Additional sources: Deborah M. Club, "Legacy of Growth: Wilson's Heirs Play Big Role in Memphis," *Memphis (TN) Commercial Appeal*, March 23, 2003, G1; Jane Roberts and Yolanda Jones, "Business Legend Lauded as Friend, Folksy Dynamo," *Memphis (TN) Commercial Appeal*, February 13, 2003, A2 (both via Factiva).

76. William F. Lucas, *Nothing Better in the Market: Brown-Forman's Century of Quality, 1870–1970* (New York: Newcomen Society in North America, 1970), 12.

77. "President Is Named by Brown-Forman," *New York Times*, July 26, 1966, 49; "Distiller is 110 and Still Growing," *New York Times*, August 1, 1980, D1.

78. David P. Garino, "Brown, Brown, Brown, Brown, Brown & Brown Rise at Brown-Forman," *Wall Street Journal*, December 21, 1970, 1.

79. Lucas, *Nothing Better*, 24.

80. Brown-Forman Annual Report, 2004, 21, available at www.brown-forman.com.

81. Anishka Clarke, "Brown-Forman's Well-Stocked Bar: The Maker of Jack Daniel's, Southern Comfort, Finlandia, Fetzer, Korbel, and More Is Thriving on Strong Demographic Trends," *BusinessWeek Online*, September 28, 2004 (via Lexis-Nexis Academic).

82. Additional source: Brown-Forman Company History Web page, www .brown-forman.com.

## Chapter 7

1. "Report of the 13th Annual Convention of the National Negro Business League held at Chicago, Illinois, Aug. 21–23, 1912, 99–101," cited in A'Lelia Perry Bundles, *On Her Own Ground: The Life and Times of Madam C. J. Walker* (New York: Scribner, 2001), 134–136.

2. Nan Robertson, "Dorothy Schiff Tells of Relationship with Roosevelt," *New York Times*, May 27, 1976, 73.

3. "Interest Centers in Congress Race," *New York Times*, October 24, 1937, 40.

4. On Dorothy Schiff Backer's assumption of leadership of the *Post*, see "Woman to Guide Oldest Paper Here," *New York Times*, April 5, 1942, 39. For an example of George

Backer's philanthropy, see "Relief Group Aids 795,000 Overseas," *New York Times*, December 5, 1942, 9. See also "George Backer, Published Post," *New York Times*, May 2, 1974, 50.

5. Jeffrey Potter, *Men, Money and Magic: The Story of Dorothy Schiff* (New York: Coward, McCann & Geohegan, 1976), 207.

6. Ibid., 11.

7. Ibid., 228.

8. George Barrett, "Harriman Loses Support of Post," *New York Times*, November 4, 1958, 1.

9. Murray Seeger, "Post Will Resume Today; Computer on Week's Trial," *New York Times*, June 24, 1965, 1.

10. Damon Stetson, "Newspapers and Printers Reach a Tentative Accord," *New York Times*, May 24, 1974, 1.

11. Potter, *Men, Money and Magic*, 275.

12. Additional sources: Deirdre Carmody, "Dorothy Schiff Agrees to Sell *Post* to Murdoch, Australian Publisher," *New York Times*, November 20, 1976, 53; "Dorothy Schiff, 86, Ex-*Post* Owner, Dies," *New York Times*, August 31, 1989, B11.

13. "Women in Business: III," *Fortune*, September 1935, 81.

14. Alfred Allan Lewis and Constance Woodworth, *Miss Elizabeth Arden* (New York: Coward, McCann & Geohegan, 1972), 38–39.

15. "Business Troubles" listing, *New York Times*, August 16, 1910, 10.

16. "I Am a Famous Woman in This Industry," *Fortune*, October 1938, 62.

17. Ibid., 64.

18. "Women in Business: III," 81.

19. Additional sources: "Elizabeth Arden Dies Here at 81," *New York Times*, October 19, 1966, 47ff.; "The Big Business of Beauty," in *50 Great Pioneers of American Industry*, edited by the staff of Newsfront and Year (Maplewood, NJ: C. S. Hammond, 1964), 182–185.

20. Sources: John N. Ingham and Lynne B. Feldman, "Herndon, Alonzo Franklin," in *African-American Business Leaders: A Biographical Dictionary* (Westport, CT: Greenwood Press, 1994), 322–338; M. S. Stuart, *An Economic Detour: A History of Insurance in the Lives of American Negroes* (New York: Wendell Malliet and Co., 1940), 117–122; Atlanta Life Web page, http://www.atlantalife.com/main.asp?urh=quickFacts.

21. Allan H. Spear, *Black Chicago: The Making of a Negro Ghetto, 1890–1920* (Chicago: University of Chicago Press, 1967), 134.

22. John H. Johnson, *Succeeding Against the Odds* (New York: Amistad Press, 1992), 57.

23. See, for example, "Flood Crest Rushes South," *New York Times*, April 28, 1927, 1.

24. Johnson, *Succeeding Against the Odds*, 53.

25. Ibid., 74.

26. Ibid., 114.

27. Ibid., 344–345.

28. Ibid., 249.

29. Peter J. W. Elstrom, "Last Black Insurance Firm Sold," *Crain's Chicago Business* 14, no. 17, section 1, (November 25, 1991): 1 (via Factiva).

30. "Linda Johnson Rice Named CEO of Johnson Publishing Company," *Jet* 101, no. 19 (April 29, 2002): 16 (via Factiva).

31. Johnson, *Succeeding Against the Odds*, 294.

32. Jim McKay, "Under Its Editor Courier Grew to Be Nation's Top Black Paper," *Pittsburgh Post-Gazette*, February 6, 1995, B1 (via LexisNexis).

33. Additional source: John N. Ingham and Lynne B. Feldman, "Vann, Robert Lee," in *African-American Business Leaders: A Biographical Dictionary* (Westport, CT: Greenwood Press, 1994), 641–654.

34. Terry Mason, "Terry Mason's Family History Site," www.tmason1.com, provides genealogical information on Shaver, particularly her maternal grandfather, Benjamin Borden. See also "Shaver, Dorothy" in *Current Biography: 1946* (New York: H. W. Wilson, 1947), 546.

35. "Fifth Avenue's First Lady," *Time* 46, no. 27 (December 31, 1945): 82.

36. Margaret B. Parkinson, "How Did She Get There?" *Charm* 83, no. 4 (December 1955): 122.

37. "How Lord & Taylor Paid Up $10,000,000," *New York Times*, November 9, 1924, 30.

38. "Small Town Men Who Succeed Here," *New York Times*, November 27, 1927, XX10.

39. "Woman to Succeed Hoving As Head of Lord & Taylor," *Wall Street Journal*, December 19, 1945, 7.

40. "Fifth Ave. 'Blizzard' Spurs Winter Trade," *New York Times*, November 15, 1938, 13.

41. Mark Albright, "Slow, Steady Make-over," *St. Petersburg Times*, September 2, 2001, 1H (via LexisNexis Academic).

42. Rea Lubar Duncan, "We Need More Incorrigible Nonconformists," *Cleveland Plain Dealer*, March 19, 1999, 9B (via LexisNexis Academic).

43. S. J. Woolf, "Miss Shaver Pictures the Store of Tomorrow," *New York Times*, January 5, 1947, SM18.

44. Jeanne Perkins, "No. 1 Career Woman," *Life* 22, no. 19 (May 12, 1947): 128.

45. Ibid., 126. Additional sources on Shaver: Dorothy Shaver Papers, Schlesinger Library, Radcliffe College, Cambridge, MA; "Miss Shaver Dead; Led Lord & Taylor," *New York Times*, June 29, 1959, 1 and 29.

46. Newcomer, *Big Business Executive*, 42.

47. Warner and Abegglen, *Big Business Leaders in America*, 5.

48. David Callahan, *Kindred Spirits: Harvard Business School's Extraordinary Class of 1949 and How They Transformed American Business* (New York: John Wiley & Sons, 2002), 37.

49. Observations are based on 1980 census statistics for comparable age brackets and are derived from data in U.S. Department of Commerce, Bureau of the Census, *1980 Census: Chapter D—Detailed Population Characteristics, U.S. Summary, Part 1* (Washington, DC: Government Printing Office, 1984), table 262, 40–41.

50. Stuart Elliott, "An Anomaly on Madison Avenue," *New York Times*, February 19, 1997, D21.

51. Bernice Kanner, "Trumpet of the Swan," *Chief Executive* 124 (June 1997): 23.

52. "Creating an Environment 'Where People Can Do Great Work': Shelly Lazarus Talks About the Challenges and Satisfactions of Her Role as CEO of Ogilvy & Mather," *Advertising Age* 69, no. 38 (September 21, 1998): C14 (via Factiva).

53. Alison Fahey, "Shelly Lazarus: Ogilvy Exec Takes 'Direct' Route to Top," *Advertising Age* 61, no. 6 (February 5, 1990): 38 (via LexisNexis Academic).

54. Stuart Elliott, "I.B.M. to Transfer Advertising Work to Single Agency," *New York Times*, May 25, 1994, A1 and D16.

55. Kanner, "Trumpet of the Swan," 23.

56. "Shelly Lazarus Talks About the Challenges," C18.

57. Ken Wheaton, "Adages," *Advertising Age* 76, no. 3 (July 25, 2005): 52.

58. Additional sources: Elizabeth Cohen, "Shelly Lazarus: Mixing Manicures and Megabuck Deals," *People* 47, no. 17 (May 5, 1997): 89ff. (via Academic Search Premier); Stuart Elliott, "From One Woman to Another, Ogilvy & Mather Is Making History," *New York Times*, September 9, 1996, D7; Ogilvy and Mather Web page, Shelly Lazarus biography, www.ogilvy.com/company.

59. Warner and Abegglen, *Big Business Leaders in America*, 227.

60. Jonathan P. Hicks, "Reginald F. Lewis, 50, Is Dead; Financier Led Beatrice Takeover," *New York Times*, January 20, 1993, A21. See also Reginald F. Lewis and Blair S. Walker, *"Why Should White Guys Have All the Fun?" How Reginald Lewis Created a Billion-Dollar Business Empire* (New York: John Wiley & Sons, 1995).

61. "Beatrice Deal a Landmark for Black Business," *USA Today*, August 11, 1987, 2B.

62. Bernard E. Anderson, "Overview: A Tale of Two Decades," *Black Enterprise* 22, no. 11 (June 1992): 207.

63. Derek T. Dingle, "Reginald Lewis: The Deal Heard 'Round the World," *Black Enterprise* 35, no. 11 (June 2005): 36 (via Factiva).

## Chapter 8

1. Carly Fiorina's statements were made at her appointment as president and CEO of Hewlett-Packard and were cited by John Markoff, "Hewlett-Packard Picks Rising Star at Lucent As Its Chief Executive," *New York Times*, July 20, 1999, C1.

2. This and the following statistics are from *2002 Catalyst Census of Women Corporate Officers and Top Earners in the Fortune 500* (New York: Catalyst, 2002).

3. Ilene Lang, Speech at Catalyst Awards Dinner, March 24, 2005, available at www.catalystwomen.org/award/files/2005/Ilene percent20Lang percent20Speech.pdf.

4. Frank Hobbs and Nicole Stoops, U.S. Census Bureau, *Demographic Trends in the 20th Century* (Washington, DC: Government Printing Office, 2002), 78, available at www.census.gov/prod/2002pubs/censr-4.pdf.

5. Proportion of Asian Americans in population was derived from U.S. Census Bureau tables online, www.census.gov/population/cen2000/phc-t08/phc-t-08.xls (those reporting Asian race alone or in combination were included in this estimate). On bachelor's degrees earned by Asian Americans, see U.S. Department of Education, National Center for Education Statistics, *Digest of Education Statistics, 2001*, table 268, available at http://nces.ed.gov/programs/digest/d01/dt268.asp.

6. Jeff Owings, Timothy Madigan, and Bruce Daniel, *Who Goes to America's Highly Ranked National Universities?* (National Center for Education Statistics, Statistics in Brief [NCES 98-095], November 1998), 4, available at http://nces.ed.gov/pubs98/98095.pdf.

7. U.S. Department of Commerce, Minority Business Development Agency, *Dynamic Diversity: Projected Changes in U.S. Race and Ethnic Composition, 1995 to 2050* (U.S.

# Notes

Department of Commerce, Minority Business Development Agency, December 1999), 11–12, available at www.mbda.gov/documents/unpubtext.pdf.

8. See, for example, see Michael Hout, "More Universalism, Less Structural Mobility: The American Occupational Structure in the 1980s," *American Journal of Sociology* 93, no. 6 (May 1988): 1391.

9. Cited by Robert B. Semple Jr., "President Signs School Aid Bill; Scores Congress," *New York Times*, June 24, 1972, 1.

10. U.S. Department of Education, National Center for Education Statistics, *Digest of Education Statistics, 2001*, table 284, available at nces.ed.gov/programs/digest/d01/dt284.asp.

11. Ann Harrington and Petra Bartosiewicz, "Who's Up? Who's Down? And Is That a New No. 1?" *Fortune*, October 18, 2004, 181.

12. Center for Women's Business Research, "Top Facts About Women-Owned Businesses," Web page, http://www.womensbusinessresearch.org/topfacts.html.

13. *The C200 Business Leadership Index, 2005: Annual Report on Women's Clout in Business* (Chicago: Committee of 200, 2005), available at http://www.c200.org/external/2005 index.pdf.

14. "Still Treading Water: African Americans at the Nation's Leading Business Schools," *Journal of Blacks in Higher Education* 36 (summer 2002): 109.

15. U.S. Department of Education, National Center for Education Statistics, *Digest of Education Statistics, 2001*, table 272, available at http://nces.ed.gov/programs/digest/d01/dt272.asp.

16. U.S. Census Bureau tables online, www.census.gov/population/cen2000/phc-t08/phc-t-08.xls (statistics for those people reporting "Black or African American" race alone or in combination were included in this figure).

17. National Black MBA Association, "Membership Demographics," Web site, www.nbmbaa.org/membership_demographics.cfm.

18. Kimberly L. Allers, "Won't It Be Grand When We Don't Need Diversity Lists?" *Fortune*, August 22, 2005, 101.

19. "Still Treading Water," 110–111.

20. "The 2002 Directory of Top 10 Business Schools," *Hispanic Business*, March 2002, 38, 40, 42.

21. National Society of Hispanic MBAs, "Who We Are," Web site, http://www.nshmba.org/whoweare.asp.

22. For MBAs, see U.S. Department of Education, National Center for Education Statistics, *Digest of Education Statistics, 2001*, table 272, available at http://nces.ed.gov/programs/digest/d01/dt272.asp. For other professional degrees, see ibid., table 278, available at http://nces.ed.gov/programs/digest/d01/dt278.asp.

23. Ibid., table 272.

24. Dennis Taylor and Erik Espe, "Immigrants Impacting Valley Economy," *Silicon Valley/San Jose Business Journal*, July 19, 1999, available at http://sanjose.bizjournals.com/sanjose/stories/1999/07/19/story1.html.

25. U.S. Census Bureau, "Minority Groups Increasing Business Ownership at Higher Rate Than National Average, Census Bureau Reports," Press Release, July 28, 2005, www.census.gov/Press-Release/www/releases/archives/business_ownership/005477.html.

26. Siobhan Morrissey, "The King of Condominiums: Jorge Perez," *Time* 166, no. 8 (August 22, 2005): 44.

27. Mary Ann Fox, Brooke A. Connolly, and Thomas D. Snyder, *Youth Indicators 2005: Trends in the Well-Being of American Youth*, publication no. NCES 2005-050 of the U.S. Department of Education, National Center for Education Statistics (Washington, DC: 2005), 50.

28. Susan Choy, *Students Whose Parents Did Not Go to College: Postsecondary Access, Persistence and Attainment*, publication no. NCES 2001-126 of the U.S. Department of Education, National Center for Education Statistics (Washington, DC: 2001), 7, available at nces.ed.gov/pubs2001/2001126.pdf.

29. Ibid., 26.

30. Ibid., 18.

31. Ibid., 27 and 29.

32. "Class-Conscious Financial Aid," *Harvard Magazine*, May–June 2004, 62.

33. William G. Bowen, Martin A. Kurzweil, and Eugene M. Tobin, "A Thumb on the Scale: The Case for Socioeconomic Affirmative Action," *Harvard Magazine*, May–June 2005, 48ff.

34. Horatio Alger Jr., *Ragged Dick, or, Street Life in New York with the Boot Blacks* (New York: Signet Classic/New American Library edition, 1990), 77.

35. For example, see Michelle Conlin, Jennifer Merritt, and Linda Himelstein, "Mommy Is Really Home from Work," *BusinessWeek*, November 25, 2002, 101–104.

36. Liana C. Sayer, "Gender, Time and Inequality: Trends in Women's and Men's Paid Work, Unpaid Work and Free Time," *Social Forces* 84 no. 1 (September 2005): 292–293.

37. Rakesh Khurana, *Searching for a Corporate Savior: The Irrational Quest for Charismatic CEOs* (Princeton, NJ: Princeton University Press, 2002), 103–117.

38. DaimlerChrysler Web page, www.daimlerchrysler.com.

39. Anthony Ferner, Phil Almond, and Trevor Colling, "Institutional theory and the cross-national transfer of employment policy: the case of 'workforce diversity' in U.S. multinationals," *Journal of International Business Studies* 36 no. 3 (May 2005): 315.

## Appendix

1. Anthony J. Mayo and Nitin Nohria, *In Their Time: The Greatest Business Leaders of the Twentieth Century* (Boston: Harvard Business School Press, 2005), 365–368.

2. Richard S. Tedlow, Courtney Purrington, and Kim Eric Bettcher, "The American CEO in the Twentieth Century: Demography and Career Path" (working paper 03-097, Harvard Business School, 2003), 7–10.

3. John J. Gabarro, *The Dynamics of Taking Charge* (Boston: Harvard Business School Press, 1987).

4. Tedlow, Purrington, and Bettcher, "The American CEO in the Twentieth Century."

As we noted in the stories of many of the leaders discussed in this book, we consulted many biographies, biographical dictionaries, and articles in compiling details regarding the journeys of individual leaders. In addition, the following books and articles served as important background materials forming our general understanding of U.S. business leaders' origins.

## Surveys and Studies of Business Leaders

Berger, Morroe. "The Business Elite: Then and Now." *Commentary* 22 (October 1956): 367–375.

Bonfield, Patricia. *U.S. Business Leaders: A Study of Opinions and Characteristics* (New York: Conference Board, 1980).

"The Corporate Elite." *Business Week* bonus issue, October 23, 1987.

Miller, William. "The Business Elite in Business Bureaucracies: Careers of Top Executives in the Early Twentieth Century," and "The Recruitment of the American Business Elite." In William Miller, ed., *Men in Business: Essays on the Historical Role of the Entrepreneur* (New York: Harper & Row, 1962).

Mills, C. Wright. "The American Business Elite: A Collective Portrait." In "The Tasks of American History," supplement to *Journal of Economic History* 5 (December 1945), 20–44.

Newcomer, Mabel. *The Big Business Executive: The Factors That Made Him, 1900–1950* (New York: Columbia University Press, 1955).

Newcomer, Mabel, Market Statistics, and Scientific American, Inc. *The Big Business Executive, 1964: A Study of His Social and Educational Background* (New York: Scientific American, 1965).

"The Nine Hundred." *Fortune* 46 (November 1952): 132ff.

Taussig, F. W., and C. S. Joslyn. *American Business Leaders: A Study in Social Origins and Stratification* (New York: Macmillan Company, 1932).

Tedlow, Richard S., Kim Eric Bettcher, and Courtney A. Purrington. "The Chief Executive Officer of the Large American Industrial Corporation in 1917." *Business History Review* 77 (Winter 2003): 687–701.

Temin, Peter. "The Stability of the American Business Elite." *Industrial and Corporate Change* 8 (June 1999): 189–210.

Useem, Michael, and Jerome Karabel. "Pathways to Top Corporate Management." *American Sociological Review* 51, no. 2 (April 1986): 184–200.

Warner, W. Lloyd, and James C. Abegglen. *Big Business Leaders in America* (New York: Harper and Brothers, 1955).

# Bibliography

## The Elite in America

Baltzell, E. Digby. *The Protestant Establishment: Aristocracy and Caste in America* (New York: Random House, 1964).

Lundberg, Ferdinand. *America's 60 Families* (New York: Vanguard Press, 1937).

Miller, William. "American Historians and the Business Elite." *Journal of Economic History* 9, no. 2 (November 1949): 184–208.

Mills, C. Wright. *The Power Elite* (New York: Oxford University Press, 1956).

Sorokin, Pitirim. "American Millionaires and Multi-Millionaires: A Comparative Statistical Study." *Journal of Social Forces* 3, no. 4 (May 1925): 627–640.

Useem, Michael. "The Inner Group of the American Capitalist Class." *Social Problems* 25, no. 3 (February 1978): 225–240.

Zweigenhaft, Richard L., and G. William Domhoff. *Diversity in the Power Elite: Have Women and Minorities Reached the Top?* (New Haven, CT: Yale University Press, 1998).

——. *Jews in the Protestant Establishment* (New York: Praeger, 1982).

## American Social and Occupational Mobility

Blau, Peter M., and Otis Dudley Duncan. *The American Occupational Structure* (New York: John Wiley & Sons, 1967).

Featherman, David L., and Robert M. Hauser. *Opportunity and Change* (New York: Academic Press, 1978).

Hout, Michael. "More Universalism, Less Structural Mobility: The American Occupational Structure in the 1980s." *American Journal of Sociology* 93, no. 6 (May 1988): 1358–1400.

Lipset, Seymour Martin, and Reinhard Bendix. *Social Mobility in Industrial Society* (Berkeley: University of California Press, 1959).

Sorensen, Aage B. "The Structure of Intragenerational Mobility." *American Sociological Review* 40, no. 4 (August 1975), 456–471.

——. "The Structure of Inequality and the Process of Attainment." *American Sociological Review* 42, no. 6 (December 1977): 965–978.

——. "A Model and a Metric for the Analysis of the Intragenerational Status Attainment Process." *American Journal of Sociology* 85, no. 2 (September 1979): 361–384.

## Sources Used in Dataset Selection and Coding

Drachman, Virginia G. *Enterprising Women, 250 Years of American Business* (Chapel Hill: University of North Carolina Press, 2002).

Forbes, B. C. *America's Fifty Foremost Business Leaders* (New York: B. C. Forbes & Sons Publishing Company, 1948).

Fucini, Joseph J., and Suzy Fucini. *Entrepreneurs: The Men and Women Behind Famous Brands Names and How They Made It* (Boston: G. K. Hall & Co., 1985).

Hamilton, Neil A. *American Business Leaders: From Colonial Times to the Present* (Santa Barbara, CA: ABC-CLIO, 1999).

# Bibliography

Ingham, John N. *Biographical Dictionary of American Business Leaders* (Westport, CT: Greenwood Press, 1983).

Ingham, John N., and Lynne B. Feldman. *Contemporary American Business Leaders: A Biographical Dictionary* (Westport, CT: Greenwood Press, 1990).

——. *African-American Business Leaders* (Westport, CT: Greenwood Press, 1994).

Junior Achievement. "Junior Achievement National Business Hall of Fame, 1975–2003." http://www.ja.org/nbhof/past_laureates.shtml.

Leavitt, Judith A. *American Women Managers and Administrators: A Selective Biographical Dictionary of Twentieth-Century Leaders in Business, Education, and Government* (Westport, CT: Greenwood Press, 1985).

Neff, Thomas J., and James M. Citrin. *Lessons from the Top: The Search for America's Best Business Leaders* (New York: Currency/Doubleday, 1999).

News Front Editors. *The 50 Great Pioneers of American Industry* (Maplewood, NJ: C. S. Hammond & Company, 1964).

"People Who Most Influenced Business This Century: The 50." *Los Angeles Times*, October 25, 1999.

"Time 100: Builders and Titans." *Time*, December 7, 1998.

# Index

# Index

# Index

*Anthony J. Mayo*  Tony Mayo is a Lecturer in the Organizational Behavior unit and is the Director of the Leadership Initiative at Harvard Business School. The Leadership Initiative is an interdisciplinary center that strives to serve as a catalyst for cutting-edge leadership research and course development (see http://www.hbs.edu/leadership). His most recent previous book, *In Their Time: The Greatest Business Leaders of the Twentieth Century*, coauthored with Nitin Nohria, provides a context-based view of historical leadership in America.

As Director of the Leadership Initiative, Tony oversees several comprehensive research projects on emerging, global, and legacy leadership and manages a number of executive education programs on leadership development. He was a cocreator of Harvard Business School's High Potentials Leadership and Leadership Best Practices programs and has been a principal contributor to the design of a number of custom leadership-development programs.

Prior to his current role, Tony pursued a career in database marketing, where he held senior general management positions at an advertising agency, Hill Holliday; a database management firm, Epsilon; and a full-service direct-marketing company, DIMAC Marketing Corporation. Previously, Tony served as the Director of MBA Program Administration at Harvard Business School.

Tony completed his MBA from Harvard Business School and received his Bachelor's Degree, summa cum laude, from Boston College. He lives in Needham, Massachusetts, with his wife, Denise, and their three children, Hannah, Alex, and Jacob.

*Nitin Nohria*  Nitin Nohria is the Richard P. Chapman Professor of Business Administration and Director of Research at the Harvard Business School. His research centers on leadership and organizational change.

In addition to coauthoring *In Their Time: The Greatest Business Leaders of the Twentieth Century*, with Anthony J. Mayo, Professor Nohria has written or edited several other critically acclaimed books, including *What Really Works: The 4+2 Formula for Sustained Business Success* (with William Joyce); *Changing Fortunes: Remaking the Industrial Corporation* (with Davis Dyer and Frederick Dalzell); *Driven: How Human Nature Shapes Our Choices* (with Paul R. Lawrence); *The Arc of Ambition: Defining the Leadership Journey* (with James Champy); *Master Passions: Emotion, Narrative, and the Development of Culture* (with Mihnea Moldoveanu); *Breaking the Code of Change* (with Michael Beer); *Beyond the Hype: Rediscovering the Essence of Management* (with Robert C. Eccles); *Building the Information-Age Organization*; *Fast Forward: The Best Ideas on Managing Business Change* (with James Champy); and *The Differentiated Network* (with Sumantra Ghoshal), the last of which won the 1998 George R. Terry Book Award, given annually for the best book by the Academy of Management. He is also the author or coauthor of more than fifty articles and cases that have appeared in journals such as *Harvard Business Review*, *Sloan Management Review*, and *Strategic Management Journal*.

Professor Nohria lectures to corporate audiences around the globe and serves on the advisory boards of several small and large firms. He has been interviewed by ABC, CNN, and NPR, and cited frequently in *BusinessWeek*, *The Economist*, the *Financial Times*, *Fortune*, the *New York Times*, and the *Wall Street Journal*.

In addition to teaching courses in Harvard's MBA and Executive Education programs, Professor Nohria is an adviser to PhD students in the school's Organizational Behavior program. He has also been a visiting faculty member of the London Business School.

Prior to joining the Harvard Business School faculty in July 1988, Professor Nohria received his PhD in Management from the Sloan School of Management, Massachusetts Institute of Technology, and a B. Tech. in Chemical Engineering from the Indian Institute of Technology, Bombay.

**Laura G. Singleton** Laura Singleton is currently a PhD student in Organizational Studies at the Carroll School of Management, Boston College. She began coauthoring this book with Anthony Mayo and Nitin Nohria while serving as a Research Associate at Harvard Business School from 2002 to 2005.

Prior to working at Harvard Business School, Singleton had a business career of approximately fifteen years in marketing and general management, primarily with the database marketing firm of Harte-Hanks Data Technologies. In addition, she has authored articles on business topics that have appeared in *Direct Marketing*, *DM News*, the *Boston Business Journal*, and Harvard Business School's alumni magazine.

Laura earned an MBA with distinction from Harvard Business School and a BS in mathematics, magna cum laude, from Davidson College. She was born in Morgantown, West Virginia, and is very proud to share that home state with five of the business leaders on our list.